THE CIVIL RIGHTS STRUGGLE:
Leaders in Profile

Contributors

Catharine A. Barnes
Jason Berger
Thomas J. Champion
Elliott Figman
Steven L. Goulden
Thomas L. Harrison
Edward W. Knappman
Michael L. Levine

Nelson N. Lichtenstein
Frank H. Milburn
Donald K. Richards
Eleanora W. Schoenebaum
Martin J. Swanson
Arthur E Scherr
James L. Wunsch
Selma Yampolsky

THE
CIVIL RIGHTS
STRUGGLE:
Leaders in Profile

by John D'Emilio

Facts On File
119 West 57th Street, New York, N.Y. 10019

THE
CIVIL RIGHTS
STRUGGLE:
Leaders in Profile

Copyright, 1979 by Facts on File, Inc.

Library of Congress Cataloging in Publication Data

D'Emilio, John.
   The civil rights struggle.

   Bibliography: p.
      Includes index.
   1. Afro-Americans—Biography. 2. Civil rights work-ers—United States—Biography. 3. Afro-Americans—Civil rights. I. Title.
E185.96.D38   301.45′19′6073022   [B]   79-18006
ISBN 0-87196-460-0

9 8 7 6 5 4 3 2 1

Printed in the United States of America

To My Mother, Sophie S. D'Emilio,
and My Father, Vincent A. D'Emilio

Contents

Preface

The civil rights movement has had a profound effect on modern America, bringing important issues of individual rights and freedoms to the foreground and changing Americans' attitudes. This book presents biographies of 83 men and women who were in the vanguard of that struggle, either as leaders of the civil rights movement or as heads of the opposition. Each portrait contains information on the individual's background and his career before becoming involved in the civil rights struggle. It then focuses on those events that gained the subject prominence in the movement. Participation in mass protests and organizational campaigns is discussed and attitudes about the philosophical disputes that divided both proponents and opponents during the postwar years are summarized.

The profiles deal only with people whose careers centered around the civil rights struggle. Men and women who may have had an important impact on the movement but whose careers were focused elsewhere are not included. Thus no Presidents are profiled; nor are such senators as Hubert Humphrey or Robert Kennedy, although they had an important impact on the movement. Supreme Court justices, too, are missing because civil rights was only one of the many issues with which they had to contend.

The introductory essay provides an overview of major trends in the civil rights movement since 1945, traces the roots of the struggle and places the movement in the context of the times. The volume also includes a chronology of important events and a detailed bibliography of works on the movement and its personalities.

Introduction

In 1944, as the prospects of an Allied victory in World War II brightened, the Swedish sociologist Gunnar Myrdal published his massive, two-volume study of race relations in the United States, *An American Dilemma*. Commissioned by the Carnegie Corporation to undertake the project because he was an "outsider," one who could bring a measure of dispassionate objectivity to his subject, Myrdal challenged American readers with his forceful, unflinching description of racial inequality. After examining in exhaustive detail the rigidly enforced segregation of the races in the South and the informal yet pervasive patterns of discrimination in the North and West, Myrdal concluded that "the treatment of the Negro is America's greatest and most conspicuous scandal." He coupled his indictment, however, with a hopeful prognosis for the future. "Not since Reconstruction," he argued, "has there been more reason to anticipate fundamental changes in American race relations, changes which will involve a development toward the American ideals."

Myrdal's assessment proved surprisingly accurate. In the postwar era racial injustice moved to center stage of American politics. First in the South and then in the North, millions of blacks and their white supporters mounted a sustained assault on segregation and other forms of discrimination. Basing itself on American ideals of democracy and equality, the civil rights movement of the 1950s and 1960s wrought a revolution in this country's race relations which, though it remains unfinished, is still being felt today.

Mass movements that challenge a society's status quo do not spring into existence suddenly. They are the products of the complex interplay of social, economic, political and cultural trends that allow movements gradually to take root and then to flourish. In this re-

1

spect, the civil rights revolution of the postwar decades was not an exception. It grew out of conditions that were in the making for at least a generation before World War II.

Almost from the moment that the South had enshrined white supremacy into law through its "Jim Crow" segregation statutes, forces that would ultimately undermine the system were set in motion. Beginning in the years prior to World War I, a small number of Southern blacks migrated northward to escape Jim Crow and the rising tide of lynchings and other forms of extra-legal intimidation. With the growing demand for workers created by the war and the curtailment of European immigration, the movement expanded rapidly as blacks sought greater freedom and economic opportunity in Northern cities. In 1910 roughly 10% of American blacks lived outside the South. By 1940 the proportion had grown to nearly one-quarter. The increase, moreover, was not evenly distributed throughout the country. Almost half of the 2.8 million blacks living in the North were concentrated in just six cities—New York, Chicago, Philadelphia, Detroit, Cleveland and Pittsburgh.

The migration from the rural South to Northern cities accelerated after World War II as Southern agriculture experienced a technological revolution. The introduction of mechanical cottonpickers during the 1940s promised greater profitability through increased productivity for landowners who consolidated their scattered tenant holdings. The number of farms in the South fell by 50% between 1925 and 1960 while the number of black families who farmed land through tenancy or sharecropping declined from 700,000 to 138,000. Displaced by the new technology, Southern blacks flowed North in ever larger numbers. Between 1940 and 1960 another 2.5 million left the land of Jim Crow.

The migration to the North opened the door to political influence for black Americans for the first time since Reconstruction. Concentrated as they were in large cities, blacks were able to elect their own representatives on the state and local level. The New Deal, moreover, brought an abrupt shift in party allegiance as blacks, along with the white working class, voiced support for the social welfare policies of the Democrats by voting for the party of Franklin D. Roosevelt. Northern blacks became a crucial component of the New Deal coalition that made the Democrats the majority party. Urban political machines sought to retain the newly won loyalty of black voters through patronage, through support of local black candidates and through improved services in black communities. The ballot proved an important tool for winning small concessions and for gradually making racial discrimination an issue that the Democratic Party in the North could no longer ignore.

The growth of large black communities in the North also made possible the establishment of organizations and institutions that would spearhead the civil rights revolution. In 1910 W.E.B. DuBois, with the support of white reformers such as Jane Addams and John Dewey, formed the National Association for the Advancement of Colored People (NAACP). Through what Myrdal called "a quite clearly conceived tactical plan," the NAACP tried to whittle away at segregation by selective court challenges of Jim Crow statutes. It also provided legal assistance to Southern blacks who were the victims of a white supremacist police and judicial system. In keeping with its legalistic approach to racial injustice, the NAACP received its greatest support from the black middle class. By 1940 it had 355 branches with 50,000 members. The National Urban League (NUL), meanwhile, was formed in 1911 to help Southern blacks adjust to urban life in the North. Emphasizing jobs, education and social services, the 46 branches of the NUL that existed in 1940 acted as a pressure group on municipal governments. Finally, the urban ghettoes provided fertile soil for an independent black press to grow and thrive. Newspapers such as the Pittsburgh *Courier,* the Chicago *Defender,* and the New York *Amsterdam News* gave powerful expression to black aspirations for equality and justice.

While the migration of blacks to the North provided the indispensable precondition for the development of a civil rights movement, World War II offered the immediate political context in which the movement emerged. The worldwide struggle against fascism brought into bold relief the horrifying results of racist ideology. American participation in World War II highlighted the contradictions between the nation's international stance and its treatment of racial minorities at home. The war heightened the race consciousness of black Americans as their leaders tied participation in the mobilization against fascism to demands for racial justice on the home front. In January 1941 the NAACP organized meetings in 23 states to protest discrimination in the armed forces, federal employment and defense industries. During the winter and early spring, A. Philip Randolph [*q.v.*], a former socialist and the most prominent black trade unionist, organized a National March on Washington Committee. On May 1, the Committee issued a "call to Negro America" to rally in the nation's capital on July 1 to demand jobs and equal participation in national defense. Randolph's action received an enthusiastic reception in the black press.

Even the threat of a march on Washington revealed the enormous potential of mass protest. Worried about the damage to America's image abroad and the disruption that a march might have on national unity and the mobilization effort, President Roosevelt conferred with Randolph and Walter White [*q.v.*], the executive secretary of the NAACP, in an attempt to have them cancel the rally. The black leaders demanded federal action against discrimination in defense employment and the armed services. As the date of the march approached, Roosevelt offered a compromise gesture. On June 25 he issued an executive order that barred discrimination in defense industries and in federal employment and authorized a Fair Employment Practices Committee (FEPC) to investigate and monitor hiring practices. In response, Randolph called off the march on Washington.

Roosevelt's action admittedly fell short of meeting black demands. His executive order did not touch upon the policies of the armed forces, and by the end of World War II, blacks still confronted discrimination in training and service in every branch of the military. The FEPC lacked enforcement powers, was plagued by inadequate appropriations and staffing, and was limited to investigating discrimination in defense industries during the wartime emergency. Nonetheless, the presidential action established an important precedent. For the first time since Reconstruction the executive branch had taken decisive action against racial discrimination. Roosevelt's order blocked Jim Crow at the factory gate, and the federal FEPC served as a model for Northern states to emulate. In the years after World War II, 19 states set up commissions to investigate and take action against discriminatory hiring practices. During the war the FEPC held five major sets of public hearings, including a series in Birmingham, Ala., in June 1942, that provided massive documentation of restrictions upon black employment opportunities. Impressive gains were scored within the federal government during the war as blacks won access to jobs previously closed to them. Finally, the FEPC served as a focus for the civil rights forces. In September 1943 Randolph formed a National Committee for a Permanent FEPC that gradually pulled together an impressive coalition of labor, church, Jewish and civil liberties groups. The impact of developments during the war on race consciousness can be gauged by the growth of the NAACP. By 1946 it had over 1,000 branches, triple its prewar number, and had increased its membership ninefold to nearly half a million.

The close of the war did not bring an end to the efforts of civil rights leaders; it simply changed the political context in which they worked. From leading the Allied nations in the fight against fascism, the United States moved into the role of spearheading a worldwide campaign to contain Communism. The country's racial policies proved as embarrassing in the Cold War as they did during wartime. Segregation and inequality severely compromised America's claim to world leadership in the eyes of the newly emerging nations of Africa and Asia. The State Department estimated that 50% of Russian statements attacking the United States focused on Southern treatment of the black. The United Nations charter and its covenant on human rights gave formal recognition on an international level to principles of equality. Thus, in the postwar era, the basic goals of the civil rights movement coincided with the requirements imposed by the nation's foreign policy.

Civil rights leaders faced the postwar era with a new man in the White House. When Harry S Truman became President in April 1945, he was largely an unknown quantity. Coming as he did from the border state of Missouri, Truman stimulated some apprehension among blacks. But the new President proved to be a far more out-spoken supporter of civil rights than his predecessor. His rise in Democratic politics came through the support of the Pendergast machine in Kansas City which courted black votes as part of its effort to retain control of the city's government. Although Truman had little opportunity to vote on civil rights issues during his Senate career, his public utterances revealed support for the principle of equality under the law. As President, Truman spoke out forcefully for civil rights, though political considerations often determined his legislative priorities.

Led by the NAACP, the civil rights coalition initially pursued a legislative strategy in the postwar era, with the fight for a permanent FEPC at the center of their calculations. In July 1945 Congress slashed appropriations for the wartime body and mandated an end to its existence by the following summer. Truman, responding to the requests of civil rights organizations, included a permanent FEPC among his list of "must legislation" in a special message to Congress in September 1945. In the Senate Dennis Chavez [q.v.] won approval of such a bill in the Education and Labor Committee. But when debate opened on the Senate floor in January, Southern members, led by the diehard segregationist from Mississippi, Theodore Bilbo [q.v.], filibustered. On Feb. 9 a cloture vote failed to shut off debate and the FEPC was dead.

The historian Monroe Billington has documented the extensive support that the wartime FEPC garnered among moderate white Southerners. But the invective and emotional outbursts with which Bilbo and other Southern politicians attacked the Chavez proposal quickly silenced proponents of the measure in the South. Worse, it stimulated a wave of violent assaults against blacks. There were six lynchings in 1946. In February 1946 Isaac Woodwar, a black veteran, was pulled from a bus in Batesburgh, S.C., and blinded by the chief of police. Later that month the Ku Klux Klan, abetted by local police, terrorized for two days black residents of Columbia, Tenn. In July two black couples were shot and killed by an armed mob in Monroe, Ga. In another Georgia town the only black man to dare to vote was gunned down by a sniper.

Alarmed by the upsurge in racially motivated violence, Walter White of the NAACP headed a delegation of civil rights leaders who met with Truman in September. Although reluctant to have the federal government intervene in the South, the President promised to take some action. In December he issued an executive order establishing a presidential committee on civil rights to investigate racial conditions and make recommendations to remedy inequality. The report which it released in October 1947, *To Secure These Rights,* described in chilling detail the violence directed at Southern blacks, and it catalogued the pervasive denial of basic civil rights and civil liberties. The committee disputed the "separate but equal" doctrine used to justify segregation. "It is almost always true," it said, "that while indeed separate, these facilities are far from equal. . . . No argument or rationalization can alter this basic fact: a law which forbids a group of American citizens to associate with other citizens in the ordinary course of daily living creates inequality by imposing a caste status on the minority group." The report concluded with a lengthy list of legislative recommendations.

The report of the presidential committee provided a solid underpinning for Truman to take a more aggressive civil rights stand. On Feb. 2, 1948 he delivered the first presidential message on civil rights to Congress. In it Truman offered as a "minimum program" a legislative package that included an anti-lynching law and the abolition of the poll tax, a permanent FEPC, a federal commission on civil rights, the creation of a civil rights division in the Justice Department, the prohibition of segregation in interstate transportation, and special federal protection to guarantee voting rights for blacks. Civil rights forces heralded Truman's speech which galvanized them into greater activity.

Although Truman's stance was motivated by sincere conviction, his message owed its timing to political considerations. In November 1947, Truman's special counsel Clark Clifford penned a 43 page memorandum on strategy for the upcoming presidential campaign. Arguing that the South was safely Democratic, Clifford assessed the main threat to Truman's reelection as coming from the left, from the expected announcement of Henry Wallace as a third party candidate. He urged Truman to rally liberal forces behind him with a legislative program in the New Deal tradition. In particular, Clifford mentioned the importance of the civil rights issue for retaining the Jewish and black vote in several key Northern states. Truman's message to Congress reflected his counsel's strategy.

The President's civil rights stand aroused the hostility of white politicians in the South. In May several Southern governors sponsored a states rights conference in Jackson, Miss., where they passed a resolution to bolt from the Democratic Party if it adopted a strong civil rights plank at its national convention. In response, Truman's strategists shifted into low gear. The Administration failed to draft any significant civil rights legislation, and the Party's platform committee adopted a weak civil rights plank without any specific legislative recommendations. But the Party's moderate center underestimated the strength and determination of the liberal civil rights coalition. Hubert Humphrey, the charismatic young mayor of Minneapolis, introduced on the convention floor a plank that endorsed legislation to establish an FEPC and to guarantee black voting rights, as well as measures against segregation in the military and against lynching. Humphrey's motion narrowly won approval, largely through the support of big city bosses in New York, Illinois, and Pennsylvania who feared the loss of crucial black votes in local elections. The most extreme Southern segregationists, meanwhile, remained true to their word. On July 17 they formed the States Rights Party, nominated South Carolina's Gov. Strom Thurmond [*q.v.*] for president, Gov. Fielding Wright of Mississippi as his running mate, and adopted a platform calling for the strict segregation of the races.

The 1948 presidential election thus became the first in which civil rights assumed a prominent role, thanks in part to the extremism of segregationist forces and in part to the growing strength of the civil rights coalition and the black vote in the North. Truman, confronted with opposition from the left and the right, decided to take the offensive. Late in July he called the Republican-controlled 80th Congress into special session, presented it with a package of liberal legislation, and then attacked it as a "do-nothing" Congress when it failed to act. He issued two executive orders aimed at eliminating racial discrimination in federal employment and in the armed forces. In the closing weeks of the campaign he spoke out forcefully for racial justice. On Oct. 29 he addressed a cheering crowd of 65,000 in Harlem. When the votes were counted, Truman had pulled off a surprising victory in which he received almost 70% of the black vote.

Civil rights forces were jubilant, but their expectations for substantial legislative gains were to be sadly disappointed. The attempt by Senate liberals early in 1949 to modify the Senate's cloture rule in order to ease passage of civil rights legislation failed miserably as Southern senators conducted a successful filibuster that threatened the President's entire legislative program. Civil rights took a back seat as the Administration gave priority to Fair Deal social welfare measures and to Senate ratification of the mutual defense pact that established the North Atlantic Treaty Organization. The NAACP tried to rally the civil rights coalition by focusing its efforts on the drive for a permanent FEPC. In January 1950 4,000 lobbyists, representing unions, churches, Jewish organizations and civil liberties groups, descended on Congress to urge passage of the bill. Although the House did approve a weakened version of the FEPC, Senate liberals could not muster enough votes to end a Southern filibuster. The outbreak of the Korean War in June 1950 and the splintering of liberal forces under the attacks of Sen. Joseph McCarthy and other right-wing politicians spelled the death of the NAACP's legislative strategy.

The rise of McCarthyism also shortcircuited the efforts of another civil rights organization, the Congress of Racial Equality (CORE). Founded in Chicago in 1942 by members of the Christian-pacifist Fellowship of Reconciliation, CORE was dedicated to the dual principles of nonviolence and interracial cooperation. During the 1940s chapters spread to about 20 Northern cities and members pioneered in the use of direct action techniques of protest. CORE chapters conducted picketing and sit-ins of public facilities such as lunch-counters, restaurants and hotel lobbies to protest segregation and won a number of important, though admittedly limited, victories. In 1947 the national headquarters of CORE sponsored a successful "Journey of Reconciliation" through the upper South to test a Supreme Court decision outlawing segregation in interstate transportation. By the early 1950s, however, fears of Communism cast a cloud of suspicion over most forms of protest, and CORE entered a period of stagnation.

Despite the deadlock in Congress and the unfavorable climate for mass protest, the Truman years were important ones for the young civil rights movement. For the first time in the Twentieth Century, racial equality had become an issue in national politics. Several Northern states passed legislation banning discrimination in employment and housing, and a presidential committee had taken an unequivocal stand against the separate-but-equal doctrine underlying segregation. Truman, moreover, though he did not press hard for civil rights legislation, did use his powers as chief executive on behalf of racial justice. During his Administration the armed services moved to abolish segregation in the military, a process that the Korean War helped to complete. Millions of American servicemen, black and white, had their first experience of integration while serving in the armed forces.

The inhospitability of the McCarthy era for reform movements led civil rights advocates to shift course, abandoning their emphasis on legislative action. In a number of decisions from the late 1930s onward, the Supreme Court had indicated a willingness to chip away at segregation. At its annual convention in 1951, the NAACP made a major decision to concentrate its resources on litigation that challenged the constitutional basis of Southern segregation statutes. Thurgood Marshall, the head of the legal division of the NAACP, called the organization's attorneys together to map out a strategy. They decided to focus on elementary school education and to move beyond the insistence that black schools be upgraded until they were equal to those provided for whites. Instead, the organization's lawyers argued the position that separate schools were inherently unequal.

During the early 1950s NAACP lawyers intiated several suits against segregation in elementary school education. Five cases reached the Supreme Court early in 1953 and, after hearing arguments, the Court put them over for reargument in the fall. In the interval Chief Justice Fred Vinson died and was replaced by Earl Warren. After the final arguments in December, Warren decided to write the opinion himself and he won unanimous concurrence from his associates. On May 17, 1954 he delivered the historic decision of *Brown v. the Board of Education.* "We conclude," Warren wrote, "that in the field of public education the doctrine of 'separate but equal' has no place. Separate educational facilities are inherently unequal." The *Brown* decision laid to rest the almost 60 year old separate-but-equal doctrine and marked a watershed in the struggle for civil rights. Thereafter, despite the intensity of the resistance to the court's ruling, the weight of the law remained on the side of the black and racial equality.

Initial reaction to the *Brown* decision from the white South was muted. Baltimore and Washington, D.C. desegregated their school systems and the border states moved slowly into compliance. During 1955 there were even a few communities in the upper South that put desegregation plans into effect. In May 1955 the Supreme Court handed down its implementation decision, ordering desegregation to proceed "with all deliberate speed," but leaving responsibility for compliance with local school boards and federal district court judges in the South. Southern segregationists were relieved, assuming as they did that local judges and school officials could be expected to resist the Supreme Court ruling. But as the year ended they recognized the extent of their miscalculation. During the summer of 1955 an emboldened NAACP filed desegregation petitions with over 170 school boards in 17 states. Of the 19 district court rulings on local school segregation laws delivered in 1955, each one had overturned the Jim Crow statute and ordered the integration of public schools.

In *The Strange Career of Jim Crow,* historian C. Vann Woodward has described how "something very much like a panic seized many parts of the South toward the beginning of 1956." White supremacists rallied their forces and launched a movement of "massive resistance" against the *Brown* decision. In July 1954 Robert Patterson, a plantation manager in Indianola, Miss., formed the first Citizens' Council, a grassroots organization composed mostly of middle-class whites determined to thwart implementation of school integration. For the next year or so, the Citizens' Councils grew slowly. But by the end of 1955, when school desegregation began to appear inevitable, the movement mushroomed, spreading throughout the Deep South. Within months membership leaped above 250,000; in April 1956, local leaders met in New Orleans and formed the Citizens' Councils of America to coordinate resistance to the *Brown* decision. Local groups, which frequently included members of the business community, retaliated against blacks who were active in the desegregation effort by denying them credit or employment. The Councils pressured politicians and school board officials into taking a hard line in favor of segregation. Whites who dared voice support for compliance found themselves ostracized by friends and neighbors. In many localities the NAACP was almost driven underground. Throughout the South the Citizens' Councils virtually silenced the voices of moderation.

With grassroots resistance intensifying, Southern political leaders joined the movement against school desegregation. Sen. Harry Byrd of Virginia called for massive resistance to the Supreme Court's decision. Sen. James Eastland [q.v.] of Mississippi demanded an investigation of the Supreme Court, alleging that Communist influence was at work. In January 1956 four Southern governors endorsed the doctrine of "interposition." They promised to use the power of the state government to prevent desegregation by placing the sovereignty of the state between local school board officials and the Supreme Court. During 1956 state legislatures in the South enacted a bewildering array of laws designed to evade integration. Four states proclaimed open resistance and imposed legal penalties for compliance with the *Brown* decision. In March 1956 massive resistance received its most impressive endorsement when 101 Southern members of Congress challenged the authority of the Supreme Court by signing the "Southern Manifesto." The document offered praise to those states which "have declared the intention to resist forced integration by any lawful means," and it attacked the Supreme Court for its use of "naked power" to overturn local law. Under this onslaught desegregation ground to a halt. The number of school districts in the South initiating integration plans fell from 362 in 1955 to 38 in 1957 and to 13 the following year.

White resistance to the *Brown* decision peaked in 1957–58 during the Little Rock crisis. A federal court had approved a desegregation proposal that would allow a few black students to enroll in Little Rock Central High School in the fall of 1957. On Sept. 2, Gov. Orval Faubus [*q.v.*] announced that the integration plan endangered public order, and he mobilized the national guard. Two days later, when nine black students attempted to enter Central High School, guardsmen blocked the effort. The local NAACP, under the leadership of Daisy Bates [*q.v.*], obtained a federal court injunction that ordered the removal of the troops. On Sept. 23, when the black students arrived at school, they were faced with an hysterical, hostile mob of jeering whites. Throughout the day the school was the site of violence as white students rampaged through the building. Bates announced that the black students would not return unless the federal government guaranteed their protection.

The violence in Little Rock focused worldwide attention on Southern race relations. The defiance of Faubus and other Arkansas officials finally forced the federal government to take action. Until the Little Rock crisis, President Dwight D. Eisenhower had never spoken out publicly in favor of compliance with the Supreme Court decision, thus depriving Southern moderates of sorely needed support. Privately he was reported to have deplored the Supreme Court ruling on the grounds that it went too far, too fast. But Faubus had posed a clear challenge to federal authority, and mob violence threatened the maintenance of civil peace. On Sept. 24 Eisenhower called out the national guard, marking the first time since Reconstruction that federal troops were dispatched to the South to protect the rights of black Americans. The black students attended school the next day while soldiers patrolled the halls of Central High School for the remainder of the school year. Faubus turned to the courts in an effort to win a postponement of further desegregation. In September 1958 when the Supreme Court rejected any delay in implementation, Faubus ordered the closing of Little Rock's high schools for the entire school year. The forces of resistance appeared to have won.

As white opposition to school desegregation in the South solidified, however, developments were occurring among Southern blacks that would change the very nature of the civil rights crusade. Until the 1954 *Brown* decision most of the pressure for civil rights had come from the North. NAACP chapters in the South tended to be based in the region's largest cities, and they restricted their activities to litigation. White racism in the South was too virulent and the threat of violence too great for Southern blacks to engage in public protest against segregation. And rural and small-town blacks remained almost untouched by the young movement. But the Supreme Court's ruling placed the law of the land on the side of racial equality while the issue of education, moreover, affected every black family with children. Its impact in arousing Southern blacks to action can be measured by the large number of desegregation petitions filed with local school boards during the summer of 1955.

The most dramatic sign of change, however, came with the Montgomery, Ala. bus boycott. On Dec. 1, 1955 Rosa Parks [*q.v.*], a black seamstress,was arrested when she refused to give up her seat to a white passenger and to move to the black section at the rear of the bus. Parks contacted her former employer, E.D. Nixon, the head of the local NAACP, who hastily convened a meeting of the city's black leaders. They decided to call for a boycott of the buses by Montgomery Negroes on Dec. 5, the day Parks was scheduled to appear in court. When the action proved over 90% effective, the leaders held a mass meeting at the Dexter Avenue Baptist Church where they formally approved a continuing boycott until the city's buses abandoned their segregated seating arrangement. They formed the Montgomery Improvement Association (MIA) to coordinate the campaign and selected the recently arrived, young and articulate minister of the Dexter congregation, the Reverend Martin Luther King, Jr. [*q.v.*] to head the association.

Throughout the next year Montgomery's black population preserved a high level of unity and the boycott remained solid in the face of mounting opposition from the city's white citizens. In January King's home was dynamited, and the following month, he and 100 other leaders were indicted on charges of conspiracy to conduct an illegal boycott. His conviction only heightened the determination of the boycotters. Neither did economic reprisals against black workers nor mounting harassment by the police weaken their resolve. Financial support for the MIA poured in from around the country, including large donations from the NAACP and the United Auto Workers. Meanwhile, a legal challenge to Montgomery's bus segregation statute was wending its way through the courts. On Nov. 13 the Supreme Court ruled the law unconstitutional. When the court order abolishing segregation reached city officials on Dec. 20, the boycott ended in victory for Montgomery's blacks.

The Montgomery boycott had a major impact on the course of the civil rights movement for a number of reasons. It marked the first successful instance of direct mass action by Southern blacks and raised up a major new leader in Martin Luther King, who received worldwide recognition for his role in the boycott. Montgomery also witnessed the emergence of Gandhian nonviolence as an ideological underpinning of the movement. And it produced a whole new breed of civil rights leaders—Southern black ministers who were indigenous to the region and whose occupation gave them both influence among the black population and independence from the reprisals of the white business community. Clergy filled the frontlines of the movement. In January 1957 King and a number of other black ministers convened in Atlanta and out of that meeting eventually emerged the Southern Christian Leadership Conference (SCLC). With King as its head, the SCLC began holding nonviolent training institutes and recruited a growing legion of ministers to civil rights activism. Slowly the groundwork was being laid for the movement's explosive expansion in the 1960s.

The events of the mid 1950s—the *Brown* decision, the Montgomery bus boycott, the massive resistance movement—also began gradually cial equality. In his 1956 State of the Union address, Eisenhower made his first request for civil rights legislation, recommending the creation of a bipartisan commission to look into the denial of the franchise on the basis of race. In August 1957 Congress completed action on a civil rights measure. The law established a federal civil rights commission and authorized the creation of a civil rights division in the Justice Department with the power to investigate violations of black voting rights. Although Eisenhower's preference for state over federal action made him reluctant to use the law aggressively, the act did represent something of a breakthrough. It was the first piece of civil rights legislation enacted by Congress since Reconstruction. In the spring of 1960 Congress passed additional legislation to close some of the loopholes in the 1957 Civil Rights Act, and that summer both the Democrats and the Republicans included strong civil rights planks in their national platforms.

The event that ignited the discontent of Southern blacks and that initiated the critical phase of the civil rights struggle came on Feb. 1, 1960 in Greensboro, N.C. Four black students from North Carolina Agricultural and Technical College entered the local Woolworth store, sat at the lunch counter that was restricted to whites, and asked for service. Despite abuse from white customers and store employees, they maintained a quiet dignity and stayed until closing time. The next day and for several days thereafter, they returned with other black students and organized shifts at the lunch counter. By the second week sit-ins had spread to six other towns in North Carolina and by the end of February to four other states. Throughout the spring and summer black college students in every Southern state conducted protests against segregation in public facilities. Their targets grew to include hotels, parks, theaters, libraries, swimming pools and beaches. By the end of the year, an estimated 70,000 blacks had participated in nonviolent direct action protests in over 100 Southern cities. Over 3,600 arrests occurred, but the actions led to the desegregation of lunch counters and other public facilities in many parts of the South. More importantly, the sit-ins convinced large numbers of people that nonviolent direct action was the quickest, most effective way to achieve desegregation.

The student sit-ins of 1960 caught most civil rights leaders and organizations by surprise. The NAACP was initially skeptical of their value, preferring to remain with its time-tested strategy of litigation. But Martin Luther King and the SCLC recognized the depth of passion that the protests stirred in Southern blacks and sought to give organizational expression to the enthusiasm of idealistic young students. In April 1960 the SCLC sponsored a conference in Raleigh, N.C. of student leaders that led eventually to the formation of the Student Non-violent Coordinating Committee (SNCC). Over the next few years SNCC grew rapidly and mobilized thousands of black college students to become involved in the civil rights movement in the South. It also prodded growing numbers of white students in the North into activism. The Northern Student Movement provided substantial financial assistance to SNCC, and its members conducted boycotts in the North that pressured chain stores like Woolworth to desegregate their Southern branches.

The sit-ins of 1960 had a profound impact on CORE. The organization, committed to non-violent direct action, had remained a small, little known organization throughout the 1950s. But when the student sit-ins stimulated an interest in direct action tactics, CORE became the organization to which nonstudents, black and white, turned. Almost overnight it became known as *the* militant, activist organization in the civil rights movement. Its national staff grew from seven in 1959 to 137 in 1964; its budget skyrocketed from $144,000 in 1959–60 to over $600,000 in 1961–62.

In February 1961 James Farmer [*q.v.*] was named national director of CORE. One of the organization's founders in 1942, the pacifist Farmer had worked for the NAACP and the United Auto Workers during the 1950s. In his first major decision as head of CORE, Farmer planned a campaign to test the Supreme Court's *Boynton* decision of December 1960 which ruled unconstitutional the segregation of bus and railway terminals. The Freedom Rides, as they were called, began on May 4, when a group of seven blacks and six whites embarked on a bus trip that would take them through the Deep South. Initially uneventful, the first Freedom Ride provoked violence on

May 14 when a white mob in Anniston, Ala., armed with iron bars, attacked the bus and set it aflame. Escorted by police to Birmingham, the riders decided to end their journey and flew to New Orleans. But student leaders from Nashville vowed to continue the ride and on May 20 a new contingent set out from Birmingham to Montgomery. Again, violence ensued, and when an angry mob of whites surrounded the church in Montgomery where Martin Luther King was leading a mass meeting, President John F. Kennedy dispatched federal marshals to the city. When the attorney general, Robert F. Kennedy, urged a "cooling off" period upon civil rights leaders, Farmer curtly replied, "We have been cooling off for one hundred years. If we get any cooler, we'll be in a deep freeze." Instead of suspending the rides all of the major civil rights organizations cooperated in an effort to coordinate them. Throughout the summer Freedom Riders poured into the Deep South, and hundreds were arrested.

The tempo of civil rights activity rose steadily during 1962. CORE launched a Freedom Highways campaign whose goal was to desegregate motels and restaurants along major roads in the South. King and the SCLC mounted a major desegregation drive in Albany, Ga. that lasted for over a year and resulted in thousands of arrests. In January 1962 a coalition of civil rights organizations announced the formation of the Voter Education Project (VEP). Supported by funds from private foundations, the VEP represented an ambitious and daring attempt to win the vote for blacks, especially in the Deep South where black registration was minimal. Over the following two years civil rights workers fanned out into small Southern towns where they engaged in door-to-door organizing and opened schools that taught basic civics and rudimentary politics to disenfranchised blacks. In the North, meanwhile, support for the Southern civil rights struggle grew rapidly. Financial contributions from sympathizers swelled the coffers of civil rights organizations while Northern students, and liberal whites organized boycotts and other forms of protest.

The nonviolent direct action strategy of the civil rights movement reached its culmination in Birmingham, Ala. in the spring of 1963. King and the Rev. Fred Shuttlesworth [q.v.], the founder of the Alabama Christian Movement for Human Rights, planned a major desegregation effort that was scheduled to begin on April 3. Called the "Johannesburg of America" by some blacks, Birmingham offered the movement its toughest challenge. The city's commissioner of public safety, Eugene "Bull" Connor [q.v.], was widely known for his tough law enforcement stance, and many blacks in Birmingham lived in terror of police brutality. The effort proceeded peacefully at first, as Connor exercised relative restraint in having the police arrest demonstrators. On May 2, however, King initiated a new phase of the campaign when elementary school children began marching. Over 900 were arrested. The next day, when the march resumed, the police responded by savagely attacking the young children with high pressure fire hoses and snarling police dogs. Similar police actions continued for several days as an outraged nation witnessed the brutality on television and through newspaper photographs. The Birmingham police riots elicited an unprecedented level of public support for the civil rights movement.

The events in Birmingham also proved a turning point for the civil rights policies of the Kennedy Administration. Black leaders had, at first, taken heart from the election of John F. Kennedy in 1960. The young liberal Senator from Massachusetts had spoken forcefully in favor of civil rights during his presidential campaign. Criticizing the record of the Eisenhower Administration, Kennedy declared that the President possessed the power to end discrimination in housing with "a stroke of the pen," implying that, if elected, he would issue such an executive order. He also led civil rights advocates to believe that legislation to guarantee the constitutional rights of black citizens would be a high priority in his Administration. In March 1961 the President did establish by executive order an Equal Employment Opportunity Commitee with the power to initiate investigations into job discrimination on the basis of race. He appointed a record number of blacks to important federal posts and under the direction of his brother, Robert Kennedy, the Justice Department made frequent use of the 1957 Civil Rights Act in support of black voting rights. The President also gave much rhetorical support to the movement.

But Kennedy's victory in 1960 was a narrow one and he was reluctant to antagonize Southern Democrats whose loyalty was critical to the passage of the Administration's legislative program. Throughout 1961 and 1962 civil rights forces waited impatiently for the Administration to introduce appropriate legislation, but none was forthcoming. It was not until November 1962 that the President issued an executive order banning discrimination in federally constructed and federally financed housing.

Civil rights leaders were most critical, however, of what they said was the Administration's failure to guarantee the safety of activists in the South where incidents of violence from the police and from private citizens were frequent and brutal. The Administration did dispatch federal marshals to Alabama during the violence that accompanied the Freedom Rides. It also called out the National Guard in the fall of 1962 after bloody riots left two dead and scores injured when James Meredith [q.v.] attempted to enroll in the all-white University of Mississippi. To growing numbers of civil rights advocates, federal action in these cases was too little and came too late. Many argued that the Kennedy Administration seemed more concerned with civil order than with civil rights. In March 1963, on the eve of the Birmingham campaign, Martin Luther King wrote an article appearing in the *Nation* that characterized the President's program for civil rights as "tokenism."

After the events in Birmingham President Kennedy committed the prestige of his Administration to the cause of racial justice. On June

11 he addressed the nation in the strongest terms ever used by a President on behalf of civil rights. Eight days later he sent a civil rights message to Congress in which he asked for passage of a comprehensive civil rights bill and urged Congress to stay in session until it approved the measure. Throughout the summer protests continued. The Justice Department reported that between May 20 and August 8 there were 978 civil rights demonstrations in 209 cities. A Harris poll in July indicated that almost 40% of American blacks had participated in at least one civil rights demonstration. On Aug. 28 over 250,000 blacks and whites assembled in the nation's capital in a massive, peaceful display of support for the pending legislation. It was the largest demonstration in the nation's history. As the autumn wore on, it became apparent that, despite the intransigence of Southern senators and representatives, the civil rights forces in Congress were gaining strength. Then, on Nov. 22, the nation was stunned by the assassination of President Kennedy in Dallas.

Five days later the new President, Lyndon Baines Johnson, addressed a joint session of Congress. He urged upon the legislators "the earliest possible passage" of the civil rights bill as the most fitting memorial to the slain President. Johnson made civil rights his top priority during his first year in office. Throughout the winter and spring he applied unrelenting pressure upon members of Congress. After seven months of debate, the introduction of hundreds of obstructionist amendments, and a filibuster by Southern senators, the Senate on June 10 shut off debate by invoking cloture, the first action of its kind on a civil rights measure. On June 19 it approved the comprehensive bill. House approval followed, and on July 2, President Johnson signed the historic legislation. The Civil Rights Act of 1964 prohibited racial discrimination in public accommodation, required equal access to public facilities, and authorized the federal government to withhold government funds from public institutions such as hospitals and schools that showed evidence of discrimination. Civil rights forces were ecstatic.

It remained, of course, for the law to be translated into social reality, but during the fall there was a lull in civil rights protest. Activists feared the possibility of a backlash in support of Barry Goldwater, the conservative Republican Senator from Arizona who was opposing Johnson in the 1964 presidential election. After Johnson's landslide victory, however, the movement prepared itself for renewed campaigns. Under King's leadership the SCLC mounted a major voter registration drive in Selma, Ala., to dramatize the continued disenfranchisement of blacks in the Deep South. On March 7, 1965 King and his supporters set out from the Selma courthouse on a 50 mile trek to the state capital of Montgomery. In what appeared to many as a replay of Birmingham, the local police and state troopers violently assaulted the defenseless marchers. Sympathizers poured in to Selma from around the country and on March 21, King renewed the march under federal protection. Of equal significance President Johnson addressed Congress on March 15 and called for the enactment of a tough bill to protect and guarantee the right of blacks to vote in the South. On Aug. 6, the Voting Rights Act of 1965 became law. It authorized federal officials to enter the South and to register qualified black voters.

The Civil Rights Act and the Voting Rights Act were the crowning achievements of the civil rights movement. Together the two laws sounded the death knell for the Jim Crow system of segregation and legally enforced racial discrimination that had governed Southern society since the turn of the century. Over the next few years the last remaining bastions of segregation fell rapidly and the number of black voters climbed sharply. The civil rights struggle had indeed accomplished a revolution in race relations in the South.

Five days after the Voting Rights Act became law, however, rioting erupted in the black ghetto of Los Angeles known as Watts. The disorders lasted for four days and resulted in 34 deaths, over a thousand injuries and four thousand arrests, and property damage estimated at more than $40 million. Succeeding summers witnessed further outbreaks of violence in the ghettoes of Northern cities, culminating in the major riots in Detroit and Newark in July 1967. The spreading urban violence marked a turning point in the crusade for racial justice. Almost at the moment of its greatest success, the movement found itself splintering in different directions. Civil rights, nonviolence and integration seemed to give way to calls for liberation, armed struggle and black nationalism and separatism.

Signs of trouble had begun to appear at least a year before the Watts riot. SNCC members, in particular, were becoming more militant and were increasingly questioning the integrationist nonviolent emphases of the civil rights movement. The young, idealistic students in SNCC, most of them from middle-class urban families, were jolted by their encounter with rural life in the Deep South. As they conducted voter registration drives and other organizing campaigns, they came face to face with the poverty and powerlessness of blacks in small Southern towns. They confronted at first hand the brutality and violence of Southern white racism.

Mississippi provided fertile soil for the growth of black militance. The poorest state in the nation, with the largest percentage of blacks in proportion to total population, it offered the strongest resistance to desegregation. Two years of sustained effort by civil rights workers netted fewer than 4,000 registered black voters. In 1963 civil rights organizations in the state banded together to form the Council of Federated Organizations (COFO), selecting Aaron Henry [q.v.] of the NAACP as president and Robert Moses [q.v.] of SNCC as director. In order to focus national attention on Mississippi, COFO planned the "Freedom Summer" of 1964. Volunteers, black and white, arrived in Mississippi from around the country for a determined assault against black disenfranchisement. It was a summer of sustained violence. On June 21 three civil rights workers disappeared; their bodies were found six weeks later. From mid-June to mid-September, white Mississippians perpetrated at least 80 serious assaults and 35 shootings. Thirty-five black churches were burned and 30 homes bombed.

As part of its voter registration drive, COFO leaders formed the Mississippi Freedom Democratic Party (MFDP). MFDP sent its own delegation to the Democratic Party's national convention in Atlantic City in August 1964. It demanded that it be seated as the official delegation from Mississippi in place of the regular Democrats whose selection occurred without the participation of blacks. When liberal party leaders offered as a compromise to seat two MFDP delegates, the group rejected the proposal, staged a demonstration on the convention floor, and then walked Out. The incident reverberated throughout the civil rights movement. Militants in SNCC and CORE felt betrayed by moderates like King and Roy Wilkins [q.v.] of the NAACP who urged acceptance of the compromise. They also interpreted the proposal as a sign of a wavering commitment on the part of white liberals who seemed to prefer party unity to racial justice.

Thus, the ghetto riots that began with Watts occurred at a time of growing disillusionment within the militant wing of the civil rights movement. To the young radicals the riots demonstrated that civil rights were not the answer. Equality under the law did not address the needs of Northern blacks for better jobs, decent housing and adequate educational opportunities. Nor did it meet the problem of de facto segregation. Racial separatism and black nationalism took hold within some parts of the movement. In May 1966 SNCC chose Stokely Carmichael [q.v.] asits new head and whites were asked to leave the organization. Soon thereafter Carmichael raised the cry of "black power." CORE, too, moved away from its commitment to nonviolence and integration and veered sharply in the direction of black nationalism and racial separatism. In California the Black Panther Party, under the leadership of Huey Newton [q.v.] and Bobby Seale [q.v.] captured headlines with its brandishing of weapons in the state legislature. The Panthers spread rapidly to other cities.

On March 2, 1968 the National Advisory Commission on Civil Disorders, appointed by President Johnson the previous year to investigate the causes of the ghetto riots, released its final report. Its conclusions made dismal reading. The Commission found that the nation was "moving toward two separate societies, one black, one white— separate and unequal." The report declared that "white racism is essentially responsible for the explosive mixture which has been accumulating in our cities." A solution, it concluded, would require "a commitment to national action—compassionate, massive and sustained, backed by the resources of the most powerful and richest nation on this earth."

Unfortunately, that commitment was not to materialize. On April 4, the country was struck by another tragedy when the Rev. Martin Luther King was assassinated in Memphis by James Earl Ray [*q.v.*]. King was the nation's most respected civil rights leader, the man most able to bring white and black together. His political philosophy and strategy had developed considerably in the last two years of his life as he focused less and less on the single issue of civil rights. During 1966 he came north and led a series of major demonstrations in Chicago for jobs and housing for the city's blacks. In 1967 he spoke out against the Vietnam War and led a major antiwar march in New York in April. Late in 1967 he began laying plans for a Poor People's March on Washington that would unite people of every race in a demand for economic justice. At the time of his death, King was in Memphis to support a strike of the city's mostly black sanitation-men.

King's assassination led to the worst outbreak of urban violence. In the weeks that followed, blacks rioted in over 100 cities; over 50,000 troops were mobilized to restore order. The renewed violence, in its turn, further alienated the white majority and deepened the backlash against the civil rights movement. The most impressive evidence of the backlash came in the 1968 presidential election. Alabama's former governor, George Wallace [*q.v.*], a symbol of Southern resistance to integration, captured 13.5% of the vote in a third party candidacy. And Republican Richard Nixon, whose commitment to civil rights was, at best, tenuous, won a narrow victory over Hubert Humphrey.

Civil rights forces and their liberal allies were clearly on the defensive during the Nixon presidency. The Administration's Southern strategy, designed to entice the South into the Republican Party, dictated a reversal of the pro-civil rights policies of the Kennedy and Johnson years. Daniel Patrick Moynihan, a close adviser to the President, penned a confidential memo in February 1970 in which he urged a policy of "benign neglect" to deal with the problem of racial inequality. The Nixon Administration tried to dismantle the Equal Employment Opportunity Commission and to weaken the 1965 Voting Rights Act. Congressional liberals had to fight hard merely to preserve the gains of the 1960s. When white opposition to court-ordered busing of school children to achieve integration grew during the early 1970s, Nixon lent his prestige to the anti-busing movement. George Wallace's strong showing in the 1972 Democratic primaries demonstrated again the depth of white dissatisfaction.

The nation's economic woes also retarded the quest for racial equality. The recession of 1970–71 and the more serious downturn of 1974–75 saw black unemployment rise sharply. By 1976 estimates of unemployment among black youth in Northern cities ran as high as 60%. The fiscal crisis that hit New York and other cities after 1975 also led to sharp cutbacks in social welfare programs that hurt blacks badly. Glaring inequality in jobs, housing and education pervaded the black population in the North and the South. In the midst of this, civil rights forces were in disarray. SNCC had disappeared from the scene, while CORE and the SCLC were racked by internal factionalism that seriously weakened both organizations. Even the venerable NAACP saw its membership and contributions drop noticeably during the 1970s.

Thus the 1970s revealed how intractable racial inequality was in America. Despite the passage of sweeping civil rights legislation and new social welfare programs in the 1960s to ameliorate poverty, much remained to be done. In the North most black Americans remained trapped in urban slums with poor educational facilities and even less satisfying job opportunities. Black income in the late 1970s was still less than 60% of the income level of whites. Increasingly the problem of racial injustice was moving from one of civil rights to a question of economic inequality. Without a renewed and massive government effort to upgrade the quality of housing and schools, to provide extensive job training, and to guarantee full employment, it appeared likely that blacks would continue to bear a disproportionate share of the burden of economic inequality.

Despite this sobering assessment, however, one should not underestimate the achievement of the civil rights movement. It truly wrought a revolution in Southern race relations. Jim Crow in the South was finally dead. Blacks enjoyed equal access to public facilities. They were actively involved in Southern politics, electing hundreds of black officials to public office, from sheriffs and school board members to mayors and congressional representatives. Employment opportunities in the South expanded considerably as jobs from which they were previously excluded, especially in manufacturing and in government service, were made available. The civil rights movement created a strong sense of racial pride in millions of American blacks and it pushed the question of racial justice to center stage of American politics. Although much remained to be done in order to reach the elusive goal of racial equality, one can hardly deny the enormity of what had already been accomplished.

Profiles

ABERNATHY, RALPH D(AVID)
b. March 11, 1926; Linden, Ala.
Financial Secretary-Treasurer, Southern Christian Leadership Conference, 1957-65; Vice-President, 1965-68; President, 1968-

Born on his parents' 500-acre farm in Marengo Co., Ala., Ralph Abernathy was the 10th of 12 children. He received a B.S. from Alabama State College in 1950 and an M.A. in sociology from Atlanta University in 1951. Ordained a Baptist minister in 1948, Abernathy became pastor of the First Baptist Church in Montgomery, Ala. in 1951.

Active in civic affairs and a member of the NAACP, Abernathy readily agreed to help organize a boycott of Montgomery's racially segregated bus system following the arrest of Rosa Parks [q.v.], a black seamstress, on Dec. 1, 1955 for violation of the city's bus segregation ordinance. Abernathy helped contact other black ministers, set up planning meetings and prepared for the boycott, which began on Dec. 5. He urged the formation of a permanent organization to manage the protest and suggested the name Montgomery Improvement Association (MIA) for the body, which was established on the first day of the boycott. Martin Luther King, Jr. [q.v.], a young Baptist minister relatively new to Montgomery, was chosen to lead the MIA. Abernathy was named to the executive board and the program committee.

Abernathy and King had already become close friends by the time the Montgomery boycott started. "From the beginning of the protest," King later declared, "[Abernathy] was my closest associate and most trusted friend. We prayed together and made important decisions together. His ready good humor lightened many tense moments." A member of the MIA's negotiating committee, Abernathy rose to King's defense at a meeting with city and bus company officials in mid-December, when several of the whites present challenged King's leadership position. He took charge of much MIA business when King was out of town, was a close adviser to King throughout the 381-day boycott and organized regular mass meetings of Montgomery's blacks.

On Nov. 13, 1956 the Supreme Court ruled that bus segregation in Montgomery was unconstitutional. Abernathy then helped organize a program of mass training in nonviolent techniques to prepare the black community for integration. On Dec. 21, 1956, the day after the Supreme Court's desegregation order arrived in Montgomery, Abernathy and King rode on an integrated bus. A month of retaliatory violence by whites followed. In the early hours of Jan. 10, 1957, while King and Abernathy were in Atlanta for a meeting, Abernathy's home and church, along with three other black churches and the home of another minister, were bombed.

The historic Montgomery boycott marked the beginning of an era of nonviolent direct action by Southern blacks against racial segregation and discrimination. It also inaugurated a partnership between King and Abernathy. Early in 1957 the two helped found the Southern Christian Leadership Conference (SCLC). Abernathy was appointed financial secretary-treasurer, while

King was named president. Under the auspices of the SCLC, the two ministers preached a philosophy of nonviolent resistance to Jim Crow practices and began organizing nonviolent training institutes and voter registration drives among Southern blacks. The burly Abernathy was regarded as less intellectual than King and as having more of a common touch in his preaching and speaking, but the two became alter egos. Beginning with Montgomery, King consulted Abernathy before making any important decision. In 1961, at King's urging, Abernathy moved to Atlanta in order to be closer to King, who had moved there the year before, and to the SCLC's Atlanta headquarters.

During the 1961 Freedom Rides, Abernathy, then still in Montgomery, opened his church to the interstate riders and was arrested on May 25 when he accompanied other ministers in a protest at Montgomery's segregated bus terminal. In December 1961 Abernathy joined King in aiding a desegregation campaign in Albany, Ga. The two were arrested for leading a march there in December, found guilty of the charges stemming from that arrest in February 1962 and began serving their 45-day jail sentence together in July. They were soon released from jail when someone anonymously paid their fines. At Abernathy's urging the SCLC stepped up demonstrations in Albany, and he and King were again arrested. Both were given suspended sentences, and the Albany campaign ended inconclusively soon after.

The SCLC decided to mount a major desegregation drive in Birmingham, Ala., in 1963. With King and SCLC Executive Director Wyatt Tee Walker [q.v.], Abernathy went to Birmingham in January 1963 to plan the demonstrations and to build support for the protest among local black leaders. The massive campaign began on April 3 and on April 12, Good Friday, King, Abernathy and the Rev. Fred Shuttlesworth [q.v.], the key local leader of the protest, headed a march to city hall in defiance of a court injunction prohibiting further demonstrations. They were arrested and King and Abernathy remained in jail until April 20. Abernathy participated in negotiations

with the city's white leadership early in May; on May 10 he joined King and Shuttlesworth in announcing that an agreement had been reached ending the dramatic Birmingham campaign. Abernathy then aided a desegregation effort in Danville, Va., in the summer of 1963. After a bomb exploded at a black church in Birmingham on Sept. 15, 1963, killing four young black girls, Abernathy was one of seven black leaders who met with President Kennedy on Sept. 19 to discuss the Birmingham situation.

Beginning in March 1964 the SCLC supported a desegregation effort by the black community in St. Augustine, Fla. Abernathy was arrested on June 11 with King and 16 other protesters when the group demanded service at a segregated motel restaurant in the city. Abernathy accompanied King on a speaking tour of Europe in the fall of 1964 and returned with him in December when King was awarded the Nobel Peace Prize in Oslo, Norway.

On their return home SCLC launched a campaign focused on Selma, Ala., to secure voting rights for blacks. Abernathy joined many of the almost daily marches in Selma in January and February 1965 and was arrested with King on Feb. 1 when they led a march to the county courthouse. He helped organize and was a participant in the famous march from Selma to Montgomery which began on March 21.

In June 1967 the Supreme Court upheld the contempt of court convictions of King, Abernathy and six other ministers resulting from the 1963 Birmingham demonstrations. While serving their five-day prison terms beginning on Oct. 30, King discussed with Abernathy and other aides a plan to bring an interracial coalition of the poor to Washington to pressure the federal government into enacting far-reaching antipoverty legislation. Abernathy helped plan this Poor People's Campaign over the next few months. In the meantime King gave his support to a strike by the virtually all-black sanitationmen's union in Memphis in March 1968. On April 4 King and Abernathy were in Memphis planning a march with other SCLC officials when King was shot in the head by a sniper while standing on the balcony of his motel room.

The day after King's assassination Abernathy was named his successor as president of the SCLC. He announced that the organization's first task would be to carry out the march King had planned in support of the Memphis sanitationmen. A giant march was held on April 8, and the strike was settled eight days later.

Promising that the SCLC would be "more militant than ever" while continuing to use nonviolent methods, Abernathy also went forward with the Poor People's Campaign planned by King. For three days beginning April 29, Abernathy led an interracial "delegation of 100" in conferences with congressional leaders and cabinet members in Washington to present the grievances and demands of the poor. The first group of nine caravans of poor people arrived in Washington on May 13 and began setting up an encampment called "Resurrection City" in Potomac Park near the Lincoln Memorial. Over the next month groups of poor persons attended sessions of Congress and committee hearings and demonstrated outside the headquarters of various government departments and agencies.

The campaign showed signs of insufficient organization and disunity among staff leaders, and Resurrection City, which held 2,500 people at its peak, was plagued by inadequate facilities and some incidents of violence and crime. A Solidarity Day march on June 19 brought 50,000 supporters of the campaign to Washington. On June 23 the Interior Department refused to extend the permit for Resurrection City, and the next day the Washington police closed the encampment. Abernathy was arrested the same day while leading a demonstration on the Capitol grounds, and he remained in jail until July 13.

The Poor People's Campaign did secure an expanded food distribution program, changes in welfare eligibility requirements and new provisions for participation of the poor in local operations of several government agencies. But the campaign, as Abernathy admitted, had failed in its major goal of getting Congress "to move meaningfully against the problem of poverty" by adopting legislation for jobs, low income housing and a guaranteed annual income for the unemployed. Abernathy announced the end of the Washington phase of the campaign on July 16. In August he opened a new phase, leading demonstrations by poor people at the Republican National Convention in Miami Beach and the Democratic National Convention in Chicago.

Under Abernathy's leadership, the SCLC concentrated on broad social and economic issues other than civil rights. Still firmly committed to nonviolence, Abernathy was especially concerned with forging a coalition of all the disaffected groups rising to speak out. He regularly appeared at anti-war rallies, endorsed the grape pickers boycott sponsored by Casar Chavez [q.v.] and the United Farm Workers (UFW) and participated in a weeklong UFW march through California in May 1969. The defense efforts of anti-war activists in the Chicago and Harrisburg conspiracy trials also received his support.

Targeting unemployment and poverty as the major civil rights issues, Abernathy took a leading role in the 1969 strike of hospital workers in Charleston, S.C. The strike began on March 20 after 12 union organizers were fired from their jobs. After a court injunction was issued against picketing, Abernathy led daily marches through the city, resulting in several hundred arrests. The strikers' demands for union recognition and a living wage were endorsed by major civil rights spokesmen, liberal senators and representatives, and union leaders. The demonstrations continued into June, when Abernathy was indicted on charges of inciting to riot after some protesters had damaged property. The strike was settled, however, on June 27 when the hospitals agreed to rehire all of the workers dismissed earlier and to recognize the union.

Abernathy, meanwhile, was organizing a second Poor People's Campaign, which began on May 12. Throughout the spring and summer, delegations of poor people from all races met with congressional officials, held small demonstrations in Washington and lobbied intensively for social and economic welfare legislation. Their demands included jobs for all, a guaranteed annual income, a comprehensive health care program, quality education for all children and a shift from defense expenditures to government spending on basic human needs.

In 1969 SCLC sponsored an intensive voter registration drive in Greene County, Ala., that resulted in the election of six blacks to local office and a black majority on the school board. It initiated demonstrations in Chicago during the summer of 1969 to protest the discriminatory hiring policies of the city's construction unions. In May 1970, after police in Augusta, Ga., killed five young blacks during a protest march, Abernathy led 10,000 people on a 100-mile march to protest police violence against blacks. He supported the efforts of welfare recipients in Nevada to have arbitrary welfare cuts rescinded, and in April 1971 he was arrested in New York City during a demonstration against A & P hiring practices.

Abernathy found himself increasingly at odds with the Nixon Administration. In January 1969 he and several other black leaders met with the President, who promised to do "more for the underprivileged and more for the Negro" than any other President. Four months later Abernathy met with Nixon again and later told the press that it was "the most disappointing and most fruitless of all the meetings we have had up to this time." He opposed the Administration's proposed relaxation of school desegregation guidelines, the nominations of Clement Haynsworth [q.v.] and G. Harrold Carswell [q.v.] to the Supreme Court and the White House attempt to weaken the 1965 Voting Rights Act. By the summer of 1970 Abernathy was so disillusioned with Nixon's policies that he termed the Administration "a repressive, anti-black, anti-poor, anti-youth national government" under "fascist domination."

With other militant civil rights leaders and anti-war activists, Abernathy helped form the People's Coalition for Peace and Justice. In April and May 1971, the Coalition sponsored a series of daily demonstrations against the war, poverty, and government repression. On April 29 Abernathy conducted a "teach-in" at HEW and led a mule train from the Department's offices to the White House. The following day he read a "poor people's bill of particulars" against the Justice Department. The police began making mass arrests a few days later and held over 7,000 demonstrators in make-shift jails. The arrests and convictions were later overturned because of widespread violations of constitutional rights.

Despite Abernathy's energetic leadership, the SCLC was plagued by internal difficulties during the 1970s. In December 1971, its board of directors suspended the Rev. Jesse Jackson [q.v.], head of SCLC's Operation "Breadbasket," in a dispute over the use of funds. Jackson responded by resigning, announced the formation of his own organization, Operation PUSH (People United to Save Humanity), and took most of SCLC's Chicago chapter with him. The following year SCLC fired 21 workers at its national headquarters in Atlanta due to budget difficulties. Although in the late 1960s the SCLC had easily raised over $2 million a year, by 1973 income had fallen to half a million dollars. On July 9, 1973 Abernathy announced his resignation as the organization's president. He blamed SCLC's problems on middle-class blacks who "feel they have 'arrived' simply because they now occupy high positions, but will not support SCLC financially." When the board of directors rejected his resignation Abernathy agreed to stay on. By the mid 1970s, however, SCLC was only a shadow of its former self and had ceased to play a leading role in the struggle for racial justice.

In 1977 Abernathy ran unsuccessfully to fill the Georgia congressional seat vacated when President Carter appointed Representative Andrew Young [q.v.] as U.S. ambassador to the United Nations. He continued to serve as SCLC president.

ALEXANDER, CLIFFORD L.
b. Sept. 21, 1933; New York, N.Y.
Chairman, Equal Employment Opportunities Commission, June 1967-April 1969.

After graduating from Harvard in 1955 and from Yale Law School in 1958, Alexander served as assistant district attorney for New York County. He then entered private law practice in New York City. Alexander served in several antipoverty programs, including Haryou, Inc., where he was executive and program director from 1962 to 1963. At the request of McGeorge Bundy, Alexander joined the staff of the National Security Council in 1963. From 1964 to 1967 he successively held posts as deputy special assistant, associate special counsel and deputy special counsel to the President, serving as an adviser to Johnson on various domestic problems, including civil rights.

On June 27, 1967 Alexander was named chairman of the Equal Employment Opportunities Commission (EEOC), the agency established by the 1964 Civil Rights Act to help end job discrimination by unions and industry. With Senate confirmation of his appointment on Aug. 2, Alexander became the first black to head the Commission. Because the agency lacked the power to force industries to end discrimination and could use only conciliation to settle disputes, Alexander relied on publicity and pressure to prompt businesses to hire minorities. In two October 1967 studies, for example, the Commission reported the existence of widespread discrimination against blacks in the nation's drug industry and in white-collar jobs. During January 1968 Alexander held four days of hearings documenting discrimination in New York City's white-collar occupations, particularly in the financial and communications industries. At the conclusion of the investigation, he charged: "If future intentions were gauged by the past standard of performance, it would mean that Negroes and Puerto Ricans would probably be waiting until the year 2164 for a democracy to say what he or she shall have."

Alexander's efforts led to criticism from business and congressional leaders. In March 1969 Sen. Everett M. Dirksen (R, Ill.) threatened to "get somebody fired" if the Commission did not stop "punitive harassment" of businessmen. On April 9 Alexander resigned as chairman of the EEOC because of what he termed "a crippling lack of [Nixon] Administration support." However, he remained a member of the Commission. Two weeks later Jerris Leonard, head of the Justice Department civil rights division, charged that the Commission had been ineffective under Alexander, and without naming him directly, called for his resignation as a member of the agency. Alexander remained on the panel until Aug. 8, when he resigned to become a partner in the Washington, D.C. law firm of Arnold & Porter. In September 1974 he made an unsuccessful attempt to win the Democratic mayoral nomination in Washington.

ALMOND, J(AMES) LINDSAY, JR.
b. June 15, 1898; Charlottesville, Va.
Governor, Va., 1958-62.

After earning his LL.B. at the University of Virginia in 1923, J. Lindsay Almond practiced law in Roanoke for the next nine years. In 1932 he was elected judge of Roanoke's Hustings Court and served until 1945. He then successfully ran as a Democrat to fill a House seat vacated by the resignation of Clifton A. Woodrum (D, Va.). Reelected to a full term in 1946, Almond compiled a generally conservative record, voting to extend the draft and override President Harry S. Truman's veto of the Taft-Hartley bill. He resigned from Congress in April 1948 to complete a term as state attorney general after the occupant died in office.

Almond campaigned for a four-year term as attorney general in 1949 on a platform supporting an amendment that would have repealed the poll tax and placed increased restrictions on the right to vote. Although the amendment was defeated, Almond won handily. As attorney general, he expected to be the Byrd organization candidate for governor, but in January 1953 he withdrew his name at Sen. Harry F. Byrd's (D. Va.) request. He was elected to a second term as attorney general in November.

During 1952 Almond pleaded the state's case in *Davis v. County School Board of Prince Edward County*. The suit had been brought by blacks demanding that the state law requiring segregated schools be struck down. Although privately conceding that blacks had received an inferior education in the state, Almond opposed demands for school integration and rejected the NAACP's contention that separate but equal facilities were inherently discriminatory. Instead, he supported a "separated equality" and recommended the use of funds to equalize black facilities. A three-member federal court upheld the constitutionality of the Virginia statute but ordered the unequal facilities remedied. The case was later taken to the Supreme Court, where it became one of several argued as *Brown v. Board of Education*. Almond helped present Virginia's case before the high tribunal. In May 1954 the Supreme Court unanimously declared segregated schools unconstitutional.

In the wake of the decision, Virginia Gov. Thomas B. Stanley appointed a commission, headed by Garland Gray, to seek means to preserve the status quo in Virginia's schools. The Gray Commission's November 1955 report recommended that local authorities be permitted to close public schools threatened with integration. The state would then pay tuition for private schooling. These recommendations were approved in a March 1956 referendum. Interpreting approval of local option as total support for segregation, Sen. Byrd called for "massive resistance" to the Supreme Court decision through a policy of interposition. The state would close schools threatened with integration regardless of local feeling. During the dispute over the *Brown* decision, Almond maintained a moderate stand, in April 1956 stating that interposition had no legal validity. While such prominent Southerners as Texas Gov. Alan Shivers were recommending a regional candidate for President in 1956 and the Byrd machine remained neutral, Al-

mond worked for the 1956 Democratic national ticket.

When Almond announced for governor in late 1956, Byrd concluded he could not stop the attorney general and so endorsed him. Running as the organization candidate, and recognizing a rightward drift in public sentiment, Almond campaigned on a massive resistance platform. Yet, he remained skeptical of that position and surprised segregationists in October 1957 by saying there would be a degree of forced integration under federal mandate. Despite the statement, Almond went on to win the governorship two-to-one over Republican Ted Dalton the following month.

In his inaugural address Almond gave unqualified support for opposition to the *Brown* decision. "Against massive attacks," he stated, "we must marshall massive resistance." He warned that "integration anywhere means destruction everywhere." Sensing rising segregationist sentiment, in April Almond sponsored legislation consolidating state control of pupil assignments and strengthening the governor's school closing authority. In September Almond closed nine schools that were under court order to integrate.

During the fall of 1958 moderate forces began demanding a change of position on school integration. In October the Virginia Parent-Teacher Association urged abandonment of interposition and adoption of local option. Shortly thereafter city newspapers began to withdraw support for massive resistance. By Dec. 29 leading industrialists were sufficiently alarmed by declining out-of-state investment to call on Almond and urge him to drop interposition. Attempting to stall until the direction of public opinion was clear, Almond refused to invoke laws that permitted him to reopen closed schools as segregated institutions. He also directed his attorney general to prepare a test case for the Virginia courts. According to historian Numan Bartley, Almond presumed that federal courts would strike down massive resistance and felt it would be better received if the decision came from a state court. On Jan. 19, 1959 both a federal district court and the Virginia Supreme Court of Appeals ruled closing schools and withholding state funds from integrated institutions unconstitutional.

While denouncing the decision, the Governor maneuvered Virginia toward compliance with the order. He called a special session of the legislature in January and cautiously sounded a retreat from massive resistance. Closed schools were reopened and three city systems began at least token desegregation. In the legislature Almond prevented a resurgence of extremist forces led by the Byrd organization. A report by the Perrow Commission, packed with Almond appointed moderates, recommended a 15-bill program to develop a policy of local option that held integration to token levels. In April the legislature enacted the measures dispite bitter opposition.

During the remaining years of his term, the breech between Almond and Byrd hardened, and the Governor purged Byrd supporters at every opportunity. Forbidden by law to succeed himself, Almond ran his own anti-organization candidate for governor in the July 1961 Democratic primary. His effort failed, and Byrd maintained control of the statehouse. In 1962 Almond was appointed a judge of the Federal Patents Court, where he served until his retirement in 1973.

For further information:
Numan Bartley, *The Rise of Massive Resistance* (Baton Rouge, 1969).

ASHMORE, HARRY S(COTT)
b. July 27, 1916; Greenville, S.C.
Executive Editor, *Arkansas Gazette*, 1948-59.

Harry Ashmore was the son of a Greenville merchant whose ancestors served in the Confederate Army. Ashmore became acquainted with the plight of the Southern black when, as a teenager, he worked on a cotton farm during the summer. In 1937 he graduated from Clemson Agricultural College and began a career in journalism, covering the local courthouse for the Green-ville *Piedmont*. In the late 1930s he toured poverty areas above the Mason-Dixon line to do a series on Northern "Tobacco Roads." Following service in the Army during World War II, Ashmore was named associate editor of the Charlotte, N.C., *News*. He wrote editorials advocating two-party politics in the South, racial and religious tolerance and the enfranchisement of blacks. The *Arkansas Gazette* hired Ashmore as editor in 1947. He became executive editor the following year.

In 1953 the Ford Foundation commissioned Ashmore to head a team of scholars studying biracial education in the U.S. The report, entitled *The Negro and the School* (1954), was published the day before the Supreme Court handed down its decision in *Brown v. Board of Education* outlawing segregation in public schools. The Ashmore study revealed that blacks in segregated schools were getting an inferior education; it also noted that a gap existed in the North between the quality of education blacks were getting compared to whites. The report cautioned that desegregation was an explosive issue because of Americans' intense interest in education. It pointed to community attitudes as the most important factor in integration but noted that gradual desegregation had often proved more volatile than immediate integration. The study was used by both integrationists and segregationists to support their positions.

In September 1957, when Arkansas Gov. Orval Faubus [*q.v.*] ordered National Guardsmen to Little Rock to prevent the integration of Central High School, Ashmore endorsed President Eisenhower's use of federal troops to ensure desegregation. In an editorial he wrote, "We are going to have to decide what kind of people we are—whether we obey the law only when we approve of it, or whether we obey it no matter how distasteful we find it." By mid-October Ashmore had written more than 40 pro-integration editorials and appeared on television and radio pleading for compliance. Faubus denounced him as an "ardent integrationist" while the White Citizens' Councils branded him "Public Enemy No. 1." In December 1957 segregationists attempted a boycott of *Gazette* advertisers to induce a change in the paper's editorial policies. Its circulation did drop for a short time, but throughout the incident Hugh B. Patterson, Jr., the paper's publisher, backed Ashmore. In May 1958 Ashmore received the Pulitzer Prize for editorial writing. The *Gazette* also received a Prize for carrying his work.

Ashmore's book, *An Epitaph for Dixie* (1958), appeared following the Little Rock crisis. As the title indicated, he argued that the old South was dying. He predicted that its reliance on agriculture, its one-party political system and its racial policies would crumble in the face of the demands of a growing, Northern-oriented, industrialized society. Ashmore observed that a developing industrial elite would replace the old agrarian-based Southern high society. These new leaders, anxious for immediate economic growth, would realize that a prosperous black citizenry was essential for Southern prosperity and therefore would accept integration. Segregation, with all its political, social and economic consequences, must end so that blacks could be integrated into the new system. Ashmore also predicted that, in the future, blacks would be more aggressive in demanding their rights.

From 1955 to 1956 Ashmore took a leave of absence to work in Adlai Stevenson's presidential campaign. In September 1959 he left the *Gazette* to become a director of the Center for the Study of Democratic Institutions. At the Center he concentrated his attention on race relations and the press, defending the growing militancy of the civil rights movement in the mid-1960s. He was also a prominent critic of the Johnson Administration's Vietnam policy. Ashmore left the Center in 1974 amidst a financial crisis which curbed its activities.

BALDWIN, JAMES A(RTHUR)
b. Aug. 12, 1924; New York, N.Y.
Author.

The son of a minister, Baldwin described his Harlem childhood as a "bleak fantasy." As an adolescent he tried preaching but gave up at age 17 and left home shortly thereafter. Taking odd jobs to support himself, Baldwin worked on a novel, won two fellowships and at the age of 24 went to live in France. There, in 1953, he finished *Go Tell It On the Mountain*, his highly praised novel of religious experience in Harlem. Baldwin's most widely acclaimed work during the 1950s was *Notes of a Native Son*, a collection of personal essays that probed what one reviewer called "the peculiar dilemma of Northern Negro intellectuals who can claim neither Western nor African heritage as their own."

During the 1960s Baldwin was probably the most successful black writer in America. His novel *Another Country* and a collection of essays, *Nobody Knows My Name*, were among the leading paperback best-sellers in 1963. Baldwin's literary skills and large audience also made him a major presence in the early civil rights movement. In *The Crisis of the Negro Intellectual* Harold Cruse described Baldwin as "the chief spokesman for the Negro among the intellectual class" during the Kennedy years.

Shortly after the January 1963 publication of *The Fire Next Time*, two essays by Baldwin on the imminent escalation of America's racial crisis, Assistant Attorney General Burke Marshall [*q.v.*] arranged a private breakfast meeting between Baldwin and Attorney General Robert Kennedy, who was then concerned about rising black protest against discrimination.

Baldwin later arranged for Kennedy to meet with a dozen prominent black leaders including singer Lena Horne, playwright Lorraine Hansberry and Dr. Kenneth Clark, the distinguished psychologist, in New York on May 24. According to David Lewis, a biographer of Dr. Martin Luther King, Jr. [*q.v.*], the well publicized meeting was an "unmitigated failure." Robert Kennedy was upset that Baldwin had selected mostly artists and entertainers for the meeting and was incensed at their disrespect for the Administration's civil rights accomplishments. After the meeting Baldwin stated that the group felt it had failed to impress Kennedy "with the extremity of the racial situation" in the North and their view that the Administration's civil rights activity was not sufficient to avert a deepening crisis.

A week before the Aug. 28, 1963 March on Washington, Baldwin led a group of 80 American artists in Paris who presented a petition to the U.S. embassy supporting the Washington demonstration. Later, Baldwin flew to Washington to deliver an address to the marchers.

Baldwin was also among the speakers at a Sept. 22, 1963 rally at New York's Foley Square, where 10,000 people gathered to protest the Sept. 15 Birmingham, Ala., church bombing, which killed four black children. At the rally Baldwin called for a nationwide campaign to boycott Christmas shopping as a protest against the bombing. On Oct. 7 Baldwin addressed a Student Nonviolent Coordinating Committee (SNCC) voter registration rally in Selma, Ala. A week after President Kennedy was assassinated, Baldwin gave the keynote address at SNCC's annual conference and lauded the late President for breaking the traditional compact between the South and North that had let Southern whites do as they wished with "their niggers."

In *The Fire Next Time*, two essays published in 1963, Baldwin argued that black people in America "are very well placed indeed to precipitate chaos and ring down the curtain on the American dream." He went on to predict that "if we do not dare everything, the fulfillment of that prophecy, recreated from the Bible in song by a slave, is upon us: 'God gave Noah the rainbow sign, no more water, the fire next time.'" Read in light of the 1965 Watts riot and later violence in black ghettos across the nation, *The Fire Next Time* came to be regarded as a prophetic and insightful study of American race relations. In his history of the civil rights movement, Thomas Brooks wrote that no one else predicted the events "with such verve and before such a wide audience."

Baldwin returned from Europe in March 1965 to participate in the march from Selma to Montgomery, Ala., led by Martin Luther King, [*q.v.*]. Although Baldwin lived abroad and devoted most of his energies to creative writing, he continued to take an active interest in the course of the black movement in America. In February 1967 he resigned from the advisory board of *Liberator*, a black nationalist monthly he had been associated with since 1961, in protest against the magazine's publication of allegedly anti-Semitic articles. Baldwin also contributed the introductory essay to *If They Come In The Morning*, a collection of essays that assessed the significance of the trial of Angela Davis's trial, which was published in 1971.

BARNETT, ROSS R(OBERT)
b. Jan. 22, 1898; Standing Pine, Miss.
Governor, Miss., 1960-64.

The youngest son of a Confederate veteran, Barnett worked his way through Mississippi College and the University of Mississippi Law School, receiving his law degree in 1926. He then began private practice in Jackson, served as president of the State Bar Association in 1943 and 1944 and made two unsuccessful attempts for the governorship in 1951 and 1955. He tried again in 1959, this time placing first in the Aug. 5 Democratic primary and winning the Aug. 25 runoff by a wide margin. A member of the segregationist Citizens Councils, Barnett preached white supremacy during his campaign with what one observer called a "Bible-pounding evangelistic fervor." Repeatedly promising he would "rot in jail" before he would "let one Negro ever darken the sacred threshold of our white schools," Barnett won the November election easily and was inaugurated on Jan. 19, 1960.

In Barnett's first 10 weeks in office, 24 new segregation bills were introduced in the state legislature and circuit clerks were ordered not to give the Justice Department any voter registration figures. As chairman of the State Sovereignty Commission, Barnett subsidized the Mississippi Association of Citizens Councils throughout his term, awarding it over $100,000 in state grants in 1962 alone. Labeling the civil rights plank adopted at the Democratic National Convention in 1960 "repulsive," Barnett tried to organize a third party movement comparable to the Dixiecrats of 1948 but won little support from other

Southern governors. Barnett then put forward a slate of unpledged Democratic electors, which defeated the Mississippi slate pledged to support Kennedy in November. They ultimately cast the state's eight electoral votes for Sen. Harry F. Byrd (D, Va.).

All these events were a prelude to Barnett's defiance of federal court orders mandating the admission of James Meredith [q.v.] to the University of Mississippi in September 1962. There had been no desegregation in any of the state's public schools until then, and shortly after the final court order for Meredith's admission was handed down on Sept. 10, Barnett promised to oppose it, declaring, "We will not surrender to the evil and illegal forces of tyranny." Appointed special registrar for Meredith by the University's Board of Trustees, Barnett met Meredith in Oxford when he came to register on Sept. 20 and read him and accompanying federal officials a lengthy proclamation denying Meredith entry. On Sept. 25 the Fifth Circuit Court issued an injunction prohibiting Barnett from interfering with Meredith's enrollment, but when Meredith tried to register at the trustees' office in Jackson that day, Barnett refused to accept a copy of the injunction and once again denied Meredith admission. Acting under Barnett's orders, Lt. Gov. Paul B. Johnson [q.v.] blocked Meredith's third registration attempt in Oxford on Sept. 26. Two days later the Fifth Circuit Court found Barnett guilty of civil contempt and required him to comply with court orders by Oct. 2 or face a $10,000 per day fine.

Beginning Sept. 15 Attorney General Robert F. Kennedy negotiated with Barnett in a series of phone conversations, hoping to persuade the Governor to comply with the court orders and thus obviate the need to call in federal troops. Barnett did work out a plan with the Justice Department on Sept. 27 in which the Governor would physically block Meredith and a force of U.S. marshals when they came on the campus that day, but would step aside when the marshals drew guns. This plan was canceled, however, when a gathering crowd in Oxford made Barnett and federal officials fearful that violence would result. President Kennedy entered the behind-the-scenes negotiations on Sept. 29 and, in three phone conversations with Barnett, worked out a new arrangement in which Barnett would go to Oxford on Oct. 1, ostensibly planning to deny Meredith admission again, while Meredith would quietly register in Jackson. Late that evening Barnett canceled the deal and on Sept. 30, after President Kennedy had federalized the Mississippi National Guard, Barnett suggested staging a dramatic show of force at Oxford in which state forces would give way to the U.S. Army. The Attorney General dismissed the idea as, "foolish and dangerous" and added that the President, in a television address that night, intended to reveal the plans Barnett had agreed to on the 29th and announce that the Governor had gone back on his word. In response Barnett now suggested that Meredith be taken quietly onto campus that day before the President's address. Barnett promised that state police would aid federal marshals in protecting Meredith and maintaining order, and it was agreed he would issue a statement saying he was yielding to force but condemning any talk of violence.

Federal marshals and state police entered the campus late that afternoon, while Meredith was flown in from Memphis and taken to his dormitory room around 6 p.m. At 9 p.m. Barnett issued a statement declaring that the state was "surrounded by armed forces" and "physically overpowered" but calling on Mississippians to "preserve the peace and avoid bloodshed." A riot had already erupted on the campus, however, and at a crucial point the state police were suddenly ordered away from the University. It was never clear who gave the order, but the troopers returned after the Kennedys urged Barnett to get them back onto the campus. Shortly before midnight Barnett issued a second statement accusing the federal government of "trampling on the sovereignty of this great state" and asserting that Mississippi "will never surrender." The riot lasted into the early morning hours and ended only after President Kennedy called in both the National Guard and the Army. Two men died during the night of violence and over 350 were injured. At 8 a.m. on Oct. 1, Meredith finally registered at the University.

In the aftermath of what was termed the most serious clash between federal and state authority since the Civil War, Barnett blamed the riot on "inexperienced, nervous and trigger-happy federal marshals" and said Mississippians were "enraged, incensed—and rightly so" by federal intervention. Although Meredith had at last enrolled, the Fifth Circuit Court refused to drop the contempt charges against Barnett. Late in 1962, at the explicit request of the Court, the Justice Department added criminal contempt-of-court charges to the pending civil contempt action against the Governor. The Kennedys were reportedly averse to prosecuting Barnett once the September crisis was past and did not want him arrested and imprisoned for fear of touching off another confrontation. The case remained in court until May 1965 when the Fifth Circuit, in a 4-3 ruling, dismissed the contempt charges against Barnett.

Barnett meanwhile denounced civil rights workers in Mississippi as "alien agitators, provocateurs and mercenaries," testified in Senate hearings against the 1964 Civil Rights Act and called for continuation of voter literacy tests and poll taxes so that there would not be "a government of the ignorant, by the ignorant, and for the ignorant." He acquiesced in the enrollment of a second black student at the University of Mississippi in June 1963 only because it was forced on him, he said, by "the armed might of the federal government."

Aside from his defense of Southern segregation policy, Barnett made an all-out drive during his administration to bring new industry into the state. He lowered the state income tax, offered special tax exemptions to new plants and emphasized the low level of wages in Mississippi. Total state income grew 9% in 1962, the fourth highest increase of any state, but Mississippi still had the lowest per capita income level in the nation in 1963. When his term ended in January 1964, Barnett returned to his private law practice. He entered a 1967 Democratic gubernatorial primary but polled only 11% of the vote and did not qualify for the runoff.

For further information:
Walter Lord, *The Past That Would Not Die* (New York, 1965).

BATES, DAISY (GATSON)
b. 1922; Huttig, Ark.
President, Arkansas NAACP, 1953-61.

Daisy Gatson grew up on farms in eastern Arkansas. She attended Philander Smith College and Shorter College in Little Rock, Ark., and in 1941 founded the Arkansas *State Press* with her husband, L.C. Bates, to advance the cause of black rights. Daisy Bates first became known in the civil rights movement in 1946, when she was found guilty on contempt charges in circuit court for criticizing the trial of a black defendant. This conviction was overturned by the Arkansas Supreme Court.

When the U.S. Supreme Court ruled public school segregation unconstitutional in May 1954, a number of Arkansas school districts desegregated voluntarily. This process was supported by Gov. Francis A. Cherry, who promised compliance with the law. In November 1954 Orval Faubus [*q.v.*] was elected governor, pledging not to "force" integration on those communities who opposed it. Several attempts to delay integrating Little Rock schools were challenged by Mrs. Bates and the NAACP and nullified in federal court.

Little Rock's school board prepared to integrate Central High School in September 1957. Nine black students were selected by the NAACP and coached in Daisy Bates's home on nonviolent reaction to expected segregationist abuse. Beginning in August 1957 and for the next two years, Daisy Bates was regarded as the driving force behind Little Rock's integration effort. Her life was repeatedly threatened. In September Gov. Faubus uttered his famous warning that "blood will run in the streets" if integration were attempted, and he called out the National Guard to keep black students from entering Central. Later in the month President Dwight D. Eisenhower federalized the Arkansas Guard. He dispatched federal troops to maintain order and escort the blacks through hostile mobs to Central High. Central was forcibly integrated, but in October Little Rock's City Council ordered the arrest of Daisy Bates and other civil rights activitists on charges of failing to register as NAACP members under a new law. The defendants were convicted and fined in municipal court in December 1957. This conviction was overturned by the Supreme Court in 1960.

Little Rock remained under court order to desegregate all of its schools. Faubus closed all Little Rock high schools in September 1958. As they prepared to reopen on an integrated basis, Daisy Bates's home was bombed in July 1959. She escaped injury and wired Attorney General William P. Rogers requesting federal protection. When this was denied she telegraphed President Eisenhower, who referred her back to the Justice Department. All Little Rock's high schools reopened on an integrated basis in September 1959, and the tide of violence began to ebb.

Daisy Bates told her story in a book, *The Long Shadow of Little Rock* (1962). She continued to be an activist and 10 years later denounced President Richard Nixon's cutoff of Office of Economic Opportunity funds for an Arkansas community as "economic genocide." In 1974 Bates was honored for her role in Little Rock by the National Black Political Convention. She remained a trustee of the NAACP.

BEVEL, JAMES L(UTHER)
b. Oct. 19, 1936; Itta Bena, Miss.
Organizer and Project Coordinator for Southern Christian Leadership Conference, 1963- .

Bevel became a Baptist minister in 1959 and shortly afterwards became active in the civil rights movement. While studying at the American Baptist Theological Seminary in Nashville, Bevel worked as an organizer for the Student Nonviolent Coordinating Committee (SNCC). In 1962 SNCC members joined with Martin Luther King's [*q.v.*] Southern Christian Leadership Conference (SCLC) to protest the trial of freedom riders in Albany, Ga. This was Bevel's first close contact with the SCLC; one year later, he joined King's organization as Alabama project coordinator.

Bevel was closely associated with King during the most important civil rights struggles of the mid-1960s. In April and May 1963 he helped organize the SCLC campaign to end segregation in Birmingham, Ala. Bevel also directed the statewide drive to register black voters in the spring and summer of 1965. Many of the marches that he led were broken up by police, and Bevel himself suffered cranial injuries at the hands of Selma police in March 1965. Bevel aided King at this time not only as an organizer but also as a contact man with SNCC and other civil rights groups that increasingly objected to the nonviolent strategy of SCLC.

When King decided in 1966 to expand civil rights activity in Northern cities, Bevel was chosen head of the SCLC Chicago program. His main task was to coordinate the activities of 100 neighborhood improvement and community action organizations in the city's large west side ghetto. Bevel soon came to believe that the ghetto's condition resulted from "internal colonialism," which he defined as the efforts of businessmen and city officials to take money from blacks without reinvesting it in the black community. Attempting to reverse this pattern, he formed an association of welfare recipients in Chicago and directed a boycott of four local dairy companies that had refused to hire black workers. Bevel also helped organize several marches into all-white ethnic neighborhoods in May 1966, dramatizing black demands for an end to housing discrimination. The practical effects of the SCLC Chicago campaign were not great, but it did publicize the problems of black communities in the North.

In addition to his civil rights activities, Bevel became a strong opponent of the Vietnam war during the mid-1960s. As early as 1965 he urged the formation of an "international peace army" in which civil rights groups would share tactics and organizers with the anti-war movement. Bevel attacked American involvement in Vietnam as a "war of oppression against a foreign colored people," paralleling the oppression of blacks in the U.S. According to sources in SCLC, Bevel persuaded King in early 1967 to come out openly in support of the anti-war movement. This stand drew the criticism of several black leaders, including Roy Wilkins [q.v.] and Whitney Young [q.v.], who wanted to keep civil rights separate from issues of foreign policy. But Bevel continued working to bring the two together. In January 1967 he became head of the Spring Mobilization Committee to End the War in Vietnam, and he helped organize the large anti-war demonstrations of April 15 in New York and San Francisco. In New York 125,000 participated, including King himself.

Bevel took a leave of absence from the SCLC in 1967 to devote himself to further anti-war activities. By the time of King's assassination in April 1968, however, Bevel had returned to the civil rights movement. He was present in Memphis when King died, and he led the march King had planned in support of the city's striking sanitation workers. One month later Bevel was a leader of the SCLC Poor People's Campaign in Washington, a series of demonstrations to demand greater government attention to poverty problems. He subsequently coordinated SCLC activities in Philadelphia and worked as an aide for Ralph Abernathy [q.v.], King's successor as head of the SCLC.

BILBO, THEODORE G(ILMORE)
b. Oct. 13, 1877; Poplarville, Miss.
d. Aug. 21, 1947; New Orleans, La.
Democratic Senator, Miss., 1935-47.

Theodore Bilbo became a part-time Baptist preacher at 19 and later attended the University of Nashville and Vanderbilt University. He entered politics in his twenties as a protege of James K. Vardaman, a charismatic demagogue who was known to his followers as the "Great White Chief." Vardaman's election to the governorship in 1904 ended the era in which state government had been dominated by the aristocratic planter families of the delta region. In 1907 Bilbo won a seat in the state Senate. Like Vardaman, he had campaigned as an enemy of the rich and educated and as a violent advocate of white supremacy. He perfected a style of oratory, combining profanity with biblical allusions, that appealed strongly to the poor tenant farmers and sharecroppers of Mississippi's hill country.

Bilbo first achieved notoriety three years later, when he admitted accepting a bribe. The Senate declared him "unfit to sit with honest, upright men in a respectable legislative body." Nevertheless, Bilbo's backwoods supporters elected him lieutenant governor in 1911 and governor in 1915. Unable to succeed himself, he ran unsuccessfully for the U. S. House in 1920. Eight years later Bilbo was again elected to the governorship after a campaign in which he condemned his opponent for having called out state troopers to prevent a black from being lynched.

In 1934 Bilbo won a U.S. Senate seat. He supported the New Deal but retained the loyalty of his constituents by crusading against anti-lynching legislation and proposing to solve unemployment by deporting blacks to Africa. During World War II, when equality in the hiring of blacks was considered necessary to overcome the manpower shortage, Bilbo opposed the Fair Employment Practices Act. Repeatedly his prolonged filibusters against the measure impeded other important legislation.

In September 1945 President Truman asked Congress to reconstitute the wartime Fair Employment Practices Commission (FEPC) on a permanent basis. When a bill to establish the panel was brought before the Senate early the following year, Southerners responded with a filibuster lasting three weeks. Bilbo insisted that the FEPC was "nothing but a plot to put [blacks] to work next to your daughters . . ." and called its supporters "Quislings of the white race." Finally, the Senate leadership was forced to remove the item from the agenda.

Threatened by new civil rights initiatives from Washington, Bilbo's former opponents among Mississippi's conservative elite rallied in support of his reelection in 1946. Prior to the voting Bilbo issued inflammatory statements aimed at discouraging Mississippi blacks from exercising their right—recently upheld by the Supreme Court—to participate in the primaries. In an apparent invitation to terrorism which received nationwide publicity, he declared, "I call on every red-blooded white man to use any means to keep [blacks] away from the polls. If you don't understand what that means you are just plain dumb." Northerners with Italian or Jewish surnames who wrote letters of protest to Bilbo received replies filled with ethnic epithets.

On Jan. 1, 1947 the Department of Justice announced that it was investigating charges that Bilbo had intimidated blacks to prevent them from voting. Additional allegations suggested that the Senator had been involved in influence peddling with Mississippi war contractors. On the following day the Congressional War Investigating Committee declared that evidence it had received "clearly indicated that Sen. Bilbo improperly used his high office . . . for his personal gain." As a result, at the initiative of Sen. Robert A. Taft (R, Ohio), the Senate's Republican leadership recommended that when the chamber convened, Bilbo be barred at the door and thus prevented from taking the oath of office. When the Senate met, Southern supporters of Bilbo began a filibuster that deadlocked the body and prevented any senator from being sworn in. On Jan. 15 Bilbo settled the issue by leaving Washington for a clinic in New Orleans, where he was undergoing treatment for cancer of the mouth. The Senate simply passed over his name in the subsequent swearing-in ceremonies. Bilbo's condition steadily worsened, and he died in New Orleans on Aug. 21.

BOND, (HORACE) JULIAN
b. Jan. 14, 1940; Nashville, Tenn.
Communications Director, Student Nonviolent Coordinating Committee, 1961-66; Member, Georgia House of Representatives, 1966-   .

Bond grew up on the campuses of Fort Valley State College in central Georgia and Lincoln University in Pennsylvania where his father, historian Horace Mann Bond, served as president. He enrolled in Atlanta's black Morehouse College in 1957, and when the sit-in movement began in February 1960, Bond co-founded the Committee on Appeal for Human Rights (COHAR), which organized a series of student sit-ins in Atlanta. Bond was arrested in the first sit-in at the City Hall cafeteria in March, but he soon left sit-in campaigns to do communications and publicity work for COHAR and to report for the Atlanta *Inquirer*, a newspaper Bond and other students founded in 1960. COHAR coalesced with other student groups in April 1960 to form the Student Nonviolent Coordinating Committee (SNCC), and in the spring of 1961 Bond became communications director for SNCC. Working mainly at SNCC's Atlanta headquarters, Bond edited its newspaper, *The Student Voice*, prepared radio tapes and news releases for the press and supervised publicity for SNCC voter registration and civil rights drives.

Early in 1965 Bond entered the Democratic primary for the Georgia House of Representatives in the 136th district, a new and predominantly black Atlanta district created as the result of a court-ordered reapportionment of the state legislature. Bond swept both the May primary and the general election in November. On Jan. 6, 1966, four days before Bond was to be sworn in as a House member, SNCC issued a policy statement condemning the Vietnam war and expressing support for men who resisted the draft. Bond endorsed the statement the same day. On the grounds that the statement was "un-American," the Georgia House voted 184-12 on Jan. 10 not to seat him. Bond immediately filed suit in federal court to challenge his exclusion, but a three-judge court ruled 2-1 on Jan. 31 that the House's action was constitutional. While this decision was on appeal to the Supreme Court, Bond ran unopposed in a Feb. 23 special election in his district but was again denied his seat by the House Rules Committee on May 23.

Bond ran a third time for the House seat in a September Democratic primary and this time won in a very close race. On Sept. 8, just before the primary, he resigned from SNCC for "personal reasons." In later years Bond said economic necessity, the desire to start a new career and SNCC's growing emphasis on the North rather than the South contributed to this decision. According to Roger M. Williams, who wrote a biography of the Bond family, Julian also felt that SNCC was no longer doing enough constructive and concrete work under its new chairman, Stokely Carmichael [q.v.]. Carmichael's presence in Atlanta during riots on Sept. 6 and 7 and his arrest on Sept. 8 on a charge of inciting to riot may also have forced Bond to disassociate himself from SNCC in order to win the primary. Bond won the November general election, and on Dec. 5, 1966 the Supreme Court ruled unanimously that the Georgia House had violated Bond's First Amendment right to free expression in expelling him for his anti-war statements. On Jan. 9, 1967 Bond was finally sworn in as a member of the Georgia House of Representatives. During the year-long fight for his seat, Bond became a national political figure. He spoke at numerous anti-war rallies and in June 1966 was elected cochairman of the National Conference for New Politics.

Bond was cochairman of an insurgent delegation called the Georgia Loyal National Democrats at the Democratic National Convention in Chicago in August 1968. Before the Credentials Committee Bond argued that Georgia's regular delegation, led by Gov. Lester Maddox, should not be seated because blacks were excluded from any real participation in the regular Democratic Party in the state. A majority on the Credentials Committee recommended a compromise in which Georgia's votes would be split between the regular and insurgent groups. After a floor fight in which Bond's delegation came very close to unseating the regular delegation entirely, the compromise was accepted by the Convention on Aug. 27.

At the Convention Bond delivered one of two seconding speeches for anti-war presidential candidate Sen. Eugene McCarthy (D, Minn.), and on Aug. 29 Bond's own name was placed in nomination for the vice presidency. His nomination, Bond later explained, was "a diversionary effort" to extend the Convention and give those who opposed the Vietnam war and the tactics used by Chicago police against anti-war demonstrators a chance to speak in protest. Bond received 48½ votes for the nomination before withdrawing his name during the course of the balloting. Bond continued to serve in the Georgia House of Representatives after 1968 and maintained an extensive speaking schedule as the national spokesman for a liberal political coalition of the black and white poor.

For further information:
Roger M. Williams, *The Bonds: An American Family* (New York, 1971).

BOUTWELL, ALBERT B(URTON)
b. Nov. 13, 1904; Montgomery, Ala.
Lieutenant Governor, Ala. 1959-63;
Mayor, Birmingham, Ala., 1963-67.

Boutwell was admitted to the Alabama bar in 1928 and opened a legal practice in Birmingham. He served as a member of the state Senate from 1946 to 1958. Chosen as the state's lieutenant governor in 1958, he filled that office for four years and gained a reputation as a moderate on racial issues.

In the Birmingham municipal elections held on April 2, 1963, Boutwell was elected mayor, leading a ticket that defeated the incumbent city administration of Mayor Arthur Hane and Police Commissioner Eugene "Bull" Connor [q.v.], both of whom were unyielding opponents of the civil rights movement. On the following day Martin Luther King [q.v.] and Fred L. Shuttlesworth [q.v.], both of the Southern Christian Leadership Conference, initiated a series of civil rights demonstrations in the city. During the month-and-a-half between the election and the new city administration's assumption of power, Mayor-elect Boutwell and local white leaders began quiet negotiations with King and other civil rights leaders. They also attempted to restrain Connor's use of force, but early in May the police began to employ dogs, nightsticks and pressure hoses against the civil rights marchers.

After these public attacks and the national and worldwide protest which ensued, the Kennedy Administration began to exert strong pressure on the local business elite to reach agreement with the civil rights leaders. On May 10 Shuttlesworth announced that a compromise plan to desegregate some public facilities and ease job discrimination had been devised. Mayor Hane denounced the white negotiators as a "bunch of quisling, gutless traitors," but Boutwell, although a segregationist, accepted the results. Contrasting the Mayor-elect with Hane and Connor, Martin Luther King said that Boutwell was at least "responsible enough to see the futility of massive resistance to desegregation."

On May 23, the day he took office, Boutwell announced his desire to meet with local blacks, and in mid-July the Mayor led a conference of black and white civic leaders. The meeting, which was picketed by the Ku Klux Klan and the White Citizens Council, created a biracial commission to recommend solutions for the city's racial problems. During the same month a U.S. district judge ordered the desegregation of Birmingham's schools in the fall. Boutwell, who opposed Gov. George Wallace's [q.v.] threats to block school desegregation in Alabama, was primarily concerned with maintaining order. He warned all outsiders, whether for or against integration, not to interfere in Birmingham's affairs. When protests directed against school integration culminated in the bombing of a Negro church in September 1963, killing four black girls, Boutwell described the incident as "just sickening."

During the remainder of Boutwell's administration, blacks gained access to the city's major public accommodations and to a modest number of jobs previously reserved for whites. About 600 black children attended formerly all-white schools. After protests flared over allegations of police brutality in early 1966, the Mayor urged black leaders to recruit qualified persons for employment on the all-white police force, and within a year a few blacks had been hired. In April 1965 an undetonated bomb, reputedly planted by white extremists, was discovered outside the Mayor's home on

the same day that another exploded in the city. While some whites rejected any steps towards integration, Birmingham's growing black electorate rejected the slow pace of change. As a result, Boutwell was eliminated in the first round of the mayoral election of October 1967.

BROWN, H(UBERT) RAP (GEROID)
b. Oct. 4, 1943; Baton Rouge, La.
Chairman, Student Nonviolent Coordinating Committee, May 1967-June 1968.

Brown grew up in Baton Rouge and enrolled at Southern University there in 1960. He spent the summers of 1962 and 1963 in Washington, D.C., where he joined demonstrations organized by the Nonviolent Action Group (NAG), an affiliate of the Student Nonviolent Coordinating Committee (SNCC). Brown quit school in 1964 and moved to Washington, where he became chairman of NAG in the fall of 1964 and a neighborhood worker in a local antipoverty program during 1965. He began working as a SNCC organizer in Greene County, Ala., in 1966 and was named SNCC's state project director in Alabama late that year. In 1967 Brown was elected chairman of SNCC, replacing Stokely Carmichael [q.v.].

The militant Carmichael told reporters at the time of Brown's election that "people will be happy to have me back when they hear him." As SNCC chairman Brown quickly captured media attention for his statements in support of black power, his condemnation of American society and government and his advocacy of violence and revolution. He repeatedly accused white America of conspiring "to commit genocide against black people" and counseled blacks to "get yourself some guns." Brown called President Johnson a "wild, mad dog, an outlaw from Texas" who sent "honky, cracker federal troops into Negro communities to kill black people." He applauded ghetto riots and called on blacks to celebrate Aug. 18, the day the 1965 Watts riot had begun, as their "day of independence." He warned that the riots were only "dress rehearsals for revolution" and predicted that "the rebellions will continue and escalate." Violence "is necessary," Brown asserted. "It is as American as cherry pie."

Brown became controversial not only for his public statements but also for the role he allegedly played in instigating riots in 1967. Rioting erupted in Dayton, Ohio, in June and in East St. Louis, Ill., in September shortly after speeches by Brown in each city. In a widely publicized incident Brown addressed a rally of blacks in Cambridge, Md., on July 24, reportedly telling his audience that they should get their guns and that they "should've burned . . . down long ago" a 50-year-old all-black elementary school in the city. Later that night a fire broke out in the school and quickly spread throughout the black business district, destroying nearly 20 buildings.

Brown was arrested in Washington on July 26 by federal officials and taken to Alexandria, Va., where he was rearrested by state authorities on a fugitive warrant, charged by Maryland with arson and inciting to riot. Released on bond on July 27, Brown was again arrested in New York City on Aug. 19 on a warrant issued by a federal court in New Orleans and charged with violating the Federal Firearms Act by carrying a gun across state lines while under indictment. He was also arrested in February 1968 for violating travel restrictions imposed on him by a federal judge while he was out on bond. From the time of his July 1967 arrest on, Brown spent various periods of time in jail while raising bail ranging from $10,000 to $100,000 on different charges.

Brown, who repeatedly insisted that the charges against him were trumped-up, was often singled out by proponents of a federal anti-riot bill as one of their major targets. The 1968 Civil Rights Act included a section making it a crime to cross state lines with intent to incite a riot, and the controversial provision was popularly known as the "Rap Brown amendment." In May 1968 Brown was convicted of violating the federal firearms law and given the maximum sentence of five years and a $2,000 fine, but

he was released on bond pending appeal.

From February to July 1968, while SNCC and the Black Panther Party were allied with each other, Brown served as the Black Panthers' minister of justice. He was replaced as SNCC chairman in June 1968 but then reelected to the post in July 1969 at a meeting where SNCC also changed its name to the Student National Coordinating Committee. Brown's trial on the Maryland charges was scheduled for March 16, 1970 but was twice postponed when Brown failed to appear in court. Brown disappeared in March 1970, and in May he was placed on the FBI's ten-most-wanted list. He was not seen until October 1971, when he was shot and captured by police in New York City. The police charged that Brown had participated in the armed robbery of a Manhattan bar and was shot while trying to make a getaway. In March 1973 Brown was found guilty of armed robbery in New York and was sentenced to a term of 5 to 15 years. Maryland dropped its riot and arson charges against Brown in November when he pleaded guilty to a lesser charge of failing to appear for trial in 1970.

For further information:
H. Rap Brown, *Die Nigger Die!* (New York, 1969).

CARMICHAEL, STOKELY
b. June 29, 1941; Port-of-Spain, Trinidad.
Chairman, Student Nonviolent Coordinating Committee, May 1966-May 1967; Prime Minister, Black Panther Party, February 1968-July 1969.

Carmichael grew up in Trinidad and New York City and then enrolled at Howard University in Washington, D.C., in 1960. There he joined an affiliate of the Student Nonviolent Coordinating Committee (SNCC) known as the Nonviolent Action Group (NAG), which organized sit-ins and demonstrations to desegregate public facilities in the Washington area. Carmichael also participated in the 1961 Freedom Rides, and following his graduation from Howard in 1964, he became a full time worker for SNCC. During the 1964 Mississippi Freedom Summer, he served as project director in the state's second congressional district. Carmichael also became director in 1965 of a SNCC voter registration project in Lowndes County, Ala., where he organized the Lowndes County Freedom Organization, an independent political party with a black panther as its emblem. Carmichael's work in Alabama made him a symbol of the greater militance and emphasis on blackness that many SNCC members were advocating by 1965, and he was elected SNCC chairman in May 1966.

Little known outside of SNCC at the time of his election, Carmichael soon became a much-publicized and highly controversial figure. He first attracted nationwide attention on a June 1966 protest march in Mississippi. The march was begun by James Meredith [q.v.] but continued by other civil rights leaders after Meredith was shot from ambush. When the march reached Greenwood, Miss., Carmichael raised the cry of "Black Power." The phrase, voiced repeatedly on the rest of the march, quickly captured national attention and generated great debate over its meaning. No one definition of black power was ever established. Depending upon the speaker, it could mean pride in blackness and in black history and culture, more political officeholding by blacks, greater black control of economic institutions, black nationalism and separatism or violence and revolution by blacks. At the outset black power was frequently alleged to be "racism in reverse" or black "extremism." It was often identified with black militants in the civil rights movement who were turning away from interracial cooperation, integration and nonviolence.

A prominent advocate of black power, Carmichael gave his most complete statement of its meaning in *Black Power: The Politics of Liberation in America*, written with Charles V. Hamilton and published in November 1967. Black power, the authors wrote, meant first that blacks would redefine themselves, developing a positive self-image based on a "recognition of the virtues

in themselves as black people." Black power also meant a rejection of the traditional civil rights goal of integration on the grounds that that goal was based on the erroneous notion that there was nothing of value in the black community and because it required acceptance of the white middle class values and institutions which were actually the mainstays of racism. Within the framework of black power, blacks would "reject the racist institutions and values" of American society, "define their own goals" and establish independent organizations to serve as "power bases . . . from which black people can press to change local or nationwide patterns of oppression." This organized black power would result in control of community institutions by blacks where they were in the majority and "full participation" by blacks in "the decision-making processes" affecting their lives.

Aside from his advocacy of black power, Carmichael generated controversy for frequently denouncing the Democratic Party as the "most treacherous enemy the Negro people have," for opposing the Vietnam war and for encouraging black men to resist the draft. Carmichael was also considered by some a professional agitator and an instigator of ghetto riots. He was in Atlanta in September 1966 when riots broke out there and was arrested on charges of inciting to riot. He spoke at a symposium in Nashville in April 1967, and riots erupted less than an hour after he left the city. He was again in Atlanta during disorders in June 1967 and in Washington during April 1968 riots there. Whether Carmichael's presence encouraged the riots remained debatable, but Carmichael and his successor as SNCC chairman, H. Rap Brown [q.v.], were the two figures most often cited as targets of anti-riot bills by congressmen who favored such legislation in the late 1960s.

Carmichael did not seek reelection as SNCC chairman in May 1967, and from July to December he traveled extensively in Europe and Africa and made trips to North Vietnam and to Cuba. During his travels Carmichael adopted a revolutionary position that went beyond the program outlined in his book on black power. At a conference of the Organization of Latin American Solidarity held in August 1967 in Havana, for example, Carmichael said that American blacks were fighting to change the "imperialist, capitalist and racialist structure" of the U.S. "We have no other alternative," he proclaimed, "but to take up arms and struggle for our total liberation and total revolution in the United States." Carmichael also advocated guerrilla warfare and armed struggle at various times after his return to the U.S., further inflaming the controversy which surrounded him.

In January 1968 Carmichael helped establish the Black United Front to organize Washington's blacks, and he began working as a community organizer in that city. When SNCC established an alliance in February 1968 with the Black Panther Party founded by Huey P. Newton [q.v.] and Bobby Seale [q.v.], Carmichael was named prime minister of the Party. The alliance was broken in July, but Carmichael stayed on as the Black Panther prime minister and was expelled from SNCC shortly afterwards. He resigned from the Black Panther Party in July 1969, denouncing it for its "dogmatic" party line and its willingness to ally itself with white radicals. Late in 1968 Carmichael left the U.S. and began living in self-imposed exile in Guinea.

CHAVEZ, DENNIS
b. April 8, 1888; Los Chavez, N.M.
d. Nov. 18, 1962; Washington, D.C.
Democratic Senator, N.M., 1935-62.

A descendant of Spanish colonial governors, Dennis Chavez dropped out of school at the age of 13 to help support his family. In 1916 he served as a Spanish interpreter for Sen. A. A. Jones (D, N.M.) and was rewarded with a job as a Senate clerk. Upon passing a special entrance examination, he was admitted to Georgetown University Law School. He obtained his degree in 1920 and subsequently established a practice in Albuquerque, N.M. During the 1920s Chavez served in the New Mexico House of Representatives and in 1930 won a seat in the U.S. House. He lost the race for

U.S. Senate in 1934 but was appointed to the seat following the death of the incumbent. He won election to a complete term in 1936.

Chavez established a liberal reputation as a supporter of New and Fair Deal programs. He often voted for civil rights legislation and for measures granting equal rights to women. Although he urged strict neutrality before Pearl Harbor, he supported Roosevelt's war policies following the attack. During the postwar period Chavez backed the President's plans for the containment of the Soviet Union, including the Truman Doctrine and the Marshall Plan. The only Spanish-surnamed senator, he pressed for recognition of Franco's Spain, urged increased aid to Latin America and sought to improve conditions in Puerto Rico.

Chavez was the leader for the fight for a permanent Fair Employment Practices Commission (FEPC). As head of the Education and Labor Committee's subcommittee on the FEPC, he pushed the bill through committee in May 1945. At the same time Chavez led the fight against the filibuster staged to prevent restoration of funds to the temporary Commission. He was able only to gain a compromise, giving the agency half the amount originally recommended. Chavez succeeded in bringing his bill for a permanent FEPC to the floor in January 1946. The measure prevented discrimination by an employer or union on the basis of race, creed or color. It called for a five-person panel, appointed by the President, to carry out the bill's provisions. Southern senators again led a filibuster against the proposal. Attempts at cloture were unsuccessful, and the measure died.

That same year Chavez fought a bill that would have facilitated the recruitment of Mexican farm laborers, claiming it would have reinstated a form of slavery. An amendment suggested by Chavez, giving U.S. farm workers priority in government benefits, was rejected. A year later he helped write a bill that increased unemployement and sickness benefits for railroad workers. This measure was passed over strenuous opposition from members of the railroad industry.

During the Eisenhower Administration Chavez gained prominence as an opponent of the President's national defense policies. He died of cancer in November 1962.

CLARK, JIM (JAMES) (GARDNER),
b. 1921; Elba, Ala.
Sheriff, Dallas County, Ala., 1955-67.

A political protege of Alabama Gov. Jim Folsom, Clark was the state's assistant revenue commissioner in Folsom's administration. He became sheriff of Dallas County in 1955. Clark gained national prominence during the first three months of 1965, when Rev. Martin Luther King's [q.v.] Southern Christian Leadership Conference (SCLC) sponsored a series of demonstrations in Selma, Ala. These actions culminated in a march from Selma to Montgomery to protest racial discrimination in the registration of voters and to demand federal action to end this practice. Blacks constituted a majority of the population of Dallas County, of which Selma was the seat, but only 300 were registered to vote.

Wilson Baker, Selma's director of public safety, followed a conciliatory policy towards the demonstrators. Clark, a militant segregationist who denounced civil rights leaders as "the lowest form of humanity," dealt with the protestors in a harsher fashion. Responding to charges of Clark's brutality by protest leaders, a federal district judge on Jan. 23 enjoined the sheriff from employing intimidation and harassment. On Feb. 10 Clark and his posse led black children and teenagers, who had been peacefully demonstrating at the Selma courthouse, on a forced march into the Dallas County countryside. Clubs and electric cattle prods were used by the sheriff's men. That night King said, "Selma will never get right . . . until we get rid of Jim Clark." Later in the year Clark was fined $1,500 for violating the January injunction. On March 7 state troopers and Clark's men lined up near the Edmund

Pettis bridge and used teargas, nightsticks and whips to block an attempted march from Selma to Montgomery. These incidents produced a national outcry that spurred Congress's passage of the Voting Rights Act of 1965.

Baker challenged Clark in the May 1966 primary for the Democratic nomination for sheriff. Baker stressed his commitment to fair and efficient law enforcement while the incumbent emphasized his belief that the civil rights movement was a Communist-inspired uprising. Thousands of blacks had been registered since the beginning of SCLC's activities in Dallas County, and civil rights leaders regarded the primary as an important test of the strength of the new voters. Baker, who received almost all of the black votes, defeated Clark. Clark ran a write-in campaign in the general election but was again defeated by Baker, 7,249 to 6,742.

After his defeat Clark served as a speaker for the John Birch Society and other right-wing organizations.

CLARK, KENNETH B(ANCROFT)
b. July 24, 1914, Canal Zone.
Educator, psychologist.

Clark was born in the Panama Canal Zone, where his father was a passenger agent for the United Fruit Company. When he was five years old, his parents separated and his mother took him and his sister to live in Harlem. He attended New York City public schools, received a B.A. from Howard University in 1935 and earned a doctorate in experimental psychology from Columbia in 1940. From 1939 to 1941 he worked under Gunnar Myrdal on the Swedish sociologist's famous study of the Negro in America. Clark became an instructor in psychology at City College in 1942 and 18 years later was granted tenure, making him the first black to receive a permanent teaching appointment in the city university system. In February 1966 he became the first black member of the New York State Board of Regents.

Clark specialized in childhood personality disorders and was particularly interested in those related to racial discrimination and the problems of ghetto life. He published a report in 1950 suggesting that racial discrimination adversely affected the emotional development of white as well as black children. This report was cited by the U.S. Supreme Court in its 1954 decision ordering school desegregation. Following that decision Clark pointed out that, although New York City had not deliberately created a segregated school system, such a system had in fact emerged as a result of the city's segregated housing patterns. Throughout the 1950s Clark worked with a variety of groups which urged the city's Board of Education to begin to integrate its schools, but the Board was reluctant to act.

During the 1960s Clark remained a strong advocate of integration but expressed doubt that the goal could be achieved in the foreseeable future. Unlike many civil rights leaders in the early 1960s, Clark opposed forced long-distance busing to achieve integration. Middle class parents, he said, would not permit their children to attend schools in the ghetto. According to Clark, poor blacks therefore should not wait passively for the arrival of integration. They would not receive help from the New York City Board of Education, an over-grown bureaucracy incapable of effecting real change in the quality of education. If blacks and Puerto Ricans wanted better schools, he said, they would have to assume for themselves the responsibility of school management.

Clark also urged blacks to develop a broad range of community service organizations to help compensate for feelings of powerlessness in the ghetto. In June 1962 he helped organize Harlem Youth Activities Unlimited (HARYOU), a group that sponsored retraining and work programs for unemployed youths, dropouts and delinquents. This group became a prototype for antipoverty organizations funded by the Johnson Administration under legislation passed in 1964 and 1965. Many ghetto residents picketed the Board of Education in support of the Clark plan. To qualify for increased federal funding, HARYOU in June 1964 merged with Associated Community Teams (ACT), another Harlem antipoverty group associated with Rep. Adam Clayton Powell, Jr. (D, N.Y.) [q.v.]. When former Powell aide Livingston Wingate was elected director of HARYOU-ACT, Clark resigned from the board, charging that Wingate intended to use the agency to advance Powell's political influence. To Clark's regret, HARYOU-ACT, plagued by internal dissension and fiscal mismanagement, failed to become a force in Harlem life.

As an eloquent spokesman for school decentralization, Clark was invited by a community parent group in October 1966 to draw up plans for the management of experimental Intermediate School 201 and three nearby primary schools in Harlem. He proposed that these schools be run by a group of parents and university educators rather than the city's Central Board of Education. The plan won the enthusiastic endorsement of Mayor John Lindsay, State Commissioner of Education James E. Allen [q.v.] and most civil rights groups. It was denounced by Albert Shanker, head of the United Federation of Teachers (UFT), who charged that establishment of autonomous neighborhood school boards would lead to the abrogation of teachers' rights and protection against punitive transfers. The Clark plan was rejected by the Board of Education on the grounds that it could not delegate authority to any outside agency. A HARYOU report released in February 1964 documented the "massive deterioration" of Harlem schools and pointed out that student performance in the ghetto actually decreased with length of schooling. Late in 1966, however, the Ford Foundation proposed that teachers be given representation on neighborhood boards. The proposal won the tentative approval of the UFT and became the basis for the establishment of local boards in Harlem, the Lower East Side and the Ocean Hill-Brownsville section in Brooklyn.

In April 1968 the Ocean Hill-Brownsville board announced the dismissal of 13 teachers, five assistant principals and one principal from district schools. Three hundred teachers in the district walked off their jobs in protest, and in the fall the UFT called a series of city-wide strikes that lasted nearly two and a half months. Clark was sympathetic to the Ocean Hill-Brownsville board and attempted to bring about a settlement through the offices of State Education Commissioner Allen. As the strike wore on, however, Allen was forced to suspend the board and replace it with a special three-man state supervisory committee.

By the early 1970s Clark had become thoroughly disillusioned with the decentralization experiments in Brooklyn, Harlem and the Lower East Side. Local boards, torn by internal dissension and excessively concerned with politics, had failed, he said, to improve the quality of education in the ghetto.

CLEAVER, L(EROY) ELDRIDGE
b. 1935; Wabbaseka, Ark.
Black Panther Party Leader, 1967-71.

The son of a dining car waiter, Cleaver was born in a small town near Little Rock, Ark. He grew up in Phoenix, Ariz., and in the Watts section of Los Angeles, where his parents separated. Cleaver spent much of the early 1950s in state reformatories and prisons for marijuana-related crimes. In 1957 he began a 2-14 year prison term for assault with intent to murder. The next year Cleaver joined the Black Muslims and became a leader among Muslim prisoners campaigning for religious freedom. When Muslim founder Elijah Muhammad and his charismatic spokesman Malcom X [q.v.] split in March 1964, Cleaver sided with Malcolm and renounced Muhammad's racial demonology. Expressing his ideological debt to Malcolm X, Cleaver later wrote: "I have, so to speak, washed my hands in the blood of the martyr, Malcolm X, whose retreat from the precipice of madness created new room for others to turn around in, and I am now caught up in that tiny space, attempting a maneuver of my own."

In mid-1965 Cleaver wrote to Beverly Axelrod, a prominent San Francisco attorney specializing in civil liberties cases, to request that she plead his case for parole.

Axelrod took his case and also showed Cleaver's manuscripts to the editor of *Ramparts* magazine, which began publishing autobiographical essays and critical pieces by Cleaver in June 1966. In February 1968 these articles were published in a book entitled *Soul On Ice,* which won immediate critical acclaim. A review published in the *New Republic* placed the book "at the exact resonant center of the new Negro writing." Critic Maxwell Geismar described it as having a "true moral affinity with the *Autobiography of Malcolm X."* *Soul On Ice* became an immediate best-seller and established Cleaver as a leading literary spokesman for black militancy in the late 1960s.

Supported by prominent literary figures such as Norman Mailer and with the promise of a job at *Ramparts,* Cleaver was paroled in December 1966. In February 1967 he first met Huey P. Newton [q.v.] and Bobby Seale [q.v.], the cofounders of the Black Panther Party. A short time later Cleaver joined the Party as its minister of information.

On April 6, 1968 a 90-minute gun battle took place between the Panthers and the Oakland police in which Panther Treasurer Bobby Hutton was killed and four others, including Cleaver, were wounded. Cleaver's parole was immediately rescinded, and he remained in jail until June 12, when Superior Court Judge Raymond J. Sherwin ordered him freed on $50,000 bail. The state successfully appealed Judge Sherwin's decision to the District Court of Appeals, which ruled that Sherwin had acted beyond his authority in ordering Cleaver's release. Cleaver exhausted his last legal remedy Nov. 26 when U.S. Supreme Court Justice Thurgood Marshall [q.v.] denied his request for a stay to prohibit state officials from taking him into custody.

Throughout this appeal process Cleaver maintained his militant posture. The radical Peace and Freedom Party chose Cleaver as its presidential candidate in August 1968, and Cleaver campaigned on a program calling for an alliance of black and white radicals. In the fall he became embroiled in a dispute with California Gov. Ronald Reagan

(R) and the State Board of Regents over a series of lectures he was slated to deliver at the University of California, Berkeley. Gov. Reagan denounced Cleaver Sept. 17 as an advocate of "racism and violence" and sought to prevent him from lecturing at Berkeley. Three days later the Regents voted to limit Cleaver to one guest lecture and censured the faculty Board of Educational Development for having "abused a trust" in approving Cleaver's lecture series.

Over 2,000 students met Sept. 24 and demanded that the Regents rescind their restrictions on Cleaver's appearances. On Oct. 3 the faculty voted to repudiate the Regent's action, and four days later Berkeley Chancellor Roger W. Heyns announced that a lecture hall would be made available to Cleaver but that no course credit would be given to those attending the series. After Cleaver's first lecture Gov. Reagan submitted a resolution to the Regents barring university facilities for "a program of instruction . . . in which Mr. Cleaver appears more than once as a lecturer." Although Reagan's resolution was rejected by the Regents on Oct. 18, student demonstrations and sit-ins in support of course-credit status for Cleaver's lecture series took place Oct. 23 and 24 and resulted in about 200 arrests.

Having exhausted all legal appeals, Cleaver fled the country on Nov. 28, 1968. He lived in Cuba until July 1969 and then moved to Algiers where he founded the first international section of the Black Panther Party in September 1970. Cleaver was expelled from the Party in February 1971, after he attacked the national leadership's lack of militance.

By the mid 1970s Cleaver had moderated his political views considerably. He returned to the United States in November 1975 and voluntarily surrendered to federal authorities.

For further information:
Eldridge Cleaver, *Soul on Ice* (New York, 1968).
———, *Post-Prison Writings and Speeches*, ed. Robert Sheer (New York, 1969).

COLEMAN, JAMES P(LEMON)
b. Jan. 9, 1914; Ackerman, Miss.
Governor, Miss., 1956-60.

Born on a red dirt farm, James P. Coleman worked his way through the University of Mississippi and George Washington University law school. He received his LL.B. in 1939. While in Washington Coleman worked as secretary to Rep. Aaron L. Ford (D, Miss.) and became friends with **Rep. Lyndon B. Johnson (D, Tex.).** Coleman returned to Mississippi and served first as a district attorney and then a circuit judge between 1939 and 1950. In October 1950 he was elected state attorney general. Coleman served as Democratic national committeeman in 1952 and kept the Mississippi delegation from bolting the Democratic National Convention over a proposed requirement that delegates promise to support the Convention's ticket regardless of its stand on civil rights.

Following the May 1954 Supreme Court decision outlawing segregation in public schools, Coleman asked for restraint. He cautioned against adoption of a strategy of "massive resistance," which called for the interposition of state power to prevent enforcement of the decision. Coleman avoided Negro-baiting and restored stability after the murder of Emmett Till [*q.v.*] in August 1955. On Sept. 1 U.S. Attorney General **Herbert Brownell** announced an inquiry into alleged intimidation of black voters in Mississippi. Coleman denied any violations. In the tense atmosphere following Till's murder and Brownell's inquiry, Coleman's approach was cool and legalistic. He told a White Citizens' Council meeting that eliminating segregation through court action would take the government 2,000 years. In 1955 Coleman ran for governor on a platform pledging continued segregation by legal means. He was unopposed in the November election. When the Interstate Commerce Commission decreed an end to segregated terminals the same month, he announced a $50 fine for mixing races in the depots.

Coleman's attempts to maintain moderation met with only limited success in the face of an increasing rightward trend. The Governor was therefore pushed to adopt a more segreationist position. He endorsed interposition in a January 1956 conference convened by Virginia's Gov. Thomas Stanley but refused to join a call for nullification. The following month Coleman obtained legislative approval for a $78 million school budget—the largest in state history—to upgrade black schools and silence Northern critics. He also urged a bill to keep blacks out of white society by giving businesses the right to choose their customers and providing segregated waiting rooms in intrastate travel.

The segregation laws failed to allay fears of integration, and the Governor faced a restive state Party divided over political strategy in the 1956 presidential election. In May the Association of Citizens' Councils, a group of white supremacist organizations, formulated a resolution demanding that the state delegation to the Democratic National Convention accept only a presidential candidate who supported interposition. Coleman continued to counsel moderation. He insisted that the South concentrate on finding a solution to the school desegregation dilemma in private meetings and avoid public quarrels which would force delegates into rigid positions. Coleman predicted that this attitude would encourage compromise. Supported by Sen. John Stennis (D, Miss.), he won his pleas for an unpledged delegation. Coleman's stand became the basis for Southern convention strategy and resulted in the Democrats adoption of a moderate civil rights platform.

In keeping with his desire to use "friendly persuasion" to convince critics of the validity of Mississippi's moderate stand and prevent racial hysteria, Coleman created a State Sovereignty Commission in June 1956. The Commission was given virtually blank-check authority to "perform any . . . acts . . . necessary and proper to protect the sovereignty of the State of Mississippi." It was granted unlimited powers of investigation and authorized to prevent "provocations," such as desegregation petitions, and to dispel the atmosphere created by the Citizens' Councils.

Coleman's public relations effort bore fruit. Reporters from 18 New England newspapers toured the state writing generally sympathetic accounts of social conditions. However his attempts to lead Mississippi into the mainstream of American life met with deepening suspicion. When he supported a new constitution that did not mention race, it was narrowly defeated in the legislature. He prevented white Citizens' Councils from obtaining tax money and in April 1959 called in the FBI after the lynching of Mack Parker. At the end of his term, Coleman supported Sen. John F. Kennedy (D, Mass.) for President. A more rigidly segregationist governor followed him. In a 1963 gubernatorial comeback attempt, Coleman was called a Kennedy liberal and was defeated im the primary. President Lyndon Johnson appointed him a judge on the U.S. Court of Appeals in 1965.

For further information:
Numan V. Bartley, *The Rise of Massive Resistance* (Baton Rouge, 1969).

CONNOR, (THEOPHILUS) EUGENE "BULL"

b. July 11, 1897; Selma, Ala.
d. March 10, 1973; Birmingham, Ala.
Commissioner of Public Safety, Birmingham, Ala., 1937-53, 1957-63.

Between 1926 and 1936 Connor acquired a large following as a radio sports broadcaster in Birmingham and received his nickname from the deep tone of his voice. Banking on his personal popularity, Connor was elected to the state legislature for one term in the mid-1930s and then won four consecutive terms as Birmingham's commissioner of public safety, serving from 1937 to 1953. He filled that post again from 1957 to 1963. As one of only three elected city officials, Connor, with his lengthy tenure in office, established himself as Birmingham's major public figure. According to the *New York Times*, he enhanced his influence by using his power to appoint temporary judges as a device for controlling the city's court system.

In the late 1950s and early 1960s Birmingham was known as one of the South's most rigidly segregated cities. And Connor earned a reputation as the unenlightened leader of its resistance to the civil rights movement. When an integrated Freedom Ride bus entered Birmingham on Mother's Day, May 14, 1961, it was received by a hostile white mob. Asked why the police were not present to prevent violence, Connor stated that most of the policemen were off duty to visit their mothers. Later in the year, when the manager of the city's bus terminal attempted to comply with an anti-discrimination directive of the Interstate Commerce Commission, Connor had him arrested.

In the fall of 1962 Birmingham's voters chose to replace the existing commissioner form of government with the mayor-city council system. Connor ran for mayor the following year but was defeated 29,000 to 21,000 by Albert Boutwell [q.v.] on April 2. However, Boutwell and the city councilmen did not assume their offices until May 23, 1963. During the interim Martin Luther King, Jr. [q.v.] and Fred Shuttlesworth [q.v.] led a series of civil rights demonstrations in Birmingham. Connor initially employed restraint in dealing with the protesters, but in early May his men began to use dogs, nightsticks and pressure hoses in an effort to crush the integration drive. After Shuttlesworth was injured and removed from the scene by ambulance, Connor remarked, "I waited a week to see Shuttlesworth get hit with a hose: I'm sorry I missed it. I wish they'd carried him away in a hearse."

Connor's strategy backfired. Many local white leaders were frightened by his methods and wanted a truce. The Kennedy Administration, responding to national and worldwide indignation against his methods, exerted strong pressure upon Birmingham's business community to negotiate with black leaders. On May 10 Shuttlesworth announced an agreement which provided for gradual desegregation of the city's major public accommodations and the hiring of blacks in jobs previously reserved for whites. President Kennedy, in a conversation with civil rights leaders shortly afterwards said, "I don't think you should be totally harsh on 'Bull' Connor. He has done more for civil rights than almost anybody else."

Connor remained an unyielding foe of integration after his defeat in Birmingham's municipal election. When Martin Luther King won the Nobel Peace Prize in 1964, Connor asserted, "They're scraping the bottom of the barrel. . . ." Three years later he defended his use of dogs against demonstrators in 1963 and urged they be employed against black rioters in the North. In 1964 Connor won a libel suit begun four years earlier against the *New York Times* over two April 1960 articles which depicted him as a repressive force in Birmingham's racial politics. The judgment was ultimately overturned by the U.S. Supreme Court on freedom-of-the-press grounds. Elected president of Alabama's Public Service Commission in 1964 and 1968, he was defeated in 1972 after the state's attorney general accused him of being a "tool" of the utility companies whose rates were regulated by the Commission. Connor died on March 10, 1973, shortly after suffering a stroke.

COX, W(ILLIAM) HAROLD

b. June 23, 1901; Indianola, Miss.
U.S. District Judge, Southern District of Mississippi, June 1961- .

Cox received his B.S. and LL.B. from the University of Mississippi and was admitted to the Mississippi bar in 1924. He practiced in Jackson until 1961 and served as chairman of the Hinds County Democratic Executive Committee from 1950 to 1961.

A long-time personal friend of Senator James O. Eastland (D, Miss.) [q.v.]—the two had been college roommates—Cox was named a district court judge in Mississippi in June of 1961. Both the President and Attorney General Robert Kennedy reportedly hoped Cox's appointment would placate Eastland, the powerful chairman of the Senate Judiciary Committee, and prepare the Senator to accept their selection of Thurgood

Marshall [*q.v.*] the director of the NAACP Legal Defense and Educational Fund, for a Circuit Court judgeship. (Marshall was appointed to the Second Circuit Court in October 1961, but lengthy hearings by Eastland's Judiciary Committee postponed Senate confirmation of the nomination for nearly a year.) Although Eastland was an ardent segregationist, Cox himself had no public record on civil rights at the time of his nomination, and he assured Robert Kennedy in a private interview that he would uphold the Constitution in the realm of civil rights.

The meeting apparently convinced the Attorney General that Cox would rise above segregationist sentiments in dealing with civil rights cases. Once on the bench, however, Judge Cox handed down a string of anti-civil rights decisions and became the most famous of the segregationist Southern judges in the 1960s. Cox refused to overturn the conviction of five freedom riders in August, 1961, arguing that "their destination was Jackson but their objective was trouble." He issued an injunction barring the Congress of Racial Equality from encouraging blacks to use the McComb, Miss. interstate bus terminal, even after a 1961 Interstate Commerce Commission order required that all such facilities be integrated. Cox did hand down a temporary restraining order against race discrimination in an April 1962 voting rights case, but he generally ruled against blacks in voting rights suits brought by the Justice Department. In one instance, he attributed the fact that no blacks in a certain Mississippi county were registered though nearly 2,500 blacks of voting age lived there, to "the fact that Negros have not been interested to vote," and privately, he complained of having to spend most of his time "fooling with lousy cases" brought by the Justice Department's Civil Rights Division. As of March 1964, all but one of Cox's civil rights decisions had been reversed on appeal.

Cox did order the integration of a Jackson restaurant chain in January 1966, and in a suit for damages against the Ku Klux Klan brought by relatives of a black man murdered in 1966, the judge condemned the murder and directed a verdict for the plaintiffs.

These were exceptions, however, to Cox's usual pattern of rulings in civil rights cases. On March 6, 1964 he voted to uphold the constitutionality of Mississippi's voting laws in a Justice Department suit challenging the statutes as discriminatory. The *New York Times* reported on March 9, 1964 that Cox referred to blacks trying to register to vote in Canton, Miss., as "a bunch of niggers" and said they were "acting like a bunch of chimpanzees." The remarks prompted an unsuccessful attempt by NAACP official Aaron Henry [*q.v.*] and other Mississippi civil rights leaders to have Cox disqualified from handling any more civil rights cases.

During a suit involving voter discrimination in Clarke County, Miss., Cox wanted perjury charges pressed against two black witnesses he felt were lying. After a probe by the Federal Bureau of Investigation, the Justice Department advised Cox that there was no basis for prosecution. When Cox insisted on the prosecution, Attorney General Nicholas Katzenbach ordered the U.S. attorney in Mississippi not to sign indictments against the two blacks. Cox responded in October 1964 by holding the local U.S. attorney in contempt of court and threatening Katzenbach with the same. In January 1965 the Fifth Circuit Court overturned Cox's action. The judge dismissed a Justice Department suit to integrate a Gulf Coast beach in March 1966, asserting that the beach was privately owned, and in December he voted to hold federal school desegration guidelines unconstitutional.

Cox's most famous case grew out of the murder of Andrew Goodman, Michael Schwerner and James Chaney, three civil rights workers who were reported missing on June 21, 1964. After a massive federal investigation their bodies were uncovered six weeks later in an earthen dam near Philadelphia, Miss. In January 1965 a federal grand jury in Jackson indicted eighteen men, including the county sheriff, for the murders on charges of violating federal civil rights laws. A month later Cox dismissed most counts of the indictment, causing an outcry among civil rights activists. The U.S. Supreme Court unanimously reversed Cox's decision and reinstated the charges in March 1966. The charges were again dropped for technical reasons at the Justice Department's request, but a new indictment against 19 men was handed down in February 1967. In October an all-white jury convicted seven of the defendants. Cox sentenced them to prison terms ranging from three to ten years, but he also made all the sentences "indeterminate," thus qualifying all seven for immediate consideration for parole.

DOAR, JOHN M(ICHAEL)

b. Dec. 3, 1921; Minneapolis, Minn.
U.S. Assistant Attorney General, 1960-65; U.S. Assistant Attorney General in charge of Civil Rights Division, 1965-67.

A graduate of Princeton and the University of California, Berkeley Law School, Doar practiced law in New Richmond, Wisc., the town where he grew up, from 1950 to 1960. In the spring of 1960 he was appointed first assistant in the Civil Rights Division of the Justice Department, and although a Republican, he was retained in that post by the Kennedy Administration.

During the Freedom Rides in the summer of 1961, Doar won an injunction from the federal courts barring the Ku Klux Klan from interfering with the riders as they attempted to integrate interstate bus terminals. Throughout the Kennedy years Doar supervised many of the Justice Department's suits in the South to secure voting rights for blacks and to desegregate public schools and juries. Doar personally conducted the investigations which gathered evidence for court hearings in a number of these cases, developing a reputation for careful research and close attention to details.

Aside from litigation Doar became directly involved in several civil rights crises in the South. He was with James Meredith [q.v.] during three of Meredith's unsuccessful attempts to register at the University of Mississippi at Oxford in September 1962. On Sept. 30 he accompanied Meredith onto the University campus and stayed with him in his dormitory room that night while federal marshals and the National Guard quelled a riot outside. The next morning Doar escorted Meredith to the registrar's office where he was finally enrolled at the University.

Doar was also on hand on June 11, 1963, when two black students integrated the University of Alabama at Tuscaloosa. He accompanied one of the students onto campus and to his dormitory while Gov. George C. Wallace [q.v.] stood in the doorway of the University's registration hall in a final and futile attempt to block the entry of the students.

Four days later Doar was in Jackson, Miss., for the funeral of Medgar Evers [q.v.], the Mississippi NAACP field secretary who had been shot by a sniper outside his home on June 12. After the funeral several thousand blacks participated in a march of mourning in Jackson. Near its end a group of young blacks broke from the ranks and went down another street where they met a line of police who ordered them to disperse. As the crowd grew, some rocks and bottles were thrown, and the police moved forward and began making arrests. At this point Doar strode down the middle of the street between the line of police and the gathering of blacks, urging the crowd to remain calm, to stop the rock throwing and to leave the area. Several black leaders joined in Doar's appeal, and the crowd moved out without further violence.

In December 1964 Doar was named head of the Civil Rights Division following Burke Marshall's [q.v.] resignation. In that position he supervised all Justice Department cases dealing with civil rights and continued to spend much of his time in the South, often turning up during critical situations.

In March 1965, when Martin Luther King [q.v.] led a march from Selma to Montgomery, Ala., to protest the denial of voting rights to blacks, Doar was present throughout the march to help coordinate the federal government's activities and to see that court orders barring state authorities from interfering with the march were followed. Doar went to Bogalusa, La., in July 1965 after several months of civil rights demonstrations there had flared into racial violence. As President Johnson's personal representative Doar met with rights leaders and with local and state officials, and he initiated a legal suit against the Ku Klux Klan to prevent it from harassing civil rights workers. Doar was also in Canton, Miss., on June 23, 1966 when the local police ordered some 250 people who were part of a protest march going to Jackson, Miss., to move away from their campsite. When the marchers refused to leave, the police fired tear gas at them, and Doar made a futile effort to restrain the police as they moved in with clubs to clear the area.

Doar personally led the Justice Department's prosecution in two major cases against men charged with the murder of civil rights workers in the South. On March 25, 1965, at the end of the Selma march, Viola Liuzzo, a civil rights worker from Detroit, was shot 20 miles outside of Selma. In his first criminal case in the Justice Department, Doar prosecuted the three Klan members believed responsible for her murder under an 1870 federal law making it a crime to conspire to violate an individual's civil rights. In December 1965 an all-white jury in the federal district court in Montgomery, Ala., found the three men guilty of violating the law, and each received the maximum 10-year sentence. Doar also headed the prosecution of 18 men charged with conspiracy in the June 1964 killing of three civil rights workers near Philadelphia, Miss. Once again Doar won his case. On Oct. 20, 1967 another all-white federal jury in Meridian, Miss., convicted seven of the defendants.

Doar resigned from the Justice Department in December 1967 to become executive director of the Development and Service Corporation, a private company formed to redevelop New York's Bedford-Stuyvesant ghetto. He also served as president of the New York City Board of Education in 1968 and 1969, emerging as an advocate of decentralized control of schools. In December 1973 Doar was appointed majority counsel to the House Judiciary Committee for its inquiry into the impeachment of President Richard Nixon.

EASTLAND, JAMES O(LIVER)
b. Nov. 28, 1904; Doddsville, Miss.
Democratic Senator, Miss., 1941, 1943-   ; Chairman, Judiciary Committee, 1956- .

Eastland was born into a well-to-do, politically influencial family in rural Mississippi. After attending Vanderbilt University and the University of Mississippi, he began a legal practice in Sunflower Co., Miss. From 1928 to 1932 he served as a representative in the Mississippi State Legislature and then practiced law and ran the family's 5,400 acre cotton plantation. In 1941 Eastland was appointed to a temporary 90-day term in the U.S. Senate. He won the seat outright in the 1942 election.

A vigorous opponent of civil rights, Eastland voted against anti-lynching and anti-poll tax legislation. In 1945 he opposed the extension of the Fair Employment Practices Commission, alleging that its efforts to improve the status of blacks were associated with Communism. Following the Supreme Court's ruling in 1947 that Oklahoma had to provide legal training for blacks, Eastman asserted that the Court was "not judicially honest." In January 1948 Eastland advocated that Southern Democrats withhold their electoral votes from the Party in the upcoming presidential election in order to force the election into the House of Representatives, where he believed a Southerner would emerge as President. Following the adoption of a strong civil rights platform by the Democratic Party at its 1948 National Convention, Eastland joined other Southerners at the States Rights Convention in Birmingham, Ala., that July. He supported South Carolina's Gov. J. Strom Thurmond [q.v.] for President. Eastland, himself, ran unopposed for re-election that November.

Eastland continued his unrelenting opposition to civil rights during the 1950s. In 1955 he denounced the Supreme Court school desegregation decision of the previous year, asking, "Who is obligated morally or legally to obey a decision whose authorities rest not on law but upon the writings and teachings of pro-Communist agitators?" That year he played a major role in the formation of the Federation for Constitutional Government, a short-lived attempt to unite the white Citizens' Councils and other local white supremacist groups. He was a frequent and popular speaker before those organizations.

After becoming chairman of the Judiciary Committee in March 1956, Eastland posed a formidable obstacle to the passage of civil rights bills, which were within the jurisdiction of that panel. The Administration's 1957 civil rights measure was passed only after the Senate, in June, voted to bypass the Committee and place the measure on the chamber's calendar. Throughout 1959 Eastland delayed another civil rights bill in committee. Liberals pressed Majority Leader Lyndon B. Johnson (D, Tex.) and Minority Leader Everett M. Dirksen (R, Ill.) to bring the measure to the floor, and the leaders announced in September that they would act early the following year to bring the legislation up for debate. On March 24, 1960 the Senate, over Eastland's opposition, voted to require the panel to report the measure by March 30. The bill became law the following May. During 1960 Eastland bottled up an anti-poll tax amendment to the Constitution. He asserted in January that "a person who does not care enough for the franchise to desire to pay a poll tax as a qualification should not be permitted to vote. . . ."

Eastland maintained a vociferous opposition to civil rights in the early 1960s. He voted against the confirmation of Robert C. Weaver as administrator of the Housing and Home Finance Agency in 1961 alleging that Weaver, a black, had "a pro-Communist background." Eastland's Judiciary Committee handled all federal judicial appointments, and he was thus able to delay Senate confirmation of Thurgood Marshall's [q.v.] nomination to a circuit court judgeship for nearly a year. Eastland voted against a constitutional amendment to abolish the poll tax for federal elections in March 1962. He supported Mississippi

Gov. Ross Barnett's [q.v.] efforts to prevent James Meredith's [q.v.] entry into the University of Mississippi in September 1962 and threatened a Judiciary Committee investigation of the federal government's intervention during the "Ole Miss" crisis. In January 1963 the Justice Department brought suit to end voting discrimination in Sunflower County, Miss., the site of Eastland's plantation, alleging that only 114 of more than 13,000 eligible blacks were registered to vote. Eastland decried the move, asserting that there was "no foundation in fact" for the charges of discrimination. He also denounced the Administration civil rights bill, introduced in Congress in June 1963, as a "grasp for power." One version of the bill was referred to the Judiciary Committee, which had never voluntarily reported out a civil rights measure during Eastland's chairmanship. After several days of hearings between July and September 1963, the Committee took no further action on the proposal. Eastland voted against an October 1963 bill to extend the life of the Civil Rights Commission for one year, claiming that the Commission "spews forth an unending series of fantastic and unconstitutional recommendations which would destroy our republican form of government."

As chairman of the Judiciary Committee, which had jurisdiction over civil rights legislation, Eastland had the power to bottle up civil rights bills. As of 1964 the Judiciary Committee, under his chairmanship, had never voluntarily reported out a civil rights bill, and in 1966 Eastland claimed to have defeated 127 such bills during his Senate years. To keep Eastland from blocking the Johnson Administration's civil rights measures, the Democratic leadership won Senate approval of a motion to place the 1964 Civil Rights Act directly on the Senate calendar, bypassing the Judiciary Committee altogether. The 1965 Voting Rights Act and later civil rights bills were referred to the Judiciary Committee but with orders from the Senate to report the measures back by set deadlines. Eastland objected to both maneuvers and claimed that the time-limit provisions amounted to "legislative lynching."

Eastland also opposed the appointment of Thurgood Marshall [q.v.] to the Supreme Court and of Constance Baker Motley to a district court judgeship. He was a strong critic of black militants and supported federal anti-riot legislation. When the Judiciary Committee, meeting a Senate deadline, reported out a bill to protect civil rights workers from injury and intimidation in November 1967, Eastland denounced the move, claiming that the bill would give "added protection to roving fomenters of violence, such as Stokely Carmichael [q.v.] and H. Rap Brown [q.v.]." He voted to add an anti-riot provision to the 1968 Civil Rights Act.

Eastland was floor manager for the cotton title of an Administration-backed farm bill in 1964. The cotton section provided for subsidies to domestic textile mills to decrease the price they paid for domestic cotton. As Eastland explained in the Senate, cheaper imported cotton textiles and synthetic fibers were destroying the market for domestic cotton. This bill, which he successfully steered through the Senate, was designed to make domestic cotton competitive in price, thus aiding both the textile industry and cotton farmers. Eastland's own cotton plantation became a source of increasing controversy in the Johnson years. Civil rights activists criticized the fact that Eastland received over $100,000 per year in cotton price supports and diversion cash payments from the government. In July 1965 a representative of the Mississippi Freedom Labor Union denounced the working conditions of black sharecroppers on Eastland's plantation in testimony before a House Education and Labor Subcommittee. In July 1967 a team of six physicians who had investigated malnutrition in Mississippi reported to a Senate Labor and Public Welfare Subcommittee that conditions in the delta region, where Eastland's plantation was located, approached starvation. Eastland and his colleague Sen. John C. Stennis (D, Miss.) immediately denied that there was mass malnutrition in the Mississippi delta.

During the Nixon years Eastland supported all of Nixon's Supreme Court appointments, including the nominations of Clement F. Haynsworth and G. Harrold Carswell. He voted against the Equal Rights Amendment, home rule for the District of Columbia and fought busing for school desegregation. He remained a strong supporter of the war in Southeast Asia, voting against the Cooper-Church amendment to limit American military involvement in Cambodia in June 1970.

EVERS, (JAMES) CHARLES
b. Sept. 11, 1922; Decatur, Miss.
Field Secretary, Mississippi NAACP.
1963-69.

Evers grew up in Decatur and received a B.A. from Alcorn A & M College in 1950. He moved to Philadelphia, Miss., the next year and established several successful businesses, including a funeral parlor, hotel, cafe and taxi service, all of which catered to the local black community. Evers also worked closely with his brother Medgar, who became state field secretary for the NAACP in 1954. As a result of his civil rights work, white segregationists put such severe economic pressures on Charles Evers that he was forced to leave Mississippi in 1956. He moved to Chicago and there held a variety of jobs. As he later disclosed in his autobiography, he also ran a small policy game and a brothel.

Medgar Evers was assassinated by a sniper outside his home in Jackson, Miss., on June 12, 1963. Charles returned to the state immediately and asked the NAACP to let him succeed his brother as the organization's Mississippi field secretary. Assuming the job on June 16, Evers worked in campaigns to desegregate public accommodations and register black voters, concentrating on McComb, during 1964. He was arrested in Jackson in June 1965 for leading demonstrations to protest a special state legislative session called to rewrite Mississippi's voting and registation laws.

Following passage of the federal Voting Rights Act in August 1965, Evers moved his office to Fayette in Jefferson County, one of several predominantly black counties in southwest Mississippi. From the fall of 1965 through early 1967, he organized highly effective boycotts by the black communities in Natchez, Fayette, Port Gibson and other towns in the area. In each place black demands included the integration of schools, hospitals and public accommodations, increased employment of blacks by city agencies and private businesses, the use of courtesy titles for blacks by city employes and black representation on juries and school boards. A boycott of white merchants, mass marches and picketing continued in each town until black demands were met. At the same time Evers and NAACP state president Aaron Henry [q.v.] organized local NAACP chapters and took advantage of the federal voting rights law to increase dramatically voter registration among blacks. Between 1963 and 1971 the number of blacks registered in Mississippi rose from 28,000 to over 250,000.

When James Meredith [q.v.] was shot on June 6, 1966 while on a solitary protest march from Memphis, Tenn., to Jackson, Miss., Evers joined national civil rights leaders in continuing the march. However, Evers repudiated a strongly worded march manifesto issued June 8, declaring it "too critical of President Johnson." He also complained that the highly publicized march could "turn into another Selma, where everyone goes home with the cameramen and leaves us holding the bag." After other march leaders announced on June 11 that they would encourage black voter registration while en route to Jackson, Evers supported the march's objectives and labeled the protest a "good thing." Evers led demonstrations in Natchez in February and March 1967 to protest the murder of a local NAACP official. He also led marches in Jackson in June after police shot and killed a black delivery man during disturbances at Jackson State College.

Evers ran for Congress in a 1968 special election to fill the seat vacated by John Bell Williams after he became Mississippi governor in January. Running against six white opponents, Evers won a plurality in the Feb. 27 election but lost the runoff on March 12 by over 40,000 votes. He supported Sen. Robert F. Kennedy (D, N.Y.) in his bid for the Democratic presidential nomination in 1968, serving as state

cochairman for the Kennedy campaign in Mississippi. Evers campaigned for Kennedy in California and was with the Senator when he was assassinated on June 5.

The regular Mississippi Democratic Party selected Evers in July 1968 as one of four blacks in its 68-member delegation to the August Democratic National Convention (DNC). Evers rejected the offer as "tokenism," helped organize a biracial challenge delegation, the Loyal Democrats of Mississippi, and testified before the DNC Credentials Committee. On Aug. 20 the Committee voted overwhelmingly to unseat the regular state delegation and give all of Mississippi's Convention seats to the challengers. Following the Convention Evers was chosen the Democratic national committeeman from Mississippi.

A candid, extroverted and self-confident figure, Evers remained a shrewd businessman as well as a tireless activist and organizer in Mississippi. He repeatedly argued that economic independence, with increased black employment and black-owned businesses, was a crucial underpinning for black political advancement in the South. In 1966 Evers opened the Medgar Evers Shopping Center in Fayette, and in 1970 he added a motel with a restaurant and lounge to the complex.

Evers ran for mayor of Fayette in 1969, organizing a strong drive to get out the black vote. He won the May 13 Democratic primary, was unopposed in the June election and resigned his post as NAACP state field secretary before he was sworn in as mayor on July 7. The first black mayor of a biracial community in Mississippi since Reconstruction, Evers successfully lobbied with the federal government, foundations and businesses to secure grants and new industry for Fayette. In April 1971 he was nominated to run for governor by the Loyal Democrats, but he was defeated in the November election.

For further information:
Charles Evers, *Evers*, ed. Grace Halsell (New York, 1971).

EVERS, MEDGAR W(ILEY)
b. July 2, 1925; Decatur, Miss.
d. June 12, 1963; Jackson, Miss.
Mississippi Field Secretary, NAACP,
December 1954-June 1963.

After graduating from Alcorn A & M College in 1952, Evers took a job with a black-owned insurance company in Mound Bayou, Miss. At the same time he joined the NAACP and began organizing chapters of the Association in the Mississippi Delta. At an NAACP meeting late in 1953, Evers volunteered to try to desegregate the University of Mississippi. He applied to the University's Law School in January 1954, but when his application was rejected in September, Evers and the NAACP decided not to take his case to court.

Evers became the Association's first state field secretary in Mississippi in December 1954, and he opened an office in Jackson, the state capital, in January 1955. Over the next nine years Evers worked to increase NAACP membership and to encourage voter registration among Mississippi's blacks. He traveled throughout the state explaining the Supreme Court's 1954 school desegregation decision, showing black parents how to file petitions for desegregation with local school boards, the first step in implementing the Supreme Court ruling. While he organized the school board petition campaign, Evers also coordinated aid for black parents who signed petitions and were then subjected to economic reprisal for their action. He investigated the August 1955 lynching of 14-year-old Emmett Till, the murders of civil rights workers such as Lamar Smith in 1955 and Herbert Lee in 1961, and the charges of personal harassment and threats his office received from blacks throughout the state.

Once described as "the heartbeat of any integration activity in the state of Mississippi," Evers kept in touch with the increased tempo of civil rights work in the state during the Kennedy years. After 1960 the Student Nonviolent Coordinating Committee and the Congress of Racial Equality began voter registration drives in Mississippi. The Justice Department filed several voting discrimination suits and black students from colleges and high schools staged occasional sit-ins and protests. James Meredith [q.v.] called on Evers in the fall of 1960 and said he wanted to enter the University of Mississippi at Oxford, still an all-white institution. Evers encouraged him, put him in touch with NAACP attorneys and counseled and supported him until his graduation in 1963. Evers and his wife also signed a petition to the Jackson school board asking for desegregation of the city's schools in August 1962. When the board took no action, they joined in a federal court suit to integrate the schools, the first such case to be filed by individuals in Mississippi.

The next year Evers led a major antisegregation drive in Jackson. On May 12, 1963 a mass meeting called by the NAACP adopted a resolution demanding fair employment opportunities for blacks in city jobs, the desegregation of all public facilities and accommodations in Jackson, an end to discriminatory business practices and the appointment of a biracial committee to achieve these goals. Jackson Mayor Allen Thompson rejected all the demands the next day, and on May 17 Evers called for a consumer boycott which quickly spread from a few local products and one department store to all the stores in Jackson's main shopping area. The Mayor finally met with an NAACP committee on May 28, but when black leaders reported afterwards that he had agreed to several of their key demands, the Mayor denied their statements. Black college students in Jackson began sitting in at local lunch counters that day, and on May 30 a student march was attacked by the police and 600 were arrested.

According to his wife Evers was initially wary of the student protests and wanted the time and place of demonstrations carefully chosen and their purpose made clear. Evers and other adults in the black community were won over by the students' courage, however, and Evers was soon organizing protests and arranging bail for the jailed students. On June 1 he was arrested for picketing. Released from jail soon after, Evers led a daily campaign of mass meetings, marches, picketing and prayer vigils. On the evening of June 11, with the

Jackson protests still in high gear, Evers listened to President Kennedy's nationwide address on civil rights, spoke at a mass rally in Jackson and then drove home. Around 12:20 a.m., as he walked from his car to the door of his house, Evers was shot in the back by a sniper. He died within an hour.

Evers had received little publicity for his work while alive, but his death made him a celebrated martyr of the civil rights movement. Funeral services were held in Jackson on June 15, and some 3,000 blacks marched that day behind a hearse bearing Evers's body. On June 19 Evers was buried in Arlington National Cemetery. The Jackson demonstrations he had led were suspended on June 17 while another local black leader met with President Kennedy in Washington. After a call from the President and Attorney General Robert Kennedy, Mayor Thompson met with a committee of black leaders on June 18. Later he announced that the city would hire six blacks as policemen and eight as school crossing guards and would promote another eight blacks in the sanitation department. On June 23 the Federal Bureau of Investigation arrested Byron de la Beckwith, a fertilizer salesman from Greenwood, Miss., and a member of the segregationist White Citizens Council. He was indicted by a country grand jury in July in connection with Evers's murder and was tried twice early in 1964. After both trials ended in hung juries, he was free.

For further information:
Mrs. Medgar Evers with William Peters, *For Us, the Living* (Garden City, 1967).

FARMER, JAMES L(EONARD)
b. Jan. 12, 1920; Marshall, Tex.
National Director, Congress of Racial Equality, February 1961-March 1966.
Assistant Secretary of Health, Education and Welfare, March 1969-December 1970.

After graduating from Wiley College in Texas in 1938, Farmer enrolled at the School of Religion at Howard University where he became well versed in pacifist thought. He received a Bachelor of Divinity degree in 1941 and then served as race relations secretary for the Fellowship of Reconciliation, a Christian pacifist organization, until 1945. While in this post he helped found the Congress of Racial Equality (CORE), first as a local Chicago group in the spring of 1942 and then as a national organization in June 1943. An interracial association, CORE applied Gandhian techniques of nonviolent direct action to racial segregation and discrimination in the U.S., pioneering the use of sit-ins and other forms of nonviolent protest. Farmer later worked as an organizer for several unions and as program director for the NAACP, but he remained in touch with CORE and its activities.

Farmer became national director of CORE on Feb. 1, 1961, and on March 13 he issued a call for a Freedom Ride through the South to challenge segregation at interstate bus terminals. Thirteen riders, including Farmer, left Washington by bus on May 4 with New Orleans as their destination. The first ride ended on May 14, however, after one bus was burned in Anniston, Ala., and several riders were severely beaten there and in Birmingham, Ala. On May 23, in Montgomery, Ala., Farmer and other rights leaders announced that the rides would continue despite threats of violence. Farmer and 26 other riders left for Jackson, Miss. the next day in two heavily guarded buses. There they were arrested when they tried to use the white waiting room at the bus terminal and, when found guilty of breach of the peace, elected to go to jail rather than pay their fines. Farmer spent 39 days in jail and then continued organizing more rides through the summer. As Farmer later noted, the Freedom Rides "catapulted CORE into fame," making it a major civil rights organization and Farmer a black leader of national stature. The rides ended after the Interstate Commerce Commission issued an order on Sept. 22 prohibiting segregation in all interstate bus terminals.

As CORE national director, Farmer traveled extensively to raise money, organize new CORE chapters and assist local action projects. In May 1963 he went to North Carolina to lead demonstrations and help coordinate protest movements in Greensboro, Durham and High Point. In each city Farmer led mass marches and boycotts until a biracial committee was appointed to work for the desegregation of public accommodations. Farmer went to Plaquemines, La., in August 1963 where local blacks aided by CORE workers had begun demonstrations to achieve desegregation in the town. The protests intensified on Aug. 19 when Farmer led a mass march of 500 blacks that was broken up by police. Farmer was arrested along with key local leaders and remained in jail until Aug. 29. He led another march of 600 blacks to the county courthouse on Sept. 1. This was also broken up by police using tear gas, fire hoses and electric cattle prods. State troopers then began a house-to-house search for the demonstration leaders, especially Farmer. Fearing that he would be killed if found, several local blacks hid Farmer in a hearse and took him over back roads to New Orleans. Farmer later described his escape during that "night of wild terror" as "a story book escape that was no story while I was living it."

Under Farmer CORE became known as one of the most militant and creative groups in the civil rights movement and he developed a reputation as a tough and audacious rights leader of great physical courage. Farmer was a co-chairman of the 1963 March on Washington, but he missed the Aug. 28 march since he was then in the Plaquemine jail.

In April 1964 the Brooklyn chapter of CORE announced plans for a "stall-in" of cars on major routes leading to the New York World's Fair, set to open on April 22. The proposed demonstration, intended to protest the condition of blacks in New York City, immediately became a center of controversy. Farmer publicly opposed the idea, saying the stall-in would not be orderly or nonviolent or effective in dramatizing blacks' needs. When the Brooklyn chapter refused to drop its plans, the national CORE office suspended the branch and quickly developed its own plan for demonstrations at specific sites within the fair grounds. Only 12 cars attempted to stall-in on April 22, but several hundred people demonstrated in the fair grounds, Farmer among them.

Despite his opposition to the disruptive stall-in, Farmer refused to endorse a July 1964 statement, issued by the leaders of several other civil rights organizations, that called for a "moratorium" on mass demonstrations during the 1964 presidential campaign. Farmer asserted that "people must be allowed to protest" and said CORE would engage in "all the necessary nonviolent action" to support the challenge of the Mississippi Freedom Democratic Party (MFDP) against the seating of the regular Mississippi delegation at the Democratic National Convention in August 1964. CORE workers led a round-the-clock vigil outside the Convention hall in Atlantic City while the MFDP's challenge was being considered.

In January 1965 the all-black Voters League in Bogalusa, La., invited CORE to aid in a campaign for desegregation and increased black employment in the town. Farmer joined the highly publicized protests in April, leading mass marches to the city hall on April 9 and 20. Vice President Hubert H. Humphrey reportedly intervened in late April and convinced Farmer and CORE to accept a mediation effort and halt their demonstrations. During the Bogalusa demonstrations Farmer defended CORE's controversial association with the Deacons for Defense, a black self-defense group that often supplied protection against intimidation and assaults to civil rights workers in Louisiana. After reaffirming CORE's own commitment to nonviolence, Farmer stated that CORE had "no right to tell Negroes in Bogalusa or anywhere else that they do not have the right to defend their homes. It is a constitutional right."

At its July 1965 annual convention, CORE delegates adopted a resolution calling for the withdrawal of U.S. troops from Vietnam. Although a pacifist and opponent of the Vietnam war, Farmer objected to the resolution on the grounds that the peace and civil rights movements should remain separate. He organized a successful effort to retract the resolution before the convention's end. The same convention endorsed a continuation of the civil rights drive in Bogalusa, and the campaign there was resumed on July 7. Farmer returned to the city and led 600 people in a silent march on July 11. The demonstrations continued into early August, eventually bringing Louisiana Gov. John J. McKeithen and John Doar [q.v.], head of the Justice Department's Civil Rights Division, to Bogalusa to try to resolve the crisis. The Bogalusa campaign finally ended with desegregation of local restaurants and theaters, the employment of two black policemen and a beginning of school desegregation under court order.

CORE announced in December 1965 that Farmer would resign as national director on March 1, 1966. Farmer explained that he was planning to establish and head a private agency, the National Center for Community Action Education, which would oversee a nationwide program to improve literacy and job skills among unemployed minorities. Farmer had submitted a proposal for this project to the Office of Economic Opportunity (OEO) in August 1965, and he later said he had received "assurances" from OEO before he left CORE that OEO would fund the center. By July 1966 OEO had not approved a grant for the project, and Farmer announced he was abandoning his plan for lack of funding. According to historians August Meier and Elliott Rudwick, several big city mayors were wary of Farmer's center and its radical supporters. Their pressure allegedly kept the Johnson Administration from funding the project. In July 1966 Farmer was named a consultant to New Jersey's antipoverty program, and in September he joined the faculty of Lincoln University as a professor of social welfare.

Farmer surprised many of his friends in the civil rights movement when he joined Black Independents and Democrats for Rockefeller in July 1968. When Nixon received the Republican nomination, Farmer denounced his civil rights record as "apathetic at best and negative at worst." Shortly before his inauguration, however, Nixon met with several black leaders and promised to do "more for the underprivileged and more for the Negro than any President has ever done." He offered

Farmer the position of assistant secretary of Health, Education, and Welfare (HEW) with special responsibility for relations with black youth. Farmer accepted the offer and was confirmed by the Senate in March 1969. Of all the blacks appointed to office by Nixon, Farmer was by far the most prominent.

It quickly became apparent, however, that the Nixon Administration's policies were antagonistic to the goals of the civil rights movement. In January 1969 HEW Secretary Robert Finch [q.v.] announced that he was extending the deadline for Southern school districts to comply with desegregation guidelines. In June the Administration presented a substitute proposal for extension of the 1965 Voting Rights Act that would have seriously weakened the legislation. The nomination of Clement Haynesworth [q.v.], and G. Harrold Carswell [q.v.], both of whom had poor civil rights records, to the Supreme Court was a further blow to Farmer and others who had placed faith in the new Administration.

In late February 1970 a memo by White House adviser Daniel Patrick Moynihan [q.v.], in which he urged a policy of "benign neglect" toward blacks, was leaked to the press. Several days later Farmer and 36 other black officials in the Administration conferred with Nixon on civil rights. They reported that they were feeling heavy pressure from the black community and that only stronger presidential action on behalf of civil rights would relieve it. Farmer asked Nixon in particular "to clarify his posture" on school desegregation, one of the more volatile issues.

Farmer resigned from HEW on Dec. 7, 1970. At the time he declined to criticize Nixon and cited personal reasons for his resignation. Farmer said that the "ponderous bureaucracy" prevented him from achieving gains "sufficient, or fast enough, to satisfy my appetite for progress." In January 1973, however, Farmer acknowledged that he had had "great difficulty" remaining in the Administration because the President isolated himself from blacks and instead relied on white aides for advice on racial matters.

After resigning from government office, Farmer pursued his idea of a training program for blacks. Still unable to obtain funding for a community-organizing project, he announced in July 1973 the formation of the Public Policy Training Institute in conjunction with Howard University. The purpose, he said, was to study the impact of government policy on blacks and to bring teachers from black colleges to Washington to gain understanding of how public policy is set.

In February 1976 Farmer quit his membership in CORE after its director Roy Innis announced that CORE was recruiting black mercenaries to assist anti-Communist forces fighting in the Angolan civil war.

Throughout the late 1970s Farmer continued his involvement in civil rights causes.

[JD]

FAUBUS, ORVAL E(UGENE)
b. Jan. 7, 1910; Combs, Ark.
Governor, Ark., 1955-67.

The son of a socialist and liberal Democrat, Faubus was born in the Ozark mountains of northwestern Arkansas. He worked as a school teacher and itinerant fruit picker while attending State Vocational High School at Huntsville. Following graduation Faubus was employed in the lumber industry in Washington. In 1936 he ran unsuccessfully for the Democratic nomination for representative to the state Assembly. He was elected Madison Co. circuit clerk in 1938 and reelected in 1940. Faubus served in the Army during World War II. He returned home in 1947 and bought the local Madison Co. *Record*. His liberal editorials caught the attention of Gov. Sidney McMath, who brought the young Faubus to Little Rock as state highway director. He served at that post from 1949 to 1952.

Denouncing incumbent Gov. Francis Cherry as the tool of special interests, Faubus won the August 1954 Democratic gubernatorial primary and went on to win a two-year term in November. As governor he instituted a populist program of social and economic development. Under his direction the legislature reformed welfare laws, established a conservation commission, increased mental health facilities and formed the Arkansas Industrial Development Commission, under the chairmanship of Winthrop Rockefeller, to encourage the industrialization of the state. Faubus also began complying with the 1954 Supreme Court decision banning segregation in public schools. Six out of seven state colleges were desegregated as were schools in Fayetteville, Hoxi and Charleston.

Seeking a second term in 1956 against segregationist Jim Johnson, Faubus began to modify his stand on racial integration. Following a statewide survey indicating the 85% of the people opposed desegregation, he announced that he "could not be a party to any attempt to force acceptance of a change to which the people were so overwhelmingly opposed." During the fall the Governor campaigned for a law giving the state power to assign pupils to school by race and a resolution interposing state law against federal acts deemed illegal. Both measures passed, and Faubus won reelection. Faubus openly opposed forced integration and favored local option in the desegregation controversy. Yet none of his proposals would have penalized communities that integrated their schools, and he consistently rejected calls to nullify the Supreme Court decision.

Following the Little Rock School Board's decision to integrate Central High School in the fall of 1957, the Capital Citizens' Council launched an intensive propaganda campaign demanding the Governor intervene to prevent bloodshed and preserve segregation. On the other hand, Little Rock school superintendent Virgil Blossom asked the Governor for a public commitment to law, order and peaceful desegregation. Faubus steadfastly refused to take a stand on the issue. His last-minute call for help to the Justice Department was answered by a statement that the Administration did not wish to get involved. The Administration compounded Faubus's problems by leaking his conversation to the press.

Fearing the revelation would injure his chance for reelection, Faubus was forced into a more extreme position. After attempts to delay desegregation through court action had failed, he ordered the National Guard to prevent desegregation at Central High School on Sept. 2. Four days later President Eisenhower announced he opposed using federal troops to enforce court orders and would not exercise his option of federalizing the National Guard. Moderate Democratic Rep. Brooks Hays (D, Ark.) arranged a meeting between Faubus and Eisenhower in an attempt to reach a compromise, but the Sept. 14 conference ended inconclusively.

Responding to a federal injunction on Sept. 20, Faubus abruptly removed the Guard. The city appealed to the federal court and the Justice Department for marshals to escort black students, but its request was turned down. Desegregation began on Sept. 23, but the limited number of city police and state troopers could not control the hostile mob. Eisenhower issued a proclamation ordering obstruction of justice to cease. The following day Little Rock Mayor Woodrow Mann officially asked Eisenhower for federal intervention. The President issued a second proclamation federalizing the Arkansas National Guard and ordering the 101st Army Airborne Division to Little Rock. On Sept. 25 federal troops escorted black students through white mobs to class. The troops remained in Little Rock through November.

Faubus continued to oppose integration throughout 1958. In August he called on Little Rock's School Board to avoid desegregating the remaining high schools or resign. This time Eisenhower indicated he would enforce court decisions. When the Supreme Court reaffirmed its desegregation ruling in September, Faubus signed 14 segregation bills and closed all Little Rock high schools. Later that month Little Rock citizens backed the Governor by voting more than 70% against reopening their schools on an integrated basis. That year Faubus also disbanded the NAACP by

executive fiat on the grounds that it was delinquent in tax payments.

By early 1959 a reaction began to set in against Faubus's actions. In March the city's Chamber of Commerce called for reopening Little Rock schools on a desegregated basis. That May three moderates were elected to the school board over segregationists backed by Faubus. The city peacefully desegregated its high schools in August.

Faubus ran a moderate campaign the following year and won reelection against a strong segregationist. He went on to win two more terms and retired in 1967. Opposing school busing in 1970, he again ran for governor but lost the Democratic primary. In 1977 Faubus was reportedly employed as a bank teller.

For further information:
Numan V. Bartley, *The Rise of Massive Resistance* (Baton Rouge, 1969).
Virgil T. Blossom, *It Has Happened Here* (New York, 1959).
Corinne Silverman, *The Little Rock Story* (University, Ala., 1959).

FAUNTROY, WALTER E(DWARD)
b. Feb. 6, 1933; Washington, D.C.
Vice Chairman, District of Columbia City Council, September 1967-March 1969.

Fauntroy attended Washington public schools and graduated from the Yale Divinity School in 1958. The following year he became pastor of Washington's New Bethel Baptist Church. In 1960 Fauntroy was made the Washington bureau director of the Southern Christian Leadership Conference (SCLC), and in that post he became a close friend of Martin Luther King [q.v.]. He was a coordinator of the March on Washington in 1963. Fauntroy also participated in James Meredith's first march in Mississippi in 1965 and in the 1966 Selma-to-Montgomery march. On Sept. 6, 1967 the 34-year-old Baptist minister was appointed vice chairman of the Washington city council by President Johnson.

While councilman, Fauntroy remained active in the civil rights movement. He joined with Stokely Carmichael [q.v.] in January 1968 in an attempt to create a "Black United Front" of moderate and radical leaders to formulate a unified black political program. The next month Fauntroy refused to bow to the demands of Rep. William J. Scherle (R, Iowa) that he resign his council seat or cease his support of the Poor People's March planned by the SCLC for later in the spring of 1968. In the aftermath of Martin Luther King's assassination that year, Fauntroy urged Carmichael to disavow his call for insurrection. He appealed to blacks to refrain from rioting and later toured part of Washington with Sen. Robert F. Kennedy (D, N.Y.). In February 1969 President Nixon accepted Fauntroy's resignation from the District city council.

Fauntroy served as national coordinator of the ongoing Poor People's campaign in 1969. In March 1971 he was elected as the District of Columbia's first non-voting congressional delegate. A leading advocate of Washington home rule and the election of the city's mayor, Fauntroy was returned to his seat in 1974.

FEATHERSTONE, RALPH
b. 1939.
d. March 10, 1970.
Program Director, Student Nonviolent Coordinating Committee, 1967-69.

During the early 1960s Featherstone worked as a speech therapist in Washington, D.C. He became active in the civil rights movement in 1964, when he helped organize the Mississippi Summer Project. The Project's aim was to register black voters in the Deep South. Featherstone headed the Project's Freedom Force, which led demonstrations and attempted to raise black consciousness by organizing courses in black history and community problems. Shortly after the Project ended Featherstone began to work for the Student Nonviolent Coordinating Committee (SNCC), one of the Project's sponsors. As a SNCC field secretary in Mississippi and Alabama, he gained the reputation of being a skilled and dedicated organizer. Much of his work for SNCC was a continuation of the Summer Project—registering voters, conducting classes and leading demonstrations.

In May 1967 Featherstone became national program director of SNCC. His close friend, H. Rap Brown [q.v.], was named SNCC chairman at the same time. The two leaders shared a growing impatience over civil rights progress and sought to draw a line between their organization and its white liberal supporters. In August 1967 Featherstone caused a controversy by defending an anti-Zionist article which appeared in the SNCC Newsletter. He denied that the SNCC was anti-Semitic, but attacked "those Jews in the little Jew shops in the ghettos." Many Jewish liberals, including Theodore Bickel and Harry Golden, withdrew their support from SNCC as a result; civil rights leaders, including Whitney Young [q.v.] and Bayard Rustin [q.v.], also criticized the SNCC stand. Featherstone again alienated liberals in 1968 by attending a cultural congress in Cuba, which he called "the only free territory in America."

Featherstone left SNCC in 1969 to help establish a farm cooperative in Mississippi and a civil rights bookstore in Washington, D.C. He died in March 1970 when a bomb exploded in a car he was driving. Some blacks suspected that the Ku Klux Klan was responsible, but police claimed that Featherstone had accidentally detonated a device he was carrying in the car. Featherstone's remains were taken to Libya for interment.

FORMAN, JAMES
b. Oct. 4, 1928; Chicago, Ill.
Executive Secretary, Student Nonviolent Coordinating Committee, October 1961-May 1966.

A 1957 graduate of Roosevelt University in Chicago, Forman did graduate work in African studies at Boston University and then taught for several years in Chicago public schools. In 1960 and 1961 he helped organize aid for black sharecroppers who had been evicted from their farms in Fayette County, Tenn., after registering to vote. In Tennessee Forman got to know members of the influential Nashville chapter of the Student Nonviolent Coordinating Committee (SNCC) and joined SNCC in October 1961. Shortly afterwards Forman was named executive secretary of the organization, and he spent much of the next six years at SNCC's Atlanta headquarters developing an effective communications system among SNCC workers, handling publicity, devising fund-raising mechanisms and helping establish policy.

Forman also spent time in the field, directly participating in SNCC demonstrations and voter registration drives. With other SNCC workers he launched a desegregation drive in Albany, Ga., in November 1961. The city's bus and railroad terminals were their first target. Three attempts to integrate the bus station were made in November, and on Dec. 10 Forman led a group of four blacks and five whites in a test of railroad facilities. Ignoring a conductor's order to segregate themselves, the group sat together on a Central of Georgia train from Atlanta to Albany. On arrival all entered the white waiting room at the Albany terminal where eight, including Forman, were arrested. The test efforts and arrests galvanized the local black community to greater protest. In mid-December, the local leadership called in Martin Luther King [q.v.] to help lead and publicize the demonstrations, which continued through the summer of 1962.

Forman also joined in February 1962 demonstrations to desegregate the visitor's galleries at the state capitol building in Atlanta, Ga. He participated in a voter registration drive in Greenwood, Miss., begun by SNCC in February 1963, which resulted in several shootings and the harassment of registration workers. On March 27 Forman led 10 rights workers in a march on the county courthouse to protest the violence in Greenwood and to dramatize the right of blacks to register. The group was arrested; Forman and seven others were found guilty of disorderly conduct and given maximum sentences of four months in prison and a $200 fine. They were released from jail on April 4 after federal and city offi-

cials agreed that the federal government would postpone its voter discrimination suit against local officials in exchange for the release of the eight protesters.

Forman helped organize a May 1963 "Freedom Walk" originally undertaken in April by William Moore, a white Baltimore postal employe. Moore had planned a solitary pilgrimage from Chattanooga, Tenn., to Jackson, Miss., to deliver an appeal for integration to Mississippi Gov. Ross Barnett [q.v.]. When Moore was found murdered on April 24 near Attalla, Ala., SNCC and the Congress of Racial Equality decided to continue the march to protest Moore's murder. Ten people began the march on May 1 with Forman accompanying them to do logistical work. On May 3 they crossed into Alabama where they were arrested by state troopers on breach of peace charges.

Forman also participated in the May 1963 Birmingham demonstrations led by Martin Luther King and his Southern Christian Leadership Conference (SCLC), although by that time Forman and SNCC had become very critical of King. Forman wrote in his autobiography that King's participation in protests usually inhibited the development of local leadership and of a mass movement among Southern blacks. He charged that King and SCLC often dampened the militance of demonstrations to protect their own image and prestige. Forman joined in June 1963 protests in Danville, Va., aimed at desegregating municipal facilities and increasing municipal employment of blacks. He was present at the March on Washington in August 1963 where SNCC chairman John Lewis [q.v.] spoke as the organization's representative. When other march sponsors objected to Lewis's prepared address on the night before the march, Forman joined in the negotiations over the changes to be made in Lewis's speech and helped write the final, more moderate draft.

SNCC initiated another major voter registration drive in Selma, Ala., in September 1963. There Forman helped organize an Oct. 7 "Freedom Day" to protest voting discrimination against local blacks. Some 300 blacks came to the county courthouse in Selma and stood in line the entire day waiting to register. Local sheriff's deputies did not break up the queue, but they barred Forman and other SNCC workers from bringing any food or water to those on the registration line.

Forman participated in January 1964 demonstrations to desegregate public accommodations in Atlanta, Ga. He and SNCC chairman John Lewis [q.v.] led a Jan. 18 protest outside a segregated restaurant in which 78 were arrested. Forman himself was arrested in demonstrations at another segregated restaurant on Jan. 27. During the next few months he helped plan the 1964 Mississippi Freedom Summer, a project to increase black voter registration and to establish freedom schools and community centers for blacks in that state. He helped train the student volunteers for the project and directed SNCC's national office which was moved from Atlanta to Greenwood, Miss., for the summer. Forman accompanied the delegates of the Mississippi Freedom Democratic Party (MFDP) to the Democratic National Convention in Atlantic City in August 1964, where they challenged the seating of Mississippi's regular Democrats. When the Party leadership offered the MFDP a compromise in which it would receive two "at-large" seats in the Convention, Forman urged the delegates to reject the proposal, which they did. Forman and SNCC also supported the MFDP's unsuccessful 1965 challenge to the seating of Mississippi's five representatives in Congress.

SNCC and the Southern Christian Leadership Conference cooperated in an intensive voter registration drive in Selma, Ala., beginning in January 1965. During the campaign Martin Luther King [q.v.] suggested a march from Selma to Montgomery to protest the denial of voting rights to Alabama blacks. Forman opposed the idea because he felt that mass marches "create the impression" that the people were forcing change while in fact they achieved almost nothing. The march began March 7 but was quickly routed when state troopers attacked the demonstrators at the Edmund Pettus Bridge in Selma. Forman, unwilling to let such violence successfully end the protest, joined a second attempt to begin the march, which was also turned back at the bridge on March 9. The next day Forman joined in a demonstration in Montgomery, organized by students from Tuskegee Institute to protest the police attacks in Selma, in which the protesters marched to the state capitol and staged a sit-in on its steps until 2 a.m. Forman led another march on the capitol on the 16th, but the 600 marchers were attacked en route by state and county police wielding ropes, nightsticks and electric cattle prods. That evening Martin Luther King addressed a rally in Montgomery and called for a mass march on the county courthouse the next day. Forman, King and John Lewis led a March 17 demonstration of 1,600 people. When they reached the courthouse, several of the rights leaders conferred with the local sheriff and John Doar [q.v.] of the Justice Department, reportedly reaching an agreement that harassment of orderly demonstrations would be ended so long as rights leaders obtained parade permits for all future marches in Montgomery. Forman and local students continued demonstrations in the city until March 21, when the final march from Selma began. Forman, whose commitment to nonviolence had been tactical rather than philosophical at the time he joined SNCC, later wrote that the Montgomery protests, especially the March 16 demonstration and the police attack, "snapped" his "ability to continue engaging in nonviolent direct action."

Forman was voted out as executive secretary of SNCC at a staff meeting in Kingston Springs, Tenn., in May 1966. According to his account in *The Making of Black Revolutionaries,* he had wanted to leave the post since the fall of 1964 to give himself more time for reading, analysis and writing and to rebuild his health. (Forman had nearly died of a bleeding ulcer in January 1963 and had recurrent health problems after that.) At the same meeting SNCC adopted a resolution introduced by Forman to stop using integrated field teams, and elected Stokely Carmichael [q.v.] chairman over John Lewis. Forman supported Carmichael's election on the grounds that his greater militance and his emphasis on blackness represented the direction in which SNCC should move. He also supported the black power concept expounded by Carmichael after his election.

Forman remained active in SNCC as administrator of its national office during the leadership transition and as its director of international affairs after the spring of 1967. He attended the National Conference for New Politics held in Chicago over Labor Day weekend in 1967. There he supported the organization of a black caucus at the Conference and the caucus's demands for 50% of the delegate votes and for endorsement of a statement condemning Israel as an aggressive, imperialist power. Addressing the Conference on Sept. 3, Forman argued for separate political action by blacks, asserting that blacks "have the responsibility to wage our own war of liberation as we see fit" and the "right to define the manner in which we will fight our aggressors." Forman was named minister of foreign affairs of the Black Panther Party in February 1968 when the Party and SNCC formed an alliance. The alliance fell apart in July 1968, and Forman resigned his Party post because of policy differences with the Panthers on questions of security, structure and organizational discipline.

In April 1969 Forman presented a "Black Manifesto" at a Detroit conference on black economic development called by the Interreligious Foundation for Community Organization. The Manifesto called for the establishment of a permanent National Black Economic Development Conference (NBEDC). It demanded that white churches give $500 million to the NBEDC as reparations for their past wrongs to blacks, with the money to be used for educational, cultural and industrial programs in the black community. NBEDC was set up as a permanent organization, and throughout the summer, Forman presented the demand for reparations at the headquarters or conventions of various religious denominations. NBEDC named Forman the director of its programs of community organization in 1970.

For further information:
James Forman, *Sammy Younge, Jr.: The First Black College Student to Die in the Black Liberation Movement* (New York, 1968).
The Making of Black Revolutionaries (New York, 1972).

GALAMISON, MILTON A(RTHUR)
b. Jan. 25, 1923; Philadelphia, Pa.
Clergyman, civil rights leader.

Son of a Philadelphia postal clerk, Galamison received a Master of Theology degree from Princeton Theological Seminary in 1949. That year he was named pastor of the Siloam Presbyterian Church in Brooklyn. Under Galamison, Siloam became an important social service center. Membership increased from 500 to 2,000, giving his church the largest Presbyterian congregation in Brooklyn.

During the 1950s, as chairman of the education committee of the Brooklyn NAACP and later as Brooklyn NAACP president, Galamison pressed the New York City Board of Education to eliminate de facto school segregation. As the civil rights movement gathered momentum in the early 1960s, Galamison founded and assumed leadership of the city-wide Coordinating Committee for Integrated Schools, which represented the NAACP, the Congress of Racial Equality (CORE), the New York Urban League and his own Parents Workshop for Equality. In December 1963 Galamison stated that the entire city school system could be desegregated within three years, beginning with the integration of the junior high schools the following September.

When the Board of Education and Superintendent of Schools Calvin Gross failed to satisfy these demands, Galamison, with the assistance of March on Washington organizer Bayard Rustin [q.v.], issued a call for a one-day boycott of New York City schools. On Feb. 3, 1964 nearly 45% of the city's pupils were absent while 3,500 demonstrators, including many children, marched on the Board of Education offices demanding integration and the resignation of board president James B. Donovan.

In response the Board of Education proposed to pair 20 white with 20 black elementary schools to achieve integration. This plan angered members of the white parents and taxpayers associations, who opposed sending their children to attend ghetto schools. The plan also failed to satisfy Galamison, who called for a second boycott, arguing that he would rather see the system destroyed than permit it to perpetuate racism. Most New York civil rights leaders counseled against this action because they believed that a second boycott would not be effective. Although the March 5, 1964 boycott was only half as effective as the first, it established Galamison as a civil rights leader with a following independent of established civil rights organizations.

Over the course of the next two years, Galamison came to doubt that integration could be achieved over white objections. Like many civil rights activists in urban areas, he began to argue that upgrading the quality of ghetto schools should take precedence over attempts to integrate them. Black education could be improved, he suggested, only if ghetto residents won full control of their schools, including the authority to determine who would teach in them. Galamison supported the efforts of a parent-community group to win control of an experimental intermediate school in Harlem and three primary schools located in the same district. When the plan was rejected by the Board of Education in December 1966, Galamison, as president of a "people's board of education," staged a three-day sit-in at the office of the Board of Education.

During the spring of 1968 Galamison called for a one-day school boycott in support of the efforts of the Ocean Hill-Brownsville (Brooklyn) school board and its administrator, Rhody McCoy, to force a number of white teachers and administrators out of the school district. Under Albert Shanker's leadership, the United Federation of Teachers (UFT) denounced the transfer of teachers without a hearing and called for a city-wide strike in the fall if the teachers were not reinstated. To head off a strike, Mayor John V. Lindsay in July 1968 appointed Galamison to the New York City Board of Education to negotiate a settlement between McCoy and Shanker. Galamison met regularly with the two men over the summer but failed to find a solution. In the fall the UFT called a series of city-wide strikes that eventually led to the total reorganization of the Ocean-Hill board without McCoy.

After leaving the Board of Education in 1971, Galamison devoted himself to clerical duties at the Siloam Church and withdrew from active educational politics in New York.

For further information:
Diane Ravitch, *The Great School Wars: New York City, 1805-1973* (New York, 1974).

GRAY, JESSE
b. May 14, 1923; Tunica, La.
Harlem rent strike leader, 1963-64.

Gray was educated at Xavier College and Southern University in Louisiana but left without a degree. He worked as a tailor in New York during the early 1950s, before becoming involved in community action and civil rights activities.

Gray was an early supporter of efforts to form tenant associations among black slum-dwellers and first became known as a tenant organizer in Harlem. In 1952 he joined the Harlem Tenants Council and five years later formed his own group, the Lower Harlem Council. This was later renamed the Community Council for Housing and merged into the National Tenants Association, which elected Gray its chairman. In 1964 the Community Council for Housing claimed a membership of 2,000.

Gray participated in an unsuccessful rent strike against Harlem tenement owners in 1959. Four years later he was ready for another attempt, relying on his own organization and the pride of Harlem residents in the civil rights struggles of Southern blacks. The new rent strike began in November 1963 and soon affected 300 buildings in an 18-square-block area of lower Harlem. Other tenant associations joined in 1964, spreading the strike to the Lower East Side of Manhattan and parts of Brooklyn. Gray hoped for a city-wide rent strike but could not achieve the necessary interest and coordination; by the end of 1964 the strike movement had disintegrated. Gray did gain a favorable court ruling, however, which allowed residents of dilapidated buildings to deposit their rent in escrow with a tenant organization until necessary repairs had been made.

Gray's prominence in the rent strike enabled him to speak out on broader issues affecting the black community. He soon became identified with the growing radical wing of the civil rights movement. When Harlem residents protested police treatment of blacks in July 1964, Gray called for "100 skilled black revolutionaries who are ready to die" to correct "the police brutality situation in Harlem." In April 1964 Gray joined other black militants in a group called ACT, which demanded a more forceful strategy from the major civil rights organizations and urged less reliance on white support. Gray spoke at the 1966 convention of the Congress of Racial Equality, which adopted a "black power" philosophy justifying the limited use of force against the white "establishment."

In keeping with his conviction that real change would come only when blacks shared in political power, Gray tried repeatedly to enter New York politics. In 1961 and 1969 he ran unsuccessfully for city council in a Harlem district. In 1970 he sought the congressional seat of Rep. Adam Clayton Powell (D, N.Y.) [q.v.] but lost again. Gray finally won election to the New York State Assembly in 1972, representing a Harlem district. Described as "a grassroots kind of guy with a finger in every pie in Harlem," Gray remained in close touch with his constituents and continued working to improve housing conditions.

GREENBERG, JACK

b. Dec. 22, 1924; New York, N.Y.
Director-Counsel, NAACP Legal Defense and Educational Fund, October 1961- .

A graduate of Columbia College and Columbia Law School, Greenberg joined the Legal Defense and Educational Fund of the NAACP in 1949. Greenberg worked on Fund cases that integrated Southern law schools and graduate schools in the early 1950s. He handled a case challenging racial

segregation in Delaware public schools that was decided by the Supreme Court in 1954 as part of its landmark ruling in *Brown v. Board of Education*. Greenberg later argued more school desegregation cases and worked on *Cooper v. Aaron*, the 1958 Supreme Court case ordering school disegregation in Little Rock, Ark. In 1960 he assisted in writing the brief for *Boynton v. Virginia* in which the Supreme Court held segregation at interstate bus terminals illegal. The decision spurred the organization of the 1961 Freedom Rides. During the 1950s Greenberg served as chief assistant to Thurgood Marshall [q.v.], then director-counsel of the Fund. When Marshall was appointed to a federal circuit court judgeship in October 1961, Greenberg was named the Fund's new director.

From 1961 through 1963 Greenberg oversaw court suits leading to James Meredith's [q.v.] admission to the University of Mississippi in September 1962 and to the desegregation of the Universities of Georgia and Alabama and Clemson College in South Carolina. The Fund also represented thousands of nonviolent civil rights demonstrators arrested in the South in the early 1960s. Greenberg argued *Garner v. Louisiana,* the first case involving sit-in demonstrators to reach the Supreme Court, and in December 1961 the Court unanimously overturned the conviction of 16 blacks arrested in Louisiana sit-ins. Over the next five years the Fund took 45 similar cases to the Supreme Court, winning virtually all of them. In 1963 the Fund also successfully challenged segregation in hospitals receiving federal funds and Southern city ordinances requiring segregation in public accommodations.

In December 1964, with some 3,000 sit-in prosecutions still pending in the South, Greenberg won a ruling from the Supreme Court that the 1964 Civil Rights Act barred state prosecution of peaceful sit-in demonstrators. The Legal Defense Fund also brought the first court suit under the public accommodations section of the 1964 act and secured a federal court order requiring Lester Maddox to serve black customers in his Atlanta restaurant. Over the next several years Greenberg and the Fund initiated numerous legal actions to ensure full implementation of the 1964 law, especially its equal employment opportunity provisions. Subsequent actions of the NAACP Legal Defense Fund were devoted largely to implementing the Voting Rights Act, passed by Congress in 1965.

A leading exponent of the strategy of using litigation to achieve social change, Greenberg launched new Fund campaigns in 1965 for the expansion of prisoners' rights and for the abolition of capital punishment. As part of its prison reform effort, the Fund brought suits challenging disciplinary procedures, inadequate medical care and censorship of mail in prisons. Along with the American Civil Liberties Union, the Fund appealed a series of criminal convictions where defendants had received the death penalty, arguing that the death penalty was both cruel and unusual punishment in violation of the Eighth Amendment and racially discriminatory. By 1968 the campaign had achieved what Greenberg called a temporary "de facto abolition" of capital punishment. In that year there were no executions. The Fund's effort ultimately led to a 1972 Supreme Court decision, *Furman v. Georgia*, in which the death penalty was held unconstitutional when the sentencing authority was free to decide between death and some lesser penalty. (In 1976 the Supreme Court affirmed that the death penalty per se was not unconstitutional.) Greenberg also founded the National Office for the Rights of the Indigent (NORI) in 1967 to assert the rights of the poor in court. With Greenberg as its director and with a million dollar grant from the Ford Foundation, NORI, like the Legal Defense Fund, sought cases likely to set legal precedents affecting large numbers of the poor.

Throughout the 1960s Greenberg oversaw several Supreme Court cases that successfully challenged various devices used to delay school desegregation. He repeatedly pressured the Department of Health, Education and Welfare to take stronger action to speed public school desegregation and to cut off federal aid to state welfare programs administered in a racially discriminatory manner.

In 1970, after the Nixon Administration began a covert attempt to delay desegregation in Southern schools, Greenberg won *Alexander v. Holmes County (Miss.) Board of Education* before the Supreme Court which ordered the dissolution of segregated school systems "at once." A year later in *Griggs v. Duke Power Company* he won an important decision stating that, "employment or promotion tests having a differential racial impact must be shown to be job related." Under Greenberg's leadership the Fund established the Earl Warren Legal Training Program in 1972 in order to provide scholarships and internship programs to black law students who would consider settling in areas where there existed a shortage of lawyers to handle cases of concern to black citizens.

Since his earliest days with the Fund, Greenberg undertook a campaign to examine the inequitable bases by which capital punishment was administered in rape cases. The majority of those put to death had been black and the alleged victims had, almost without exception, been white. In 1972 Greenberg argued one of the cases which resulted in the Supreme Court ruling which outlawed capital punishment because it had been applied arbitrarily "falling with uneven incidence on the poor, uneducated and racial minorities." The decision culminated the Fund's seven-year program to end capital punishment.

By 1974 under Greenberg's supervision, the Fund had expanded to include 25 staff and 400 affiliated attorneys in a national program of civil rights and poverty litigation. In addition to lecturing on the role of litigation in social change, Greenberg conducted a clinical seminar on civil rights at Columbia University Law School during the 1970s.

GREGORY, DICK
b. 1932; St. Louis, Mo.
Comedian, social activist.

The second of six children in a fatherless family, Gregory grew up during the Depression in extreme poverty. He ran track for his St. Louis high school and attended Southern Illinois University on an athletic scholarship. After serving in the Army and drifting through several jobs, Gregory began his career as a comedian in 1958 at a black nightclub in Chicago. By 1961 he had become a nationally known comedy star, commanding salaries of $6,500 a week. His ironic treatment of social issues in his routine won Gregory a reputation as "the Negro Mort Sahl" during the early 1960s. He was the first black social satirist to appeal to both black and white audiences.

Gregory became involved in civil rights in November 1962, when he spoke at a voter registration rally in Jackson, Miss. He became friendly with Medgar Evers, leader of the Mississippi NAACP, and subsequently toured the South, speaking at civil rights rallies and demonstrations. Gregory dropped out of the nightclub circuit entirely in 1966 to devote himself to college appearances aimed at encouraging student activism. During the late 1960s he became increasingly involved in opposition to the Vietnam war. Other issues, such as environmental protection and the rights of American Indians, also drew his attention.

Always an individualist, Gregory did not identify himself with any single civil rights or peace organization. However, his celebrity status enabled him to act alone for the causes he espoused. In November 1967 he began a series of fasts, lasting from 40 to 80 days, to dramatize his stand on the war and other issues. He also led anti-war demonstrations in Chicago during the 1968 Democratic National Convention and was jailed for crossing police lines—his 20th arrest since 1962. In 1967 Gregory ran a write-in campaign against Richard Daley in the Chicago mayoral election, gaining 22,000 votes. A second write-in campaign during the Democratic presidential primaries of 1968 brought him 150,000 votes. In 1969 Gregory attended the World Assembly of Peace in East Berlin, protesting "racism as the prime cause of war."

Gregory's independent crusading drew mixed reactions from other black leaders. James Farmer [q.v.], former leader of the Congress of Racial Equality, praised Greg-

ory for stimulating the political interest of many blacks. But Whitney Young [q.v.] of the National Urban League claimed that Gregory could do more good in the entertainment industry, opening new opportunities for black performers and writers. "There are many activists, but only one Dick Gregory," Young pointed out.

Gregory, in fact, reduced his political activism after 1969, partly for financial reasons. He resumed his nightclub performances in 1970 but left show business again in August 1973. This coincided with a change in Gregory's life style; he moved with his family from Chicago to a farm outside Boston and devoted himself to pursuing a "natural" life, including a vegetarian diet, breathing exercises and running.

Gregory published a number of books at various stages of his career, including *From the Back of the Bus* (1964), *Write Me In* (1968) and *Dick Gregory's Political Primer* (1972).

GROPPI, JAMES
b. 1931, Milwaukee, Wisc.
Adviser, Youth Council of the Milwaukee NAACP, 1964-68.

The son of an immigrant Italian grocer, Groppi grew up on the South Side of Milwaukee. He attended Milwaukee's St. Francis Seminary, where he was ordained as a priest in 1959. Groppi became interested in civil rights at this time, due in part to the discrimination against blacks that he witnessed in the Seminary. After serving as an assistant pastor in an Italian section of Milwaukee, he was transferred to the predominantly black St. Boniface parish in 1963. He also became adviser to the youth council of the local NAACP.

Groppi's first active involvement in civil rights came in 1964, when he participated in several voter registration marches in Mississippi. One year later he supported a school boycott by Milwaukee blacks protesting segregation in the city's educational system. On this occasion he came into conflict with his church superiors in Milwaukee, who opposed clerical participation in the boycott. Groppi was arrested several times in Milwaukee during the mid-1960s for leading or participating in civil rights demonstrations.

In 1967 Groppi and the youth council of the Milwaukee NAACP began to push vigorously for a local open-housing law. When rioting erupted in the city's black ghetto during late July and early August, Groppi blamed the outbreak on the city government's continued refusal to act against discrimination in housing and education. On Aug. 28 Groppi and the NAACP Youth Council began a series of open-housing demonstrations in Milwaukee. Lasting into late November, the protests attracted national attention as the most extensive campaign in the U.S. against housing bias. Most of the marches led by Groppi passed through the city's South Side, provoking violent counter-demonstrations by white residents. After one clash on Sept. 11, Milwaukee Mayor Henry Maier claimed that "the city verged on civil war." The largest of the marches involved 2,300 people, including civil rights workers and clergymen from seven Midwestern states.

On Sept. 13 Milwaukee Archbishop William Cousins abandoned his earlier neutrality to support Groppi's demand for a municipal open-housing law. Other religious groups, including the American Lutheran Church, also gave their support. As a result of the open-housing campaign, the Milwaukee City Council passed a measure on Dec. 13 outlawing discrimination in certain types of housing; this was later expanded into a strict open housing code.

Groppi left the Milwaukee NAACP youth council in November 1968, in order to concentrate on "militant social action involvement" within the St. Boniface parish. He remained active, however, in the city's civil rights movement. In September 1969 he led a group of students and welfare recipients which occupied the Wisconsin State Assembly chamber to protest reductions in state welfare payments. This action alienated Groppi from many of his liberal supporters, who objected to the "disruptive" tactics of the demonstrators.

Groppi was transferred from the St. Boniface parish in June 1970 to the racially mixed Milwaukee parish of St. Michael. In 1972 he entered the Antioch Law School in Washington, D.C., driving a taxi part-time to support himself. Groppi was excommunicated and banned from performing priestly functions when he married in May 1976.

HAMER, FANNIE LOU
b. Oct. 6, 1917; Ruleville, Miss.
d. March 14, 1977; Mound Bayou, Miss.
Vice Chairman, Mississippi Freedom Democratic Party, 1964-77.

The daughter of a sharecropper, Hamer grew up in rural Sunflower County, Miss. Her first contact with the civil rights movement came in 1962, when she led a group of 26 blacks attempting to register to vote in Ruleville, the county seat. Not only was the attempt unsuccessful, but Hamer was jailed and beaten, and her family was evicted from the farm land where they had worked for 18 years. After this experience Hamer joined the Student Nonviolent Coordinating Committee (SNCC), a militant civil rights organization, and worked to register black voters in Mississippi. In 1964 she helped organize Mississippi Freedom Summer, a massive voter registration drive sponsored by SNCC and other national civil rights organizations. At this time she was among the founders of the Mississippi Freedom Democratic Party (MFDP), formed to give newly registered black voters an alternative to the state's white-run regular Democratic Party.

Hamer gained national attention at the 1964 Democratic National Convention, where the MFDP attempted to unseat the regular Mississippi delegation. In hearings before the Convention's credentials committee, MFDP representatives claimed that the state Democratic organization did not support President Johnson and did not represent black voters. Described by historian Thomas R. Brooks as "a robust woman of great dignity," Hamer electrified the Convention when she told how police had repeatedly beaten her in jail after her first attempt at voter registration. Despite widespread sympathy for the MFDP, the credentials committee voted to recognize the regular Democratic delegation. At Hamer's urging the MFDP rejected a compromise offer to seat two MFDP representatives as "special delegates."

The 1964 Convention was an important event in the growing disillusionment of many civil rights activists with their white liberal allies. When SNCC leader Stokely Carmichael [q.v.] called for "black power" in 1966, Hamer supported him and spoke at several rallies at which black separatist principles were promoted. Nevertheless, she worked in Mississippi to broaden the base of the MFDP through cooperation with integrationist and white liberal groups, including the NAACP and the state AFL-CIO. In 1968 the MFDP joined with these groups to form a faction called the Loyal Democrats, which again challenged the regular Mississippi Democrats for recognition at the Party's national convention—this time successfully. Appearing before the 1968 Democratic National Convention as a delegate, Hamer received a standing ovation.

Hamer continued to serve the MFDP as vice chairman after 1968, working for the registration of black voters and the election of black officeseekers. Largely as a result of these efforts, nearly 60% of all black Mississippians were registered to vote in 1973. By this time Mississippi had more black elected officials (145) than any other Southern state.

HENRY, AARON E(DD)
b. July 2, 1922; Coahoma County, Miss.
President, Mississippi Conference of Branches of the NAACP, 1960-   ; President, Council of Federated Organizations, Miss., 1962-65.

Henry grew up in Clarksdale in the Mississippi delta and graduated from Xavier University in 1950. A pharmacist, he returned to Clarksdale and opened a drugstore, which became one of the leading black businesses in the city. In 1952 Henry helped organize the Clarksdale branch of the NAACP, and in 1960 he became president of the Mississippi Conference of NAACP Branches. Henry worked closely with Medgar Evers [q.v.], the NAACP's state field secretary, in efforts to register black voters, organize new NAACP branches and investigate charges of harassment and intimidation from blacks throughout the state.

As a leader of civil rights activity in Mississippi, Henry was repeatedly harassed and arrested. The windows of his drug store were broken innumerable times, and in 1963 his home and his store were both badly damaged by bomb explosions. Henry was convicted of conspiring to harm public trade in January 1962 after he led Clarksdale blacks in a citywide boycott of white merchants. Two months later he was convicted of disturbing the peace for allegedly having made indecent advances on an 18-year-old white youth who had hitched a ride in his car. When the civil rights leader accused the Clarksdale police chief and the county attorney of having concocted the charge, they sued him for libel and won $40,000 from local courts. The U.S. Supreme Court later overturned both the disturbance of the peace conviction and the libel judgment.

Henry was an early supporter of James Meredith [q.v.] in his legal battle to enter the University of Mississippi. After Meredith had finally enrolled at the University in October 1962, Henry denied charges that the NAACP had handpicked Meredith to desegregate the school.

In the spring of 1962 Henry was elected president of the Council of Federated Organizations (COFO), a coalition of the NAACP and other civil rights groups in the state established to conduct a unified voter registration campaign. Henry worked closely with Robert P. Moses [q.v.], project director of COFO and Mississippi field secretary for the Student Nonviolent Coordinating Committee, in planning and organizing voter registration projects throughout the state. COFO first concentrated its efforts in Greenwood, but late in the summer of 1963 it branched out from that delta town and began organizing a statewide "Freedom Ballot," a mock election to be held in November to coincide with the regular state elections. Open to all blacks of voting age, the COFO election was designed to call national attention to the disfranchisement of blacks in Mississippi and to educate blacks about the potential power of the vote. Henry ran as the Freedom candidate for governor on a platform declaring that poor whites as well as blacks suffered under the state's existing political and economic leadership. Some 80,000 votes were cast for Henry on the Freedom Ballot, a figure four times larger than the number of blacks then officially registered to vote in the state.

COFO organized the 1964 Mississippi Freedom Summer Project, an undertaking that brought over 1,000 volunteers into the state to set up community centers, teach in "Freedom Schools," and work on voter registration. The main vehicle for political work was the Mississippi Freedom Democratic Party (MFDP), founded at a statewide convention in April 1964 and intended as an alternative to the segregationist regular Democratic Party in the state. Henry was chosen temporary chairman of the new Party at the convention and worked during the summer on the "freedom registration," which enrolled over 60,000 people as Party members. In August Henry presided at a second MFDP state convention, which selected a 68-member delegation to send to the Democratic National Convention meeting later in the month. Henry was chairman of the group that traveled to Atlantic City to challenge the seating of Mississippi's regular delegation.

The MFDP challenge posed an explosive dilemma to Democratic Party leaders. Through Vice President Hubert Humphrey and former Pennsylvania Gov. David Lawrence, President Johnson proposed to split both Mississippi delegations and divide their votes equally. The MFDP rejected this proposal and in the next three days won support from many liberal Democrats. Henry, Fannie Lou Hamer and other MFDP delegates described Mississippi conditions to the Convention Credentials Committee. A pro-

posal offered by Rep. Edith Green (D, Ore.) to effectively oust the Mississippi regulars and replace them with the MFDP delegation was defeated when Johnson made his opposition to the proposal known.

Finally on Aug. 25 Humphrey and United Auto Workers President Walter Reuther proposed another compromise offering to seat as regular delegates Henry and the Rev. Edwin King, a white minister active in the MFDP. The rest of the delegation was to be seated as "honored guests." King and Henry favored the proposal, and the Credentials Committee quickly adopted the Humphrey-Reuther plan, but the MFDP delegation as a whole voted against accepting the compromise. Aided by sympathetic delegates from other states, MFDP members made their way into the Convention seats reserved for the Mississippi regulars. In the end the fight over the MFDP at the Convention left many civil rights activists embittered with both Democratic Party liberals and their own more moderate leaders like Henry.

In the fall of 1964 Henry was one of four candidates nominated by the MFDP to run for Congress. When the state election commission ruled that the candidates could not be included on the regular ballot, the MFDP organized an independent November election in which Henry received nearly 37,000 votes in his district. The MFDP then challenged the seating of Mississippi's five regular representatives in Congress in January 1965 and asked that its representatives be seated instead. The national NAACP favored a congressional investigation of Mississippi elections but did not endorse the MFDP's effort to seat its own members in Congress. Probably because of this, Henry was the only one of the MFDP candidates who did not join the congressional challenge. The challenge was eventually rejected by the House in September 1965, by a 228-143 vote.

In April 1965 the national office of the NAACP said it was officially withdrawing from COFO. Henry, who had been elected to the NAACP's national board of directors in January, joined in the announcement. Except for Henry's key role, the NAACP had not been heavily involved in COFO. The organization had been staffed primarily by members of the Student Nonviolent Coordinating Committee (SNCC), and the NAACP decided to end its affiliation in 1965, apparently because SNCC was becoming more radical and because policymaking differences appeared in COFO.

Henry remained active in voter registration work, however. Following passage of the federal Voting Rights Act in August 1965, the NAACP, led by Henry and state field secretary Charles Evers [q.v.], took advantage of the law to step up registration efforts among Mississippi blacks. While Henry repeatedly called for more federal examiners and for a stronger federal effort in the state, the NAACP's registration drive helped increase the proportion of voting-age blacks registered to vote from 6.7% in 1964 to 32.9% in 1966. Henry and Evers continually expanded their program, and in 1967 12 blacks won election to state offices in Mississippi.

After the regular state Democratic Party chose only four blacks to be part of its 68-member delegation to the 1968 Democratic National Convention, Henry again helped organize a challenge delegation, the Loyal Democrats of Mississippi. He was elected state chairman of a biracial coalition, which included the NAACP, the MFDP, the state Teachers' Association and the state AFL-CIO, among others. The Loyal Democrats delegation to the Convention won the endorsement of all the major contenders for the Democratic presidential nomination. With Henry as its chairman, the insurgent delegation presented its case to the Credentials Committee, which voted overwhelmingly to unseat the regular delegation and give all of Mississippi's Convention seats to the challengers.

In February 1969 Henry was named a member of a national party committee, headed by Sen. George S. McGovern (D, S.D.), charged with democratizing the 1972 Democratic National Convention. He ran for a seat in the state legislature in 1971 but lost the election by about 400 votes. Henry was made a member of the democratic National Committee in 1972 and was state·

campaign manager for the Party in that year's presidential election.

HICKS, LOUISE DAY
b. Oct. 16, 1919; Boston, Mass.
Democratic Representative, Mass., 1971–73.

The daughter of a local Democratic judge, Louise Day grew up in a tightly-knit, Irish Catholic community in South Boston. She obtained a teaching certificate from Wheelock College in 1938 and taught primary grades for two years. In 1942 she married design engineer John Hicks. Hicks completed her B.S. degree in education at Boston University in 1952 and received her law degree from the same institution in 1955.

In 1961 Hicks won a seat on the Boston School Committee on a pledge to take politics out of the school board. During her first years on the Committee, Hicks compiled a moderate record, attempting to alleviate local disputes on education. However by 1963 she had come out as a supporter of the "neighborhood school" and an opponent of forced busing to achieve integration. Until 1966 she prevented the implementation of massive busing. Hicks ran unsuccessfully for mayor of Boston in 1967 under the somewhat ambiguous slogan, "You know where I stand." She contended that the central issue in the race was the "alienated voter." Hicks lost by 10,000 votes.

In 1969 Hicks ran for and was elected to the Boston City Council. Her platform skirted the racial issue, emphasizing, instead, the problems of crowded schools, street crime and the tremendous tax burden. In 1970 she campaigned successfully for retiring House Speaker John McCormack's (D, Mass.) [q.v.] seat on a platform of law and order, contending further that money spent on military operations could be better spent on inner cities.

During her one term in Congress, Hicks focused her attention on education issues.

She supported legislation designed to postpone court-ordered busing and to permit voluntary prayer in schools. She pushed bills permitting direct federal aid to needy students and allowing tax credits to parents of nonpublic school students, both of which might have assisted the large number of segregated academies that arose during the late 1960s. As a result of redistricting, she lost her 1972 reelection bid.

While still in the House, Hicks attempted a second mayoral bid in 1971. She openly promised to seek repeal or amendment of the state's stiff desegregation laws. Hicks lost by over 40,000 votes out of the 180,000 cast. Hicks won reelection to the City Council in 1977, where she continued to oppose busing.

HILL, HERBERT
b. Jan. 24, 1924; New York, N.Y.
Labor Secretary, NAACP, 1951- .

While preparing for a career in music, his father's profession, Hill was captivated by the dramatic labor organizing struggles in the late 1930s. He soon plunged into radical politics and dropped out of New York University to help organize a local of the steel workers union. In 1948 Hill—who is white—joined the staff of the NAACP and in 1951 was named the Association's labor secretary, in charge of coordinating work against discrimination by private employers and labor unions.

With the rise of the civil rights movement in the 1950s, minority group workers pressed for access to high-paying jobs in industries where a pattern of employer or union discrimination had prevailed. During the Kennedy years, Hill used legal, political and economic tactics to open up employment opportunities for black and Puerto Rican workers. In 1961 President Kennedy issued an executive order barring discrimination by government contractors. Hill filed repeated claims with the newly created Equal Employment Opportunities Committee (EEOC) charging that large defense contractors were willfully violating the order. Assistant Labor Secretary Jerry R. Holleman met with Hill in April 1961 and pledged cancellation of contracts with any employer who refused to comply with the presidential order. Eight leading defense contractors, including Boeing, Douglas and General Electric, signed agreements with the EEOC in July 1961 guaranteeing racial equality in hiring and promotions. Eventually, 52 leading defense contractors pledged non-discrimination. The next year Hill attacked the corporate promises as producing "more publicity than progress."

Hill also increased NAACP pressure on organized labor. In 1959 Hill had sent a public memorandum to AFL-CIO President George Meany charging that the newly merged labor federation had failed to eliminate racial discrimination and segregation in several affiliated unions. Hill renewed his charges in the early 1960s, declaring that the "decade-long attempt to resolve these problems within the labor movement itself" had resulted in "negligible" progress. He cited the machinists, railway clerks, carpenters, electrical workers, operating engineers, plumbers and boilermakers among those unions that practiced "a broad pattern of racial discrimination and segregation" by excluding blacks, maintaining segregated locals, separate racial seniority lines and limiting opportunities in apprentice training for members of racial minorities. In August 1962 Hill charged before a congressional investigating committee that the traditionally liberal International Ladies Garment Workers Union discriminated against black and Puerto Rican workers in New York City. Hill began a campaign in October 1962 to convince the National Labor Relations Board to decertify those unions that rejected NAACP appeals to end discriminatory practices. He filed decertification petitions against the Seafarers International Union, the Brotherhood of Railway Trainmen and an Atlanta local of the United Steelworkers of America.

Hill's criticism and the decertification drive evoked an angry response from established labor leaders. In November 1962 George Meany, United Auto Workers President Walter Reuther, and A. Philip Randolph [q.v.], the AFL-CIO's only Negro vice president, all attacked Hill and the NAACP's union decertification project as destructive of trade unionism. Meany announced Nov. 13 that the AFL-CIO wanted to work with the NAACP but "could not under the circumstances we are faced with by their labor secretary." Charles S. Zimmerman, an ILGWU vice president, resigned as a member of the NAACP's Legal Defense and Education Fund because of Hill's criticism of the garment workers leadership.

NAACP Executive Secretary Roy Wilkins [q.v.] backed Hill in his conflict with union leaders, refusing to allow deteriorating relations between the Negro protest group and the AFL-CIO to inhibit demands for more minority hiring, especially in the nearly all-white building and construction trades. Keeping step with a rising wave of black protest, Hill announced in May 1963 that the NAACP would launch mass actions against construction trade unions that excluded blacks from membership. Picket lines were set up at construction sites in New York, Cleveland and other northern cities during the spring and summer of 1963, halting work in many instances. The protests won a rapid government response. On June 4 President Kennedy ordered a review of all federal construction programs aimed at ending discriminatory hiring practices. Labor Secretary Willard Wirtz announced the same day that "contracts will be cancelled or they will not be let" wherever he encountered opposition to the President's program. In return, Hill announced the NAACP would suspend its picketing of federal construction projects. His most important local victory in the summer of 1963 came in Cleveland where a coalition of civil rights groups reached agreement with a city-wide plumbers union substantially increasing the number of minority members admitted to the union's apprentice program and hiring hall.

As the job market continued to expand during the mid-1960s, Hill increased his efforts to gain what he viewed as a fair share of employment for minority workers. In 1964 and 1966 he led protest campaigns against promotion practices at General Motors and U.S. Steel. The entertainment industry also became a target of Hill's criticism, both for discriminating against black actors and technicians and for portraying blacks in terms of "outworn stereotypes."

Hill's main conflict of this period, however, was with the labor unions, particularly those in the highly skilled and well paid construction industry.

Hill repeatedly attacked the building trades unions for restricting minority membership. With the expansion of housing construction in the 1960s, civil rights groups demanded the creation of training programs designed to qualify blacks for apprenticeships and, eventually, for full-fledged construction jobs. This clashed, however, with the desire of many union officials to limit entry into their trades, both to maintain wages and to minimize unemployment in the event of a slump. In response to this practice, civil rights leaders called for a reform of union hiring-hall practices and, failing this, public supervision of apprenticeship programs. Union leaders in turn viewed these demands as an assault on union independence, reminiscent of earlier attempts at "union-busting."

Hill used several tactics in attempting to gain concessions from union leaders. In 1963 he led a nationwide campaign of sit-ins and demonstrations at publicly funded construction projects that did not meet NAACP standards of fair employment. This campaign, continuing into the late 1960s, was sometimes marked by violence. Hill also sued to block public funds from projects that refused to change their hiring practices, and he filed complaints with the Equal Employment Opportunity Commission against a number of unions for maintaining segregated locals.

All this effort, however, did not bring proportionate results. An NAACP suit to halt state- and city-supported construction in New York failed in 1963. The same year civil rights groups in Cleveland signed an agreement with the local plumbers' union, intended to increase black membership in apprentice programs, but Hill withdrew the NAACP and Urban League from the pact in 1966, claiming that the union continued to discriminate against blacks. A "biracial screening committee," set up to encourage minority employment in the New York building trades, also collapsed after a short time. One consequence of Hill's agitation was an effort by national union leaders to increase minority membership by "voluntary" means, such as disseminating information on training programs. Both the AFL-CIO and the Alliance for Labor Action, comprising the Teamsters and United Auto Workers, endorsed this approach in the late 1960s. However, Hill dismissed such programs as ineffectual "tokenism" in the absence of "sanctions, time-tables and enforcement apparatus."

Hill's activity with the NAACP during the 1960s helped loosen the traditional alliance between civil rights groups and labor. "I have given up long ago trying to satisfy Herbie Hill," stated AFL-CIO president George Meany at the height of the labor-civil rights conflict. In response to labor criticism, Hill wrote that "you must create a crisis to get something done." Most observers thought his efforts important in making the problem of job discrimination a major civil rights issue during the Johnson years.

Hill also promoted the development of black literature in the U.S. He edited and introduced two volumes of writings by black authors: *Soon, One Morning: New Writing by American Negroes* (1963), and *Anger and Beyond: The Negro Writer in the United States* (1966).

HOFFMAN, WALTER E(DWARD)
b. July 18, 1907; Jersey City, N.J.
U.S. District Judge, Eastern District, Va., 1954-   .

Hoffman, a 1928 graduate of the University of Pennsylvania, received his law degree from Washington and Lee University in 1931 and then entered private practice in Norfolk, Va. A Republican who made unsuccessful races for Congress and for state attorney general, he was among the first party leaders in Virginia to support Dwight D. Eisenhower for the Republican presidential nomination in 1952. At the Republican National Convention in Chicago, Hoffman's firmness in backing the General within the divided Virginia delegation reportedly contributed to Eisenhower's nomi-

nation. Eisenhower appointed Hoffman the U.S. district judge for the eastern district of Virginia in 1954. He took his seat that September.

On the bench Judge Hoffman proved to be a stalwart and forthright jurist who insisted on state and local compliance with the U.S. Supreme Court's school desegregation decision of May 1954. In September 1956 the Virginia legislature passed a series of laws designed to thwart school integration, including a pupil placement act and a measure requiring the governor to close any public school faced with a final desegregation order. Hoffman held the pupil placement law unconstitutional in January 1957. The next month, after assailing the state Assembly for adopting "obstructionist" legislation, he ruled that Norfolk, Va., must begin desegregating its schools in the coming fall term. A higher court granted a delay of this judgment, but the U.S. Supreme Court upheld Hoffman's integration order in October 1957.

Hoffman ruled in June 1958 that his 15-month-old desegregation decree for Norfolk must take effect at the opening of the 1958-59 school year. Under this order 151 black pupils applied for admission to all-white schools in the city, but the local school board rejected all the applicants. On Aug. 21 Hoffman opened a hearing on the rejections, and on Aug. 25 he gave the school board four days to reconsider its action. The board agreed on Aug. 29 to admit 17 blacks to formerly all-white schools. Over the next few weeks Judge Hoffman denied a school board plea for a one-year delay of desegregation and enjoined a state court from interfering with his desegregation ruling. After the Fourth Circuit Court upheld Hoffman's order for immediate desegregation in Norfolk on Sept. 27, Gov. J. Lindsay Almond, Jr. [q.v.], closed the six senior and junior high schools involved in the case. By the end of September some 13,000 students had been locked out of nine public schools throughout the state. With the schools closed, the pressure from moderates to end Virginia's "massive resistance" policy grew.

On Jan. 19, 1959 both a three-judge federal court in Richmond, of which Hoffman was a member, and the state Supreme Court of Appeals handed down decisions declaring Virginia's school closing law unconstitutional. The Governor then called a special session of the state legislature, which repealed the massive resistance laws but passed other, less stringent acts to try to discourage school desegregation. In Norfolk, after final orders from Hoffman, 17 black students finally began attending the reopened white public schools on Feb. 2, 1959.

Hoffman was also active in race-related cases not involving the school system. In July 1955 he ordered the integration of Virginia's Seashore State Park. In January 1958 Hoffman was a member of a three-judge federal panel that ruled three of Virginia's six anti-NAACP laws unconstitutional.

According to J.W. Peltason in *58 Lonely Men*, Hoffman's "bluntness and his open criticism of Virginia Democratic leaders" during the school desegregation controversy of the late-1950s "made him one of the major verbal targets of segregationists" in the state. Despite phone calls and letters criticizing his desegregation decisions, Hoffman refused to give way on his rulings.

In Norfolk, where only token school desegregation began in 1959, the NAACP continued to fight the city's school integration plans in court. The litigation finally ended in March 1966, when Hoffman approved an integration plan worked out in negotiations between the school board, the NAACP and the Justice Department. Hoffman served as chief judge for the Eastern District of Virginia from 1962 to 1973 and became a senior district judge in 1974.

HOWE, HAROLD II

b. Aug. 17, 1918; Hartford, Conn.
U.S. Commissioner of Education, January 1966-January 1968.

Harold Howe grew up in Hartford, Conn., attended Taft prep school and graduated from Yale in 1940. After naval service in World War II Howe received a master's degree from Columbia University in 1947. During the 1950s he served as principal of high schools in Massachusetts

and Ohio. In 1960 Howe was appointed superintendent of the Scarsdale, N.Y. school system, where his innovative methods impressed Parent-Teachers Association member John W. Gardner, who was later to be appointed Lyndon Johnson's Secretary of Health, Education and Welfare (HEW). In 1964 Howe was named director of the Learning Institute of North Carolina, a private organization that dealt with education problems, especially those related to poverty and desegregation.

On the recommendations of both Gardner and outgoing Education Commissioner Francis Keppel [q.v.], President Johnson appointed Howe commissioner of education in December 1965. Howe took office in January 1966 at a time when the power and prestige of the Office of Education (OE) had grown as a result of the passage of Johnson Administration education bills.

During his tenure as commissioner, Howe's greatest efforts were concentrated in the area of desegregation. At a March 7, 1966 news conference, he set down strict guidelines for Southern school districts to follow in order to qualify for federal funds granted under the 1965 Elementary and Secondary School Act. His action was initiated to implement Title VI of the Civil Rights Act of 1964, which prohibited racial discrimination in any program or activity receiving federal assistance.

The March HEW guidelines required that between 15% and 20% of the Negro students in a school district attend desegregated schools; that school district officials mail "free choice" notices to all pupils, who could then decide which schools they wished to attend; and that a "significant start" be made in the integration of school faculties. Howe also indicated that the Office of Education planned greater emphasis on compliance reviews, field visits and investigations. He set May 6 as the deadline for compliance.

In April Alabama Gov. George Wallace [q.v.] declared that his state would not submit to the OE guidelines because they violated "the historic right of school boards to handle their own affairs and . . . the historic right of academic freedom." Howe reiterated that school districts failing to meet the May 6 desegregation deadline would be subject to "deferral of [federal] funds." On May 7, 1966 the OE announced that 255 Southern school districts had failed to file pledges of compliance with the guidelines, but that 1,489 districts in 17 Southern and border states had done so.

In a June speech at Columbia University, Howe expressed his displeasure with the slow pace of desegregation and accused U.S. educators of having a "blind faith in gradualism." He declared that schools remained almost as segregated as they had been in 1954, at the time of the Supreme Court's *Brown vs. Board of Education* decision, which outlawed "separate but equal" public education. Howe called upon school administrators to consider redrawing school district boundaries and confederating with neighborhood districts "even though political boundaries may remain unchanged." He insisted that educators must be willing to sacrifice their jobs for desegregation.

Howe's militant position on desegregation angered many Southern congressmen. At a September 1966 House Rules Committee hearing, Rep. L. Mendel Rivers (D, S.C.) denounced him as an "idiot" and a man who "talks like a Communist." There was also considerable friction within the Administration over Howe's position. In April 1966 HEW Secretary John Gardner attempted to soften opposition to the guidelines by assuring Southern governors, congressmen and school officials that HEW was not ordering a specific degree of "racial balance" or requiring "instantaneous desegregation" of school faculties. At an October press conference President Johnson acknowledged that there had been "some harassment and some mistakes" in civil rights enforcement.

On Oct. 19, 1966 Congress passed a bill amending the 1965 Elementary and Secondary Education Act. The law's civil rights provision restricted Howe's authority to defer funds to school districts not complying with Title VI of the 1964 Civil Rights Act. The OE was only permitted to hold funds to schools for up to 60 days pending a hearing and for another 30 days after the hearing. The expanded elementary education act mainly benefited schools in poorer

states, providing them with an estimated $343 million for fiscal 1968.

In May 1967 Secretary Gardner announced that civil rights enforcement power within HEW would be transferred to the newly created Office for Civil Rights, headed by Gardner's special assistant, F. Peter Libassi. Gardner said that he had "complete confidence" in Howe and that "nothing in this change should be taken as a reflection on his standing within the Administration." However, many observers felt the move was an attempt to round up support of Southern Democrats for the 1967 school assistance bill. The measure, authorizing $9.2 billion for fiscal 1969-70, was signed into law on Jan. 2, 1968.

Shortly before his retirement as commissioner, Howe stated that progress in the integration of public schools had been "minimal." The U.S., he said, still faced a racially divided school system with "some 85% of Negro youngsters in the South still [attending] almost fully segregated schools." In a Jan. 9, 1968 interview with Norman C. Thomas, author of *Education in National Politics*, Howe described his role at the OE as "kind of a middle-level crossroads at the top of the bureaucracy." He acknowledged that during the 1960s "much policy development in education has moved from here [Office of Education] to the White House."

On Jan. 12, 1968 Howe resigned to join the Ford Foundation as a director of educational programs in India.

For further information:
Norman C. Thomas, *Education in National Politics* (New York, 1975).

INNIS, ROY
b. June 6, 1934; St. Croix, Virgin Islands.
National Director, Congress of Racial Equality, 1968- .

Innis, the son of a policeman, spent his childhood in the Virgin Islands. He moved to New York as an adolescent and attended City College after serving in the Army. In 1963, while working as a chemistry research assistant in a New York hospital, Innis joined the Harlem chapter of the Congress of Racial Equality (CORE), a militant civil rights organization. He soon became an important leader of Harlem CORE, rising in October 1965 to chapter chairman. In July 1967 Innis was elected second vice chairman of national CORE. He became the organization's acting national director one year later, after the previous director, Floyd McKissick [q.v.], resigned for health reasons. The national CORE convention in September 1968 confirmed Innis as head of the organization.

Innis's rise in CORE resulted largely from his position as a leading advocate of black power, which he embraced as a result of his impatience over the progress of civil rights during the early 1960s. Innis's conception of black power stressed preservation of a distinct black culture and greater reliance on black resources in the struggle for equality. In 1966 he and other Harlem CORE members concluded that the fight for integration of New York City schools was a failure and decided to press for community control over neighborhood schools. At this time Innis proposed an amendment to the New York State constitution providing independent school boards for ghetto areas. This was the first significant instance when integration was replaced by black separation as a civil rights goal. Innis had earlier formed a "black male caucus" as the chief policymaking body of the Harlem CORE, causing white members to leave the chapter. At the CORE national convention of 1966, he fought successfully for a resolution defining the organization's goal as "racial coexistence through black power."

By 1968 Innis, who was originally regarded as a CORE extremist, belonged to the organization's moderate wing. Radicals such as Brooklyn CORE chairman Robert Carson viewed the destruction of American capitalism as a necessary part of black liberation and demanded that CORE reject funds from foundations and other "establishment" sources. Innis countered these arguments with proposals for a program of "black capitalism," translating his separatist philosophy into economic activity. Government and foundation money, he argued,

should be used to finance black-controlled businesses in ghetto areas. In 1967 Innis succeeded in attracting federal funds to the Harlem Commonwealth Council, which encouraged the growth of small industries in Harlem and sought to employ jobless workers. CORE also urged Congress to pass a community self-determination act to attract private capital into the ghettos through tax incentives and matching federal funds. In general, however, the level of outside help for black enterprise remained far below the expectations of CORE.

Innis's rise to the CORE leadership in 1968 was a victory not only for political moderates but also for those who wanted to give the 180,000-member organization a tighter, more centralized structure. The 1968 CORE convention, which confirmed Innis as national director, also voted measures to give the organization's central office greater control over local chapters. A yearly assessment of $100 per chapter was levied for the central treasury. This gave Innis greater influence but also provoked the secession of many chapter heads and organizers who disagreed with his policies. The organization was further reduced in size by a new provision that barred whites from active membership.

Despite these organizational reforms, CORE lost influence within the civil rights movement during the late 1960s. Black power, with its emphasis on self-help, focused attention on smaller groups—community organizations, black student groups, black caucuses in churches and professional societies. CORE's local chapters, reduced to appendages of the central office, developed little significant activity of their own. Innis himself remained active in community affairs, especially in Harlem. He won national attention in 1973 by debating physicist William Shockley on the allegation that blacks are genetically inferior to whites in intelligence.

For further information see:
August Meier and Elliot Rudwick, *CORE: A Study in the Civil Rights Movement* (New York, 1973).

JACKSON, JESSE L(OUIS)
b. Oct. 8, 1941; Greenville, N.C.
National Director, Operation Breadbasket, 1966-71.

The son of a maid, Jackson grew up in the poverty of a small, semi-rural Southern black community. He attended a segregated high school in Greenville and graduated from the predominantly black Agricultural and Technical College of North Carolina at Greensboro in 1964. Jackson became active in civil rights as president of the college student body and led a campaign of sit-ins in Greensboro to desegregate public facilities in 1963. While participating in the Selma voter registration drive of 1965, he came into contact with the Southern Christian Leadership Conference (SCLC) and its leader, Martin Luther King [q.v.]. Jackson later described King as "my father figure, my brother figure and my teacher."

After the Selma campaign Jackson enrolled in the Chicago Theological Seminary, where he was ordained in 1968. While studying in Chicago he worked as an organizer for the SCLC, helping to increase cooperation among local civil rights and community groups. When King decided to open a civil rights drive in Chicago in early 1966, he chose Jackson to supervise the campaign's economic activities. These soon developed into Operation Breadbasket, an effort to improve the economic position of blacks through the coordinated use of black purchasing power. Working through a network of community and church groups, Jackson urged Chicago blacks to buy the products of black-owned companies and to boycott stores that refused to carry these products or practiced racial discrimination in hiring. Within five months nine Chicago companies had signed agreements promising to increase the number of black employees.

The early success of Operation Breadbasket encouraged King and Jackson to extend the program beyond Chicago. In late 1966 Jackson became the head of national Operation Breadbasket, which covered 16 cities. The program's greatest achievement came in 1968, when a 14-week black boycott of the A&P food chain forced the company to sign an agreement providing for increased hiring of blacks and the display of black-manufactured products in its stores. The pact also promised that A&P stores in black neighborhoods would use the services of black truckers, advertisers and other small businessmen.

In April 1968 Jackson was standing next to King in a Memphis motel when King was assassinated. Jackson continued to work for the SCLC after King's death. In May he went to Washington to help organize the Poor People's Campaign, a series of demonstrations and lobbying efforts aimed at increasing federal antipoverty funds. In 1969 Jackson organized a highly successful Black Expo in Chicago, which publicized achievements in business and culture. The interest generated encouraged him to make Black Expo an annual event. Conflicts eventually developed, however, between Jackson and Ralph Abernathy [q.v.], King's successor as SCLC leader. Jackson wanted more authority in the SCLC than Abernathy was willing to give him; Abernathy, in turn, wanted control over Operation Breadbasket funds, which Jackson used in 1971 to finance the Black Expo. In December 1971 Jackson left the SCLC, followed by most of the organization's Chicago chapter.

Jackson immediately founded a new Chicago-based organization, Operation PUSH (People United to Save Humanity), to continue his work. The program's emphasis remained on black economic self-help. In addition to sponsoring the annual Black Expo, Operation PUSH negotiated "covenants" on the hiring of black workers with several large corporations. Although active in Chicago Democratic politics, Jackson urged a reorientation of the civil rights movement from political activism to community economic development, claiming that blacks needed greater financial resources to take advantage of the political rights won in the 1960s.

JOHNSON, FRANK M(INIS), JR.
b. Oct. 30, 1918; Haleyville, Ala.
U.S. District Judge, Middle District,
Ala., 1955-   .

Born in the Republican hill country of northern Alabama, Frank Johnson worked his way through the University of Alabama, receiving his law degree in 1943. He engaged in private law practice from 1946 to 1953 and in 1952 was one of the Dwight D. Eisenhower's presidential campaign managers in Alabama. Johnson was appointed U.S. attorney for the northern district of Alabama in 1953; two years later Eisenhower named him U.S. district judge for the middle district of the state. Johnson began his judicial service on Nov. 7, 1955.

In his Montgomery courtroom Judge Johnson decided several important civil rights cases and in the process won a reputation among most observers as a fair and principled jurist. On June 6, 1956, during the Montgomery bus boycott led by Martin Luther King, Jr. [q.v.], Johnson was in the majority on a three-judge federal court that ruled Alabama's bus segregation law unconstitutional. Three years later he held racial segregation in Montgomery's public parks illegal.

In December 1958 Judge Johnson had the first of many run-ins with George C. Wallace, a former law school classmate who was then a state circuit court judge. On Dec. 8 Wallace defied a subpoena from the U.S. Civil Rights Commission and refused to turn over voter registration records in two counties under his jurisdiction. In three separate decrees issued between Dec. 11 and Jan. 9, Johnson ordered Wallace to let Commission agents examine the records. Wallace kept up his resistance but finally, on Jan. 12 and 13, gave the records to county grand juries which then let Commission employes see the data. On Jan. 26 Johnson dismissed contempt charges against Wallace, explaining that Wallace had complied with court orders, though indirectly, and that punishing him would only promote his political fortunes. Johnson also over-

turned a state court injunction blocking federal investigators from examining voter registration records in Montgomery in August 1960. At the same time he upheld the constitutionality of the 1960 Civil Rights Act against a challenge from the state.

With his even-handed, considered approach, Johnson did not always decide civil rights cases in favor of blacks or the federal government if he thought law or precedent was against them. In one of the first major tests of the 1957 Civil Rights Act, Johnson ruled in March 1959 against the Justice Department. He held that the law did not allow the federal government to bring a voting discrimination suit directly against the state of Alabama. The Fifth Circuit Court upheld his interpretation, and as a result of the adverse ruling Congress included a provision to authorize voting rights suits against the states in the 1960 Civil Rights Act. In a 1960 decision Johnson upheld the expulsion without a hearing of six black students from Alabama State College for having led sit-ins in Montgomery and Tuskegee. A higher court later reversed Johnson, who frequently seemed to disapprove of civil rights demonstrations.

Throughout the 1960s Judge Johnson's rulings pushed reluctant white Alabamans toward desegregation. In March 1961 he entered a sweeping decree, which served as a model for other federal courts, outlawing voting discrimination in Macon Co. Johnson enjoined a planned civil rights march from Selma to Montgomery in March 1965, but later in the month he authorized the march and ordered the state to supply police protection to the demonstrators. Johnson ordered officials in various counties under his jurisdiction to prepare school desegregation plans and in March 1967 was a member of a three-judge court that placed all of Alabama under a school desegregation order. During the 1960s Johnson was a frequent target of criticism from Alabama Gov. George C. Wallace. In the next decade he was further censured by Wallace for rulings requiring the state to upgrade its institutions for the mentally ill and retarded and its prison system. In 1977 President Jimmy Carter nominated him as FBI director.

JOHNSON, PAUL B(URNEY), JR.
b. Jan. 23, 1916; Hattiesburg, Miss.
Governor, Miss., 1964-68.

The son of a Mississippi congressman and governor, Johnson received his law degree from the University of Mississippi in 1940 and practiced in Jackson and Hattiesburg until 1948. In that year he supported the regular Democratic rather than the States' Rights ticket in the presidential election and was appointed an assistant U.S. attorney in Mississippi, serving until 1951. He ran for lieutenant governor in 1959 and won both the Democratic primary and the November election.

Johnson received little attention outside his state until September 1962 when he joined Mississippi Gov. Ross Barnett [q.v.] in defying federal court orders for the enrollment of James Meredith [q.v.] at the University of Mississippi. Barnett twice denied Meredith admission to the University in late September, and on Sept. 26 Johnson blocked Meredith's third attempt to register. Backed by some 35 state troopers and county sheriffs, Johnson stopped Meredith and accompanying federal officials two blocks from the entrance to the Oxford campus. Declaring he was acting in Barnett's "stead, by his direction, and under his instructions," Johnson read a proclamation denying Meredith entry to the University. Later the same day the U.S. Fifth Circuit Court of Appeals cited Johnson for contempt. The Court found him guilty of civil contempt on Sept. 29 and ordered him to comply with its desegregation orders or face a $5,000-per-day fine. Meanwhile Johnson participated in the behind-the-scenes negotiations between Barnett and Attorney General Robert F. Kennedy. On Sept. 30 Meredith entered the campus under an arrangement worked out by Barnett and Justice Department officials. Around 8 p.m., however, a riot broke out at the University, and Barnett sent Johnson to Oxford to aid in ending the disturbance. The riot, in which two men were killed, lasted into the early morning hours and was quelled only after President Kennedy called in the National Guard, 3,000 federal troops and 400 U.S. marshals.

Meredith finally enrolled on Oct. 1 at 8 a.m., but the Fifth Circuit Court refused to drop the contempt charges against Johnson. In December 1962, at the explicit request of the Court, the Justice Department filed additional criminal contempt-of-court charges against Johnson and Barnett. The Kennedys reportedly did not want to press the case against either official for fear of sparking another federal-state confrontation. In the end the Fifth Circuit Court dismissed the charges against both Johnson and Barnett in a 4-3 ruling in May 1965.

Johnson ran for governor in 1963 as a militant segregationist, emphasizing his obstructionist role in the "Ole Miss" crisis throughout the campaign. With backing from Barnett and Sen. James O. Eastland (D, Miss.) [q.v.], Johnson defeated a more moderate candidate in the Aug. 27 Democratic primary runoff and was easily elected in November. In contrast to his strong campaign statements on race, Johnson delivered a moderate inaugural address in January 1964. Concerned with improving Mississippi's national image, Johnson used legal means only to fight desegregation and civil rights measures throughout his term, abandoning the tactic of defiance used in the Meredith crisis and taking a strong stand against lawlessness and disorder.

During Johnson's first year as governor, a coalition of civil rights groups organized a Mississippi Freedom Summer Project to bring large numbers of civil rights workers into the state to conduct voter registration drives and establish freedom schools. Johnson condemned the project, at one point claiming that many project leaders had "Marxist backgrounds." However, when three rights workers disappeared near Philadelphia, Miss., on June 21, Johnson welcomed federal assistance in searching for them, promised full cooperation from the state and urged area residents to aid in the search. He also ordered a state investigation of the series of bombings and shootings that plagued the McComb area that summer, and he played a major role in ending the violence there.

Johnson denounced the 1964 Civil Rights Act and was reportedly against voluntary compliance with the public accommodations section of the law until it had been tested in court. He fought the Mississippi Freedom Democratic Party's (MFDP) challenge to the seating of the regular state delegation at the Democratic National Convention in August 1964. When the Convention adopted a compromise by which the regular delegates would be seated if they took a loyalty oath and two MFDP representatives would be seated as at-large delegates, Johnson led the regular delegation in voting against the compromise and then in walking out. By October Johnson publicly supported Sen. Barry Goldwater (R, Ariz.) for the presidency, and Goldwater carried Mississippi in the November election with 87% of the vote.

In June 1964 Johnson called a special session of the state legislature to adopt a plan of tuition grants to private schools in an effort to circumvent court-ordered school desegregation. Johnson did not physically obstruct school desegregation, however, and he sent state police into Grenada in September 1966 to protect black youths who had been attacked by a mob when they entered the city's previously all-white public schools. Early in 1965 Johnson urged the state's white leaders to testify at U.S. Civil Rights Commission hearings on complaints of discrimination in Mississippi, and he made a surprise appearance himself when the commission opened hearings in February in Jackson.

Johnson opposed the 1965 Voting Rights Act. In June, while the bill was still pending in Congress, he called a special legislative session to rewrite the state's voting and registration laws. The MFDP led demonstrations against the special session in which over 800 protesters were arrested in Jackson that month. Most of the bills and amendments Johnson introduced were passed by the legislature and ratified by the state's voters in August. The legislation liberalized Mississippi's voting and registration laws. It was an attempt, as Johnson said, to put the state "in the most advantageous position possible" with respect to the federal voting rights law.

When Martin Luther King [q.v.] and other civil rights leaders decided in June 1966 to continue a march from Memphis, Tenn., to Jackson, Miss., begun by James Meredith, Johnson labelled the march "a very, very foolish thing," but promised police protection for the demonstrators. He reduced the number of highway patrolmen escorting the march on June 16, however, asserting that the state did not intend "to wet-nurse a bunch of showmen all over the country." Johnson increased the police escort again after the marchers were attacked by a mob in Philadelphia on June 21. He ordered the National Guard onto the campus of all-black Alcorn A&M College in April 1966, when demonstrations there led to some violence, and into Jackson State College in May 1967, when the school's black student body clashed with police.

Gov. Johnson welcomed federal economic aid in Mississippi and generally approved grants from the federal Office of Economic Opportunity to community action programs throughout the state. In April 1966 a special presidential task force reported that Mississippi ranked second in per capita receipt of antipoverty funds. Despite such aid Mississippi still had one of the lowest per capita income levels in the nation. A team of doctors who studied hunger and poverty in six Mississippi counties told a Senate Labor and Public Welfare subcommittee in June 1967 that nutritional and medical conditions in the state were "shocking" with many children facing starvation. Johnson then sent a team of prominent Mississippi doctors into the same areas and reported in August that, while there was malnutrition in some localities, the physicians had found no conditions approaching starvation.

Barred by the state constitution from seeking a second consecutive term as governor, Johnson ran for lieutenant governor in 1967. He placed third in a field of six candidates in the Aug. 8 Democratic primary and was thus eliminated from the race.

JONES, E(VERETT) LEROI
(Imamu Amiri Baraka)
b. Oct. 7, 1934; Newark, N.J.
Writer, black political activist.

The son of a postal supervisor and a social worker, Jones graduated two years ahead of his class at Newark's Barringer High School and received his B.A. from Howard University in 1953. After serving in the Air Force, Jones settled in New York, where he did graduate work in comparative literature at Columbia and developed a reputation as an avant-garde writer. Jones's poetry, jazz criticism and plays displayed an extraordinary sensitivity to black culture and to what he perceived as the debilitating effect of white society on black Americans. In *Dutchman*, winner of the 1964 Obie Award, Jones depicted a subway car confrontation between a sexually provocative white woman and a black intellectual whose middle class appearance conceals an explosive hostility to white people.

In April 1965 Jones left his white wife and their two children and moved to Harlem, where he founded the Black Arts Repertory Theatre, a multifaceted cultural center. A year later Jones moved the center to a dilapidated three-story building in Newark's Central Ward which he named Spirit House. In January 1968 he founded the Black Community Development and Defense Organization. *Ebony* characterized Organization in 1969 as one "dedicated to the creation of a new value system for the Afro-American community" based on Afro-Islamic cultural principles. Members of the group adopted the Kuwaida Muslim faith and Jones, whose early vocational aspiration had been the Christian ministry, became a Kuwaida religious leader and was addressed by members as Imamu Amiri Baraka, the name which he assumed publicly in the 1970s.

A 1960 trip to Cuba stimulated Jones's first political commitments. Upon returning he wrote of the contrast between the popular enthusiasm in Cuba and the "ugly void" of American life and described white Americans as an "old people" not needed by the "new peoples in Asia, Africa [and] South America." Jones exempted "the captive African," whom he described as "the only innocent in the bankruptcy of Western culture," from his indictment of American life.

After his arrest on two counts of carrying concealed weapons during the July 1967 Newark riots, Jones's political influence in Newark increased. (P.E.N., the association of writers, and the United Black Artists came to Jones's aid when the sentencing judge stated that his disagreement with sentiments expressed in one of Jones's poems contributed to the length of Jones's prison sentence. The conviction was overturned in 1968.) While on bail he taught a course at San Francisco State College and met regularly with Ron Karenga, founder of the black politico-cultural group US. Returning to Newark in January 1968, Jones helped create the Committee for a United Newark, a coalition of black and Puerto Rican community organizations that sought to secure political power for Newark's black and Puerto Rican population. In November 1969 the Committee held a convention and nominated a slate of candidates for the June 1970 municipal elections.

During the campaign incumbent Mayor Hugh Addonizio denounced Kenneth Gibson, the convention's mayoral candidate, as a "puppet" for black extremists, notably Jones, whose 1967 arrest made him a symbol of racial militancy. Gibson defeated Addonizio to become the first elected black mayor of a large East Coast city, and Jones was credited with a major role in the victory. Jones received national recognition at the 1972 National Black Political Convention which he cochaired with Mayor Richard Hatcher of Gary, Ind., and Rep. Charles C. Diggs, Jr. (D, Mich.) [*q.v.*].

JORDAN, VERNON E(ULION)
b. Aug. 15, 1935; Atlanta, Ga.
Director, Voter Education Project, Southern Regional Council, 1964-68.

The son of a postal inspector, Jordan grew up in Atlanta. He was educated at DePauw University and the Howard University Law School, where he received an LL.B. in 1960. Jordan became involved in the civil rights movement immediately after graduation, serving as a clerk for Atlanta civil rights lawyer Donald Hollowell. In 1961, when Hollowell won a suit to desegregate the University of Georgia, Jordan gained national attention by escorting the first black student onto the University campus through a mob of angry whites. After he became field secretary for the Georgia NAACP in 1962, he expanded the organization and coordinated the activities of existing branches. In Augusta, Ga., Jordan led the South's first successful boycott of stores that refused to hire blacks.

In 1964 Jordan was named director of the Voter Education Project, an Atlanta-based effort to increase black voter registration in the South. The project was sponsored by the Southern Regional Council, a coalition of major civil rights organizations ranging from the militant Student Nonviolent Coordinating Committee to the more moderate NAACP and Southern Christian Leadership Conference. Much of Jordan's time as director was spent mediating conflicts among the various participants. The project succeeded, however, in registering between one and a half and two million Southern black voters between 1964 and 1968, fulfilling a major goal of the civil rights movement.

After leaving the Voter Education Project in 1968, Jordan worked briefly as an attorney for the Office of Economic Opportunity in Atlanta. He moved to New York in 1970 to become director of the United Negro College Fund, the financial arm of 36 black colleges in the U.S.

In January 1972 Jordan was named director of the National Urban League (NUL), succeeding the late Whitney Young. During his tenure he continued the programs begun by his predecessor. He focused on the problems of urban poverty—police-community relations, tenants' rights, welfare reform and job programs. Jordan predicted that the civil rights movement of the 1970s would be "less dramatic" and "less popular" than it had been in the 1960s. "Fair employment

opportunities, [a prominent issue in the 1960s] can no longer be separated," he said, "from full employment of black people and equal access to every kind and level of employment up to and including top policymaking jobs. The central civil rights issue of the seventies is the restructuring of America's economic and political power so that black people have their fair share of the rewards, the responsibilities, and the decisionmaking in every sector of our common society. . . ." He also called for voter registration drives in the North and an effort to deal with drug problems among blacks.

In 1975 Jordan asked for the replacement of "a welfare system that destroys families, discourages work, demeans both giver and recipient and arouses hostility and rage." Jordan called for an annual federal tax credit "to all" with "no means tests, no work requirements, no coercive local regulations or other stigmatizing elements."

KING, CORETTA SCOTT
b. April 27, 1927; Heiberger, Ala.
Civil rights activist.

Coretta Scott, the daughter of a store owner and laborer, grew up in Heiberger. After graduating from a missionary high school in nearby Marion, she continued her education at Antioch College (where she and her older sister were the first full-time black students) and at the New England Conservatory of Music in Boston. In 1953 she gave up plans for a music career to marry Martin Luther King [q.v.], a philosophy graduate student whom she had met in Boston. Both Mrs. King and her husband completed their studies in 1954 and returned to Alabama, where he took a position as minister in a black Montgomery church.

Mrs. King soon became deeply involved in her husband's civil rights activities, which began with the Montgomery bus boycott of 1955 and led to the creation of the Southern Christian Leadership Conference (SCLC) in 1957. She marched beside him in demonstrations, accompanied him on tours of Europe and Asia and sang in numerous "freedom concerts" to raise money for the SCLC. At the same time she raised the couple's four children. Coretta King also made a place for herself in the peace movement of the mid-1960s, serving on the Committee for a Sane Nuclear Policy and the Mobilization to End the War in Vietnam. In 1964 the Federal Bureau of Investigation, as part of its campaign of harassment against Martin Luther King, sent her a tape recording that purported to prove her husband's unfaithfulness. Mrs. King, nevertheless remained with her husband and continued to support his work.

In April 1968 Mrs. King won national admiration for the dignity and fortitude with which she responded to her husband's assassination. Her conduct and her position as Martin Luther King's widow made her an important civil rights figure. On April 11 she took her husband's place in Memphis at the head of a massive, orderly demonstration in support of the city's striking sanitation workers. Her speech following the march stressed the theme: "We must carry on." In May and June 1968 Mrs. King participated in the Poor People's Campaign in Washington, organized by the SCLC to press for larger federal antipoverty expenditures. Speaking before the Lincoln Memorial, she urged American women "to unite and form a solid block . . . to fight the three great evils of racism, poverty and war." Shortly afterwards she was named to the executive bodies of both the SCLC and the National Organization for Women, a major feminist group.

In the late 1960s and early 1970s Mrs. King participated in numerous civil rights and peace rallies. In early 1969 she made a tour of Europe and India, during which she accepted the Nehru Award for International Understanding on behalf of her husband. Using money raised on the trip and other contributions, she established the Martin Luther King Memorial Center in Atlanta for the study of nonviolent social change. This soon became a source of dispute between Mrs. King and Ralph Abernathy [q.v.], her husband's successor as head of the SCLC, who claimed that the funds ab-

sorbed by the Center were sorely needed by the SCLC itself.

Mrs. King took little public interest in the 1969 trial of James Earl Ray [q.v.], her husband's accused assassin, but expressed her belief that the assassination resulted from a conspiracy extending beyond Ray.

KING, MARTIN LUTHER, JR.
b. Jan. 15, 1929; Atlanta, Ga.
d. April 4, 1968; Memphis, Tenn.
President, Montgomery Improvement Association, 1956-59; President, Southern Christian Leadership Conference 1957-68.

Born into a middle class family in Atlanta, Ga., Martin Luther King, Jr., followed his father into the ministry and was ordained at his father's Ebenezer Baptist Church in 1947. He graduated from Morehouse College the next year at the age of 19 and then studied at Crozer Theological Seminary in Chester, Pa., receiving his divinity degree in 1951 with highest honors. King next enrolled at Boston University and was awarded a Ph.D. in systematic theology in June 1955.

In September 1954 King undertook his first pastorate at the Dexter Avenue Baptist Church in Montgomery, Ala. He was still relatively unknown in Montgomery's black community when, on Dec. 1, 1955, Rosa Parks [q.v.], a black seamstress, was arrested for refusing to give up her seat on a city bus to a white man. Her arrest sparked an almost total boycott of the city's segregated buses by the black community on Dec. 5. That same day the Montgomery Improvement Association (MIA) was formed to organize the protest and demand the hiring of black drivers and a fairer seating system. King, who had not been a major figure in the protest thus far, was chosen to head the organization. King was made president of the MIA because he was an educated, intelligent man and dynamic speaker who could effectively represent the protesters. He could also play a unifying role since he was not identified with any one taction in the black community and was young enough to relocate should the boycott fail and there be retaliation against its leaders.

Under King's leadership the MIA established a highly efficient car pool of some 300 vehicles to transport the city's black population. It began holding twice-weekly mass meetings to communicate the latest developments, raise funds and sustain morale as the protest lengthened and white opposition intensified. Negotiations between the MIA leadership, city officials and representatives of the financially strapped bus company broke down in December 1955. Late the next month the city inaugurated a "get tough" policy against the protesters, and on Jan. 26, 1956 King was arrested on a charge of speeding. His home was bombed on Jan. 30 and two other MIA officials' houses were bombed on Feb. 1. King and nearly 100 other blacks were indicted on Feb. 21 on a charge of conspiring to organize an illegal boycott. He was found guilty on March 22, but his $500 fine was suspended pending appeal.

The violence and arrests only heightened the resolve of Montgomery's blacks, who by this time were demanding a complete end to segregation on city buses. With the aid of NAACP lawyers, five Montgomery black women filed a suit in federal court on Feb. 1, 1956 challenging the constitutionality of the city and state laws which required segregation on local buses. On June 19 a three-judge federal court in Alabama voted two-to-one that the laws violated the Fourteenth Amendment. Segregation continued, however, while the city appealed this judgment to the U.S. Supreme Court. While the appeal was pending, city officials moved to enjoin operation of the MIA car pool. During a hearing on the issue on Nov. 13, 1956, word arrived that the Supreme Court had decided the Montgomery case and ruled bus segregation unconstitutional. Nonetheless, a local judge issued an injunction against the car pool, and the MIA disbanded it. Blacks remained off the buses for another month, walking or sharing rides, until the Supreme Court's desegregation order arrived in Montgomery on Dec. 20. The next day, at 5:55 a.m., King and

several associates boarded a bus and began the integration of Montgomery's public transit. Over a month of white retaliation and violence followed. On Jan. 10, 1957 the homes of two ministers and four black churches were bombed. More bombings followed at the end of the month, including an unsuccessful attempt to dynamite King's home. The terrorism subsided soon after this, once city officials and white community leaders took action against the violence.

The 382-day Montgomery protest was a momentous event for King and for the civil rights movement. The boycott attracted national and international attention and thrust King into prominence as a major black leader and spokesman. It also helped establish nonviolent resistance as King's basic philosophy. The young minister had been interested in Gandhian techniques of passive resistance since his student days, and from its start the Montgomery boycott was nonviolent, with King preaching the doctrine of Christian love and forgiveness to his followers. Only gradually, however, did King see a connection between this doctrine and Gandhian precepts and begin articulating a philosophy of nonviolent resistance to segregation and discrimination. By the end of the boycott, King had made nonviolent direct action the explicit ideological framework of the protest. Montgomery's blacks had proved that passive resistance could work on a mass scale. The boycott popularized nonviolent resistance, making it a major tactic of the civil rights movement. Many observers also asserted that the protest helped give blacks a new sense of dignity and self-respect. Montgomery marked the beginning of a new era of aggressive nonviolent direct action by Southern blacks.

On Jan. 10-11, 1957 King and some 60 other black leaders from 10 Southern states met in Atlanta and formed the organization that later became the Southern Christian Leadership Conference (SCLC). At a meeting in New Orleans the next month, King was chosen president of the SCLC, which was established to help coordinate direct action protests in the South. In March King traveled to Ghana at the invitation of Prime

Minister Kwame Nkrumah to attend the country's independence ceremonies.

On his return King joined other civil rights leaders in organizing a Prayer Pilgrimage to Washington, D.C., to demand federal action on school desegregation and voting rights for blacks. Held on May 17, 1957, the pilgrimage was the largest civil rights gathering to that time and was the forum for King's first truly national address. Speaking to the crowd of 15-25,000 demonstrators, King urged the federal government, Northern white liberals and Southern white moderates to take stronger action on behalf of civil rights, and he stressed the importance of the vote for Southern blacks. He met with Vice President Richard Nixon on June 13, 1957 and with President Eisenhower on June 23, 1958, both times encouraging stronger federal protection of civil rights. In September 1958 King's account of the Montgomery protest, *Stride Toward Freedom*, was published. On Sept. 20, while autographing copies of the book at a Harlem department store, King was stabbed in the chest by a woman later judged insane. He recovered from the injury and was released from the hospital on Oct. 3.

Following the Prayer Pilgrimage King and the SCLC undertook a voter registration campaign, but the minister's most significant activity between 1957 and 1960 was his further development of the philosophy of nonviolent resistance. After the Montgomery boycott King deepened his study of nonviolence, and in February 1959 he traveled to India at the invitation of the Gandhian National Memorial Fund. King and his wife Coretta were warmly received, and they met with leading students and followers of Gandhian passive resistance. The trip solidified King's commitment to nonviolence, which for him was not simply a tactic but the one valid method of social change. Beginning with the Montgomery boycott King traveled extensively throughout the U.S. speaking on nonviolence, and by 1960 he was the primary exponent of nonviolent direct action within the civil rights movement.

In January 1960 King moved from Montgomery to Atlanta, where the SCLC had established its headquarters, and became co-pastor at his father's church. He supported the sit-in movement that began the next month and was often hailed as the "spiritual father" of the protesters because they used nonviolent direct action techniques. The SCLC sponsored a meeting of sit-in leaders in Raleigh, N.C., in April 1960, which led to the formation of the Student Nonviolent Coordinating Committee (SNCC).

In October 1960 King was arrested by officials of DeKalb County, Ga., near Atlanta, for allegedly having violated the one year's probation he was serving on a charge of driving without a Georgia license, and he was sentenced to four months in a rural penal camp. On Oct. 26 Democratic presidential candidate Sen. John F. Kennedy (D, Mass.) and his brother Robert intervened to help get King released on bail the next day. The incident was widely publicized in the black community and was credited with increasing the black vote for Kennedy in the November election.

The Congress of Racial Equality (CORE) launched the Freedom Rides, a protest designed to challenge segregation at Southern bus terminals, in May 1961. When a mob attacked the riders as they arrived in Montgomery, Ala. on May 20, King rushed to the city and the next day addressed a mass meeting in support of the rides. With James Farmer [q.v.] of CORE and other civil rights leaders, he announced on May 23 that the protests would continue despite threats of more violence. King was named chairman of a Freedom Rides Coordinating Committee organized in May, and he rejected Attorney General Robert Kennedy's call for a "cooling off" period at the end of the month. King never went on one of the Freedom Rides, however, and CORE and SNCC were far more active in the protest than King and the SCLC.

In mid-December 1961 King was called into Albany, Ga. to help direct an anti-segregation campaign there. With the aid of some SNCC organizers, the city's blacks had formed the Albany Movement in November and had launched a series of demonstrations. King led a march to the county courthouse in Albany on Dec. 16. When he was arrested, he refused bond and announced he would stay in jail rather than pay a fine if convicted. Two days later, however, a truce was declared and King accepted bail. The truce, arranged by several local leaders who mistrusted King and his aides, won blacks only a promise that their grievances would be heard by the city commission. King later regretted having accepted bail for such an ineffectual agreement.

The truce collapsed in January, and King spent the next six months shuttling back and forth between Atlanta and Albany, where he oversaw a renewal of periodic demonstrations. Late in February he was tried and found guilty of the charges stemming from his December arrest. In July he was sentenced to a fine of $178 or 45 days in prison. King chose prison but was released three days later when someone anonymously paid his fine. At this juncture, with complaints about his leadership growing, King decided to concentrate on Albany. From mid-July through August, he and his top aides in the SCLC directed a series of daily marches and protests that attracted national publicity. The campaign tapered off in September, and by the end of the year the Albany movement had won no tangible gains. It was judged a clear defeat for King.

King used the lessons learned in Albany to prepare for the next major desegregation campaign in Birmingham, Ala., during the spring of 1963. Unlike Albany, the campaign in Birmingham was preceded by careful reconnaissance work and planning, by meetings with local black leaders to ensure unity and by intensive training of the black population in nonviolent techniques. King quietly raised funds and contacted other civil rights organizations, sympathetic religious leaders and reporters in the months before the campaign. The SCLC decided to focus its efforts on Birmingham's business community rather than attack all targets of segregation at once as it had in Albany. The starting date was twice delayed until city elections had been held.

The campaign began on April 3, 1963 when the SCLC issued a "Birmingham Manifesto" detailing blacks' grievances. Demonstrations began at segregated lunch counters and a boycott of downtown stores started the same day. A series of daily mass marches was begun on April 6. Four days later the city obtained an injunction against further demonstrations which specifically cited King. On April 12, Good Friday, King led a march toward city hall in defiance of the injunction, was arrested en route and was placed in solitary confinement. In prison King wrote his later famous "Letter from a Birmingham Jail." Addressed to some fellow clergymen who had publicly criticized King's tactics in Birmingham, the letter rebutted charges that the Birmingham campaign was untimely and unwise and detailed the injustices blacks suffered in that city and elsewhere. It explained the methods and goals of nonviolent direct action and criticized white moderates and the white church for their lack of moral leadership and courage on the race issue. Released on bond on April 20, King was tried six days later for defying the injunction and convicted of criminal contempt but was given time to file an appeal before having to serve his five-day sentence.

The Birmingham campaign reached a turning point on May 2 when King launched a new phase of the protests in which children, ranging in age from six to 16, began mass marches in the city. The same day the relative restraint exercised by Commissioner of Public Safety Eugene "Bull" Connor [q.v.] and his police officers ended. Over 900 children were arrested on May 2 and the next day, as nearly 1,000 demonstrators of all ages prepared to march. They were savagely attacked by police with nightsticks, by snarling police dogs and by high pressure fire hoses. Similar police actions, occurring over the next four days, were recorded by newspaper and television cameras. National public opinion shifted decisively toward King and the SCLC. President Kennedy sent Assistant Attorney General Burke Marshall [q.v.] to Birmingham on May 4 to try to negotiate a settlement but his efforts were unavailing until May 7. On that day two demonstrations involving several thousand blacks flared into an open riot in response to police assaults. Faced with the threat of continued civil disorders, white leaders in Birmingham asked for and were granted a truce that evening. On May 10 an agreement was announced which called for phased integration of the city's business facilities, the upgrading of black workers and the establishment of a permanent biracial committee. Late that evening, however, bombs exploded at the home of King's brother, the Rev. A.D. King, and at the Gaston Motel, headquarters for the SCLC campaign. As news of the bombings spread, a riot broke out in Birmingham, which lasted until the early morning hours.

The May 10 agreement survived the bombings and riot, but Birmingham's blacks achieved only limited gains from their victory. The city's white leaders tried to evade key points of the settlement and interpreted its terms as narrowly as possible. Outside Birmingham the campaign had enormous impact and significance. As historians August Meier and Elliott Rudwick have noted, Birmingham "compelled the United States to face the problem of Southern discrimination in a way it had never done before." Birmingham was a turning point for the Kennedy Administration, forcing it to take forthright action on civil rights. In a national television address on June 11, President Kennedy delivered his most positive statement to date on behalf of black Americans, publicly labeling racial discrimination a national and a moral issue. He announced that he would ask Congress for major civil rights legislation, and on June 19 he sent Congress a civil rights bill dealing with public accommodations, school desegregation, and employment. Birmingham also stirred blacks throughout the South, and over the summer of 1963 demonstrations similar to Birmingham's spread from one Southern city to the next.

Birmingham reestablished King's leadership in the civil rights movement after the failure of Albany. He went on a triumphal speaking tour from California to New York in June and aided a desegregation drive in Danville, Va. during the summer. King endorsed A. Philip Randolph's [q.v.] pro-posal for a mass March on Washington, helped plan the march and joined other rights leaders in a meeting with President Kennedy on June 22. At the Aug. 28 march, King addressed 250,000 people assembled at the Lincoln Memorial, delivering a speech which drew heavily on both Biblical and American democratic themes. His classic "I Have a Dream" speech eloquently set forth King's vision of full equality and freedom for black Americans and was the most remembered speech of the March.

On Sept. 15, 1963 a bomb exploded at a black church in Birmingham killing four young black girls. King immediately called for federal troops to be sent into the city to prevent a "racial holocaust." He threatened a resumption of demonstrations in Birmingham but was reportedly dissuaded from this by moderate black leaders in the city and by Kennedy's decision to send an advisory team to Birmingham to conduct negotiations between black and white leaders. Instead, King decided to focus on Atlanta, and in October he joined other local black leaders in a demand that the pace of desegregation in that city be increased. The rejection of the demands led to a series of demonstrations in Atlanta in December and January in which King joined.

King joined in demonstrations against segregated public facilities in Atlanta in late 1963 and early 1964 that were organized primarily by SNCC. Beginning in March 1964 King and the SCLC gave their support to a desegregation drive in St. Augustine, Fla. The almost daily demonstrations and marches were repeatedly attacked by crowds of whites. The campaign was intensified in May and June. When local police failed to provide protection for the demonstrators, King called for federal intervention but to no avail. By the end of June a stalemate had developed, and when Florida's governor appointed an emergency biracial committee to "restore communications" between the races, King agreed to a temporary truce. Following passage of the Civil Rights Act in July 1964, local black leaders secured federal court orders for desegregation of public facilities in St. Augustine, and a measure of desegregation was finally won in the city.

On July 18, when a riot erupted in Harlem, New York's Mayor Robert Wagner asked King to come to the city. King was criticized by Harlem leaders for conferring with Wagner and for touring the riot area without having contacted them first. His main recommendation to Wagner—a civilian review board to investigate charges of police brutality—was rejected by the Mayor. King abhorred the violence of the Harlem riot, but he said its sources lay in the economic and social deprivation blacks suffered in Northern ghettos. He placed the blame for the rioting, as he would repeatedly in the future, on white society's failure to remedy ghetto conditions.

Later that summer King toured Mississippi, encouraging blacks to enroll in the newly organized Mississippi Freedom Democratic Party (MFDP). He also supported an MFDP delegation when it challenged the seating of the regular Mississippi delegation at the August 1964 Democratic National Convention and testified before the credentials committee on the MFDP's behalf. When the Convention refused full recognition of the group and voted for a compromise measure, however, King urged the MDFP delegates to accept it, but they overwhelmingly rejected the compromise. King also joined several other rights leaders in a July 1964 call for a moratorium on civil rights demonstrations until after the November elections, a call which the more radical SNCC and the Congress of Racial Equality (CORE) refused to endorse.

King went on a speaking tour of Europe in the fall of 1964. Shortly after his return in mid-October, it was announced that he had been chosen as the Nobel Peace Prize winner for 1964. While preparing for a trip to Oslo, to accept the prize in December, King was attacked by FBI Director J. Edgar Hoover as "the most notorious liar in the country" for allegedly having said that FBI agents would not act on civil rights complaints in the South because they were Southerners. King replied in a telegram to Hoover that the FBI was not fully effective in the South but not because of the presence of Southerners on its staff. He called Hoover's statement "inconceivable."

There were reports after King's death that the FBI had tapped his telephone for extensive periods during the 1960s. In February 1975 Justice Department officials confirmed reports that President Johnson had ordered the agency to bug King's hotel suite at the 1964 Democratic National Convention. A Senate Select Committee on Intelligence disclosed in November 1975 that prior to King's assassination, the FBI had conducted a six-year campaign aimed at discrediting the civil rights leader. Aside from numerous telephone taps and bugs in King's hotel rooms, the program of harassment included attempts to disrupt functions at which King was to appear. In late 1964 and early 1965 the agency anonymously sent King and his wife Coretta [q.v.] two tape recordings that supposedly revealed instances of infidelity on his part and a letter implying that King should commit suicide. In testimony before the Senate committee, FBI officials acknowledged there had been no legal basis for these actions.

Awarded the Nobel Peace Prize on Dec. 10, King returned to the United States ready to launch another major campaign, this time to pressure the federal government to act to secure voting rights for blacks. He chose to focus the campaign on Selma, Ala., a Black Belt city where only one per cent of the 15,000 blacks were then registered to vote and where SNCC organizers had been at work during the previous two years. King announced a voter registration drive in Selma on Jan. 2, 1965, and during the next two months he and other SCLC and SNCC leaders led almost daily marches to the county courthouse there. Thousands of demonstrators were arrested and many were assaulted by Sheriff James Clark [q.v.] and his volunteer posse. By the end of February a stalemate was developing, and King called for a mass march to Montgomery to present black grievances to Gov. George C. Wallace [q.v.].

Wallace announced on March 6 that the demonstration would not be permitted. When some 500 people, led by SNCC's John Lewis [q.v.] and the SCLC's Hosea

Williams [*q.v.*], started the march the next day, they were met at the bridge leading out of Selma by Sheriff Clark, his possemen and state troopers. The demonstrators, given two minutes to disperse, were attacked with tear gas and by possemen on horseback using cattle prods and clubs. King, who was in Atlanta that day, vowed to return to Selma to lead a second march on March 9. The attack on the demonstrators received national publicity. While supporting marches were held throughout the country, other civil rights leaders and scores of Northern white clergy and sympathizers journeyed to Selma to join the next march.

A federal judge enjoined a march planned for March 9, and Administration officials pressured King and his aides to abide by the injunction. When the 1,500 demonstrators crossed the bridge on the outskirts of Selma, they were met once again by state troopers who ordered them to disperse. After briefly kneeling in prayer King turned the marchers around and told them to go back to Selma. King denied charges that he had made a prior agreement with federal officials to halt the march at the bridge.

Whatever his reasons for turning back, King's decision marked a key turning point in his relations with black militants, especially the youths in SNCC. Well before Selma many members of SNCC had criticized King for being too cautious, too ready to compromise and too closely allied to the federal government and the white establishment. By 1965 many SNCC workers were also questioning the efficacy of King's strategy of nonviolence. Before Selma King had served as a mediator between the militant and traditionalist wings of the black protest movement. After his new loss of credibility among the militants, it became far more difficult for King to play such a role.

On March 17 federal district Judge Frank M. Johnson authorized the Selma march, and it began on March 21 under the protection of a federalized Alabama National Guard and Army troops. Under the court order, only 300 people could march along the entire route, but 25,000 people came to Montgomery for the final leg of the march to the state capitol. Like Birmingham in 1963, the Selma demonstrations and march did not bring immediate improvement in the condition of local blacks. But Selma, and especially the March 7 assault on the demonstrators and the deaths of three civil rights workers during the campaign, aroused national protests that forced the federal government to act. On March 15 President Johnson addressed a joint session of Congress to decry the violence in Selma and announce that "We shall overcome." Johnson called for prompt passage of a voting rights bill to suspend the use of literacy tests and other devices that denied blacks the vote and to install federal registrars in the South and other areas where voter registration lagged. King was present on Aug. 6 when Johnson signed the bill into law.

After Selma King began to speak out against American involvement in Vietnam, calling for a negotiated settlement from July 1965 on. By 1966 he was outspoken in his opposition to the war, and in 1967 he openly identified himself with the anti-war movement. In addition to violating his precept of nonviolence, King argued that the war diverted money and attention from domestic programs to aid the black poor. He was strongly criticized by most other civil rights leaders for attempting to link the civil rights and anti-war movements. He also alienated President Johnson; at a White House conference on civil rights in June 1966, King was virtually ignored by Administration officials and he found the federal government increasingly less receptive to appeals for aid or intervention in his campaigns.

Although King remained a resident of Atlanta, he also began giving greater attention to the problems of the black poor in Northern ghettos. Early in 1964 he called for a federal "Bill of Rights for the Disadvantaged." The Watts riot of August 1965 reinforced King's conviction that massive federal aid to improve the economic and social conditions of blacks in the Northern ghettos was needed. With an invitation from some local community groups, the SCLC began planning a drive in Chicago in the summer of 1965. On Jan. 7, 1966 King announced the beginning of the Chicago Freedom Movement to end discrimination in housing, schools and employment. King was in and out of Chicago over the next several months while his aides, led by the Rev. James Bevel [q.v.], did the day-to-day organizing of the campaign. King announced on May 26 that a mass march on city hall would be held one month later, to be followed by "a long hot summer of peaceful nonviolence."

These plans were delayed when King learned on June 6 that James Meredith [q.v.], in the course of a solitary protest march from Memphis, Tenn., to Jackson, Miss., had been shot from ambush just over the Mississippi border. King rushed to Memphis and on June 7 he, Stokely Carmichael [q.v.], the newly elected chairman of SNCC, and Floyd McKissick [q.v.] of CORE, announced they would continue the march. Despite an attack on the demonstrators by a white mob in Philadelphia, Miss., on June 21 and by police in Canton, Miss., two days later, the protesters reached Jackson and held a final rally at the state capitol on June 26.

The most notable feature of the Meredith march was the public divisions among civil rights leaders it revealed. A manifesto issued June 8 declared the march was "a massive public indictment and protest" against the failure of American society and government to fulfill blacks' rights. Roy Wilkins [q.v.] of the NAACP and Whitney Young [q.v.] of the National Urban League refused to sign the manifesto, while King signed it with reluctance. During the march Carmichael raised the cry of "black power," a slogan that reflected the rising anti-white sentiment and militance within SNCC. King deplored the slogan, which quickly captured national attention, arguing that it carried connotations of violence; he continued to speak out against black power after the march. He later softened his opposition somewhat, saying he supported the emphasis on black pride and the call for blacks to amass political and economic strength to achieve their legitimate goals. But King remained opposed to black separatism and encouragement of violence.

King returned to Chicago after the Meredith march. Following a rally attended by some 30,000 at Soldiers' Field on July 10, he led 5,000 marchers to city hall to present the movement's demands. King met with Chicago Mayor Richard Daley the next day. On July 12 a three-day riot broke out on Chicago's West Side ghetto. In late July King launched a series of marches into white ethnic neighborhoods in the city to protest housing discrimination. Continuing through most of August, the marches resulted in repeated assaults on the demonstrators by angry crowds of whites. On Aug. 21 King announced that the protesters would march the following Sunday into Cicero, an all-white suburb considered a volatile enclave of anti-black sentiment. Two days before the march negotiations between black leaders and city business and government officials resulted in a 10-point agreement, and the demonstrations were halted.

Although King hailed the agreement as a victory, most of SCLC's staff later admitted that the Chicago Movement did not really achieve its goals. King's biographer David Lewis labeled the agreement "little more than a good-will pledge from the city, business, and realtors" to act against housing discrimination. In the months after Chicago King publicly recognized the fact that changes in black economic and social conditions would not come quickly. At the same time he became more of a political and economic radical. In the summer of 1967 King told an interviewer he had abandoned his earlier ideas of step-by-step reform of American institutions. Now, he said, "I think you've got to have a reconstruction of the entire society, a revolution of values," which would involve the rebuilding of the cities, the nationalization of some industries, a review of American foreign investments and the establishment of a guaranteed annual income. In his speeches and writings King continued to argue that nonviolent methods could bring real change, but he also displayed less optimism than in earlier years about white America.

Following the Chicago campaign King's public stature began to decline. While traditional civil rights leaders condemned his anti-war statements and activities, the militants attacked King for his adherence to nonviolence and his refusal to endorse black power. He was also losing his base of support among Northern whites. A growing number of white radicals, more sympathetic to black militants, considered King and his methods outdated. White liberals called for slowing down the pace of the civil rights movement. Contributions to the SCLC declined. Even among King's supporters there was a growing conviction that his strategy could not be successfully applied to the problems of Northern poverty and discrimination.

In June 1967 the Supreme Court upheld contempt of court convictions of King and seven other ministers resulting from the 1963 Birmingham demonstrations. While serving his five-day prison term beginning Oct. 30, King discussed with his aides a plan to assemble an interracial coalition of the poor which would pressure the federal government into enacting new antipoverty legislation. He devoted the next several months to organizing the Poor People's Campaign, an effort designed to prove the continuing viability of nonviolence in addition to seeking a massive program of federal aid for the poor. The plans for the campaign, completed in February 1968, called for a mass march on Washington by poor whites, American Indians and Mexican-Americans as well as blacks. In Washington there would be daily nonviolent protests until Congress acted to guarantee jobs to all those able to work, a viable income for those unable to work and an end to discrimination in housing and education. King's plans met strong opposition from government officials and hostility or indifference from other civil rights organizations.

In March 1968 King took time off from recruitment for the Poor People's March to aid a sanitationmen's strike in Memphis. King led a mass march in Memphis in support of the strikers on March 28. The demonstration ended in violence when some protesters broke away from the main crowd and began smashing windows and looting stores. Although the number involved in the violence was relatively small, King was troubled by the violence and angered when press reports focused on the incident, resulting in a storm of criticism from both blacks and whites. King was back in the city on April 3 to begin preparations for a second march. At about 6 p.m. the next evening, as he stood on the balcony outside his motel room in Memphis, King was shot in the head by a sniper and died almost immediately. James Earl Ray [q.v.], arrested in London in June 1968 and extradited to the United States in July, was charged with King's assassination and pleaded guilty to the charge in March 1969. In later years Ray attempted to change his plea and secure a new trial. This plus the 1975 disclosures of FBI harassment of King led many of his former associates and others to call for a new investigation of King's assassination.

King's unique position and leadership during much of his life were due in part, as David Lewis noted, to "forces external to himself." King lived in an era when the impulse toward social reform and black protest was rising and when many whites were willing to heed that protest. Still, King himself was a singular man, "a rare personality, endowed with an ample intelligence, great courage and convictions, and an arresting presence." Even as his influence declined in the last years of his life, King remained an unusual figure. He was seeking a solution to the problems of economic injustice for all the poor, not simply the black poor, at the time of his death. His opposition to the Vietnam war began well before the anti-war movement became respectable or popular and represented for King a broadening of his commitment to nonviolence from the national to the international level.

For further information:
Lerone Bennett, Jr., *What Manner of Man: A Biography of Martin Luther King, Jr.* (Chicago, 1968).
Martin Luther King, Jr., *Why We Can't Wait* (New York, 1964).
———, *Where Do We Go From Here: Chaos or Community?* (New York, 1967).
David Lewis, *King: A Critical Biography* (New York, 1970).

August Meier, "On the Role of Martin Luther King," *New Politics*, IV (Winter, 1965), 52-59.

KUNSTLER, WILLIAM M(OSES)
b. July 7, 1919; New York, N.Y.
Civil rights attorney.

Raised in a middle-class Jewish family in New York, Kunstler attended Yale University and took a law degree at Columbia in 1948. During the 1950s Kunstler joined his brother in a successful legal practice. He gradually became involved in civil liberties cases toward the end of the decade. His most important case in this period was that of William Worthy, a black reporter for the Baltimore *Afro-American*, to whom the State Department had denied passport renewal following his visit to mainland China. In the early 1960s Kunstler became deeply committed to the civil rights movement after he volunteered to defend freedom riders in Mississippi who had been arrested during their 1961 attempt to integrate interstate transportation facilities in the South.

In 1962 and 1963 Kunstler successfully appealed the conviction of the Rev. Fred L. Shuttlesworth [*q.v.*] and other blacks who had challenged segregated seating on buses in Birmingham, Ala. During the same years he tried unsuccessfully to win a court ruling favorable to Dewey Greene, a Negro student denied admission to the University of Mississippi. Later Kunstler served as special counsel for Martin Luther King [*q.v.*] and the Southern Christian Leadership Conference. He was a member of the legal advisory staff of the Council of Federated Organizations, the coalition that directed the massive voter registration drive in Mississippi in the summer of 1964. Kunstler also worked with the Mississippi Freedom Democratic Party and with the Student Nonviolent Coordinating Committee (SNCC).

In 1966 Kunstler defended SNCC chairman Stokley Carmichael [*q.v.*] on charges arising out of the civil rights demonstrations in Selma, Ala., the year before. During the same year Kunstler challenged the constitutionality of federal grand jury selection procedures in the Southern District of New York, arguing that the system of selection used intentionally excluded members of ethnic minority groups. Kunstler was also part of the team hired by Jack Ruby, accused murderer of Lee Harvey Oswald, to participate in the trial to determine whether he was sane and therefore competent to hire and dismiss his own lawyers. Kunstler participated, without fee, in the October 1966 appeal that reversed Ruby's conviction in the Oswald murder. (Lawyers for Ruby successfully argued that undue publicity had biased the jury.) The next year Kunstler was Rep. Adam Clayton Powell's (D, N.Y.) [*q.v.*] chief defense lawyer in the Congressman's fight to prevent his expulsion from Congress. Kunstler argued that to remove the Congressman would unconstitutionally deprive his constituents of the representative of their choice. The Supreme Court eventually ruled that the House had violated the Constitution in excluding Powell from his seat. During the same year that he defended Powell, Kunstler also represented black militant H. Rap Brown [*q.v.*]. Kunstler claimed that the $25,000 bail set in Brown's arraignment on federal charges of carrying a gun across state lines while under indictment was "excessive and outrageous." He also charged that the government's attempt to place Brown, then chairman of SNCC, in solitary confinement was a "political maneuver." Kunstler's motion that the high bail violated Brown's constitutional rights was rejected by an appeals court. In May 1968 Brown was convicted of violating the Federal Firearms Act. Kunstler unsuccessfully urged suspension of Brown's five-year prison sentence and $2,000 fine because of the "horrendous gap between white and black people in this country."

By the end of the 1960s Kunstler had thoroughly committed himself to legal and political support of those in the civil rights and anti-war movements who sought radical change in American society. Kunstler thought the legal profession offered the possibility of a "dedicated life" in which the "worker-lawyer is the equivalent of the worker-priest." Kunstler received little money from his many clients in the late 1960s. Most of his income came from the Law Center for Constitutional Rights, which paid him about $100 a week plus expenses, and lecture fees that brought his annual income to approximately $20,000 a year.

Kunstler became the center of national attention in late 1969 and early 1970 when he served as counsel for the Chicago Seven, a group of anti-war activists accused of conspiracy to incite a riot during the 1968 Democratic National Convention. A Chicago jury later found none of the defendents guilty of conspiracy but five guilty of incitement to riot. Judge Julius J. Hoffman found all of the defendants, including Kunstler and his co-counsel, Leonard Weinglass, guilty of contempt of court. Kunstler was sentenced to over four years in prison for his courtroom behavior. The sentence was later suspended.

LEWIS, JOHN
b. Feb. 21, 1940; Troy, Ala.
Chairman, Student Nonviolent Coordinating Committee, June 1963-May 1966.

Born on a small farm in Alabama, Lewis became a Baptist minister at age 16. He graduated from the American Baptist Seminary in Nashville and later studied philosophy at Fisk University. In 1959, while a seminary student in Nashville, Lewis met regularly with other students in a series of workshops on nonviolence sponsored by the Nashville Christian Leadership Conference and the Fellowship of Reconciliation. When the sit-in movement to desegregate Southern luncheon counters began in February 1960, Lewis immediately joined the Nashville sit-ins. He was a founder of the Student Nonviolent Coordinating Committee (SNCC), established in April 1960, which grew out of the sit-ins.

Lewis was one of 13 persons on the first Freedom Ride to challenge segregation at interstate bus terminals in May 1961. Organized by the Congress of Racial Equality, the ride began on May 4 in Washington, D.C., with New Orleans as its destination. When the riders reached Rock Hill, S.C.,

Lewis was beaten as he entered the white waiting room at the bus station. More violence, including the beating of several other riders and the burning of a bus, erupted at Anniston and Birmingham, Ala. As a result the ride was discontinued on May 15 in Birmingham. Lewis went back to Nashville where he and his SNCC colleagues decided that the ride should be resumed and continued until its original New Orleans destination was reached. Lewis and nine other students returned to Birmingham by bus on May 17 where they were arrested and driven back to the Tennessee border the next day by local police. On May 19 all 10 were back in Birmingham. This time they went on to Montgomery where Lewis was again beaten and arrested on May 20. Throughout the summer Lewis participated in more Freedom Rides, which helped produce a September 1961 order from the Interstate Commerce Commission desegregating all interstate bus terminals.

Lewis abandoned his studies at Fisk when elected chairman of SNCC in June 1963. He represented the organization at the Aug. 28, 1963 March on Washington. The address he prepared for that day labeled the Administration's civil rights bill "too little and too late" and warned that "we will march throughout the South, through the heart of Dixie, the way Sherman did. We shall pursue our own 'scorched earth' policy and burn Jim Crow to the ground—nonviolently." When this text was circulated on the evening of Aug. 27, the other march sponsors, upset by Lewis's criticism of the Kennedy Administration and his angry tone, insisted that its contents be changed. Lewis, who had been jailed over 20 times for his civil rights activities by the date of the march, complied but still delivered the most radical speech of the day. He asserted that American politics was "dominated by politicians who build their career on immoral compromising and ally themselves with open forms of political, economic and social exploitation." He also warned that if Congress failed to pass meaningful civil rights legislation, "we will march through the South, through the streets of Jackson . . . Danville . . . Cambridge . . . Birmingham" with "the spirit of love and with the spirit of dignity that we have shown here today." The same day Lewis joined nine other rights leaders in a meeting with President Kennedy where they discussed the Administration's civil rights bill, then pending in Congress.

Lewis helped lead demonstrations in January 1964 to integrate public accommodations in Atlanta, Ga. He led over 150 black high school students in a Jan. 7 protest at the mayor's office and was arrested 11 days later in a demonstration outside a segregated restaurant. He was jailed again during anti-segregation demonstrations in Nashville in April and May of 1964 and during a July 1964 march against voter discrimination in Selma, Ala. Lewis also helped organize and raise funds for the Mississippi Freedom Summer of 1964, a project to encourage community organizing and voter registration among the state's black citizens. In July 1964 Lewis met with A. Philip Randolph [q.v.] and the leaders of other rights organizations at a strategy conference in New York City. The meeting resulted in a call for a "moratorium" on mass civil rights demonstrations until after the 1964 presidential election. After consulting with other members of SNCC, Lewis refused to sign the call.

Following the election, the Southern Christian Leadership Conference (SCLC), led by Martin Luther King [q.v.], decided to make Selma, Ala., its focal point for 1965. Beginning in January it cooperated with Lewis and SNCC, which had been active in Selma since early 1963, in an intensive voter registration drive. By March the two organizations had made little headway because of strong opposition from local whites, and King called for a march to Montgomery to protest the denial of voting rights to Alabama blacks. SNCC did not endorse the march because some members insisted that voter registration work in Selma should take precedence over mass demonstrations. Lewis supported the march, however, and independent of SNCC helped organize it. On March 7 Lewis and Hosea Williams [q.v.] of the SCLC led 500 marchers from the Brown Chapel in Selma to the Edmund Pettus Bridge leading out of

town. There they were met by 200 state troopers and sheriff's deputies who ordered them to disperse. When the marchers failed to move, the troopers fired tear gas and attacked them with whips and nightsticks. Lewis suffered a concussion in the melee, yet he and Williams were able to lead many of the marchers back to Brown Chapel. Lewis then participated in marches in Harlem and in Montgomery to protest the violence in Selma and on March 21 was a leader of the final march that did go from Selma to Montgomery.

During the summer of 1965 Lewis led other voting rights demonstrations in Mississippi and Georgia. He also helped plan the challenge brought by the Mississippi Freedom Democratic Party to the seating of the state's five representatives in Congress, a move voted down by the House on Sept. 17. In January 1966 Lewis issued a SNCC policy statement that denounced the Vietnam war and supported those men unwilling to be drafted. He then helped found the Southern Coordinating Committee to End the War in Vietnam. Despite his opposition to Johnson's war policies, in February Lewis accepted an invitation to become a member of the President's council for the White House Conference on Civil Rights scheduled for June.

Lewis was ousted as chairman of SNCC in May 1966. During the previous year he had helped establish a SNCC policy that the organization and the civil rights movement should be led by blacks, but Lewis continued to support integration as the goal of the movement, with white participation in SNCC and nonviolence as the means of protest. By early 1966, however, many black members of SNCC were opposed to white involvement and were rejecting nonviolent tactics. Lewis was criticized for these policy differences and also for having supported the Selma march and for being on the council for the White House Conference. At an all-night SNCC meeting near Nashville on May 14 and 15, Lewis lost his chairmanship to the more militant Stokely Carmichael [q.v.]. At the same meeting, SNCC decided to stop using integrated field teams.

Lewis was named to a 10-member policymaking central committee in SNCC, and later that month he signed a statement in which SNCC withdrew from the White House Conference, charging that President Johnson was not serious about ensuring blacks' constitutional rights. On July 22 Lewis resigned from SNCC, by then identified with Carmichael and "black power." Publicly, Lewis refused to take issue with SNCC, but privately he was reported to be distressed by the group's turn away from integration and nonviolence.

Lewis continued his civil rights work as a staff member of the Field Foundation in 1966 and 1967 and later as director of community organization projects for the Southern Regional Council (SRC). He worked in Sen. Robert Kennedy's (D, N.Y.) 1968 presidential campaign. In March 1970 he was named director of the SRC's Voter Education Project.

LUCY, AUTHERINE J(UANITA)
b. (?) 1929: Shiloh, Ala.
School desegregation figure

The youngest of nine children, Lucy was born on her parents' farm near Shiloh in southwestern Alabama. She graduated from Miles College, a church-supported black school in Birmingham, Ala., in 1952. Soon afterwards Lucy decided to try to enter the all-white University of Alabama at Tuscaloosa to get a degree in library science. When she was refused admission, NAACP attorneys sued the University. In October 1955 the U.S. Supreme Court ordered the school to end segregation and admit Lucy. The University acquiesced and let Lucy enroll for the spring term in 1956, but it continued to bar her from the dormitories and dining halls on campus.

By the fall of 1955 blacks had entered the state universities in all but five Southern states. Desegregation at the college level had been peaceful, but after the Supreme Court's May 1954 decision holding segregation in public elementary and secondary schools unconstitutional, white resistance to integration at even the university level stiffened in the deep South, including Alabama. The first black ever admitted to any white public school in the state, Lucy attended her first class on the Tuscaloosa campus on Friday, Feb. 3, 1956. That evening a cross was burned on campus and a crowd of about 1,200 students exploded firecrackers, sang "Dixie," and marched on the school grounds. The next night a group of students again massed for demonstrations. On Monday Feb. 6 a mob of over 1,000, including many people not connected with the University, roamed the campus shouting their opposition to Lucy's enrollment. They threw rocks and eggs at Lucy when she arrived for classes and yelled threats at her through classroom windows. Lucy was finally removed from the campus under heavy police guard, and the University's board of trustees suspended her indefinitely on the ground that this was necessary to ensure her safety.

Three days later NAACP attorneys asked a federal court in Birmingham to order that Lucy be allowed to attend her classes. They also filed a contempt action against the University trustees and in their petition alleged that University officials had conspired with the mob on Feb. 6 to bar Lucy. The University's president denounced this charge as "untrue, unwarranted and outrageous," and at a court hearing later in the month, Thurgood Marshall [q.v.], head of the NAACP Legal Defense Fund, withdrew the conspiracy charge, saying that a careful investigation had failed to substantiate it. On Feb. 29, after the hearing, Judge H. Hobart Grooms dismissed the contempt action but ruled that the University had to reinstate Lucy. That evening the University's board of trustees permanently expelled Lucy on disciplinary grounds for having made the "false and baseless" conspiracy accusation against school officials in her court pleadings.

Throughout the crisis Lucy stayed with relatives in Birmingham, where she received numerous threatening phone calls. On March 1 she flew to New York City for rest and medical attention. Eight days later her attorneys began a court challenge to the University's expulsion order. On Jan. 18, 1957 Judge Grooms upheld the trustees' action in ousting Lucy. Lucy, who had married in April 1956 and was then living in Texas, officially ended her fight to enter the University soon afterwards. She dropped from public view and was reported in 1968 to be living with her husband and two children in Shreveport, La., where she taught English part-time in local public schools.

The crisis caused by Lucy's enrollment at the University of Alabama received nation-wide publicity and resulted in what was generally regarded as a victory for pro-segregation forces. Neither state nor local officials made a strong effort to prevent mob action or to disperse the rioters, and the federal government refused to intervene even though University officials reportedly appealed to Attorney General Herbert **Brownell for aid. President Eisen-**hower publicly deplored the rioters' "defiance of law" but added he would not interfere in the situation so long as the state was doing "its best to straighten it out." Many observers felt that the federal government's inaction during the Lucy crisis invited the official resistance to school desegregation that led to another crisis in Little Rock, Ark., in 1957. After Autherine Lucy, no blacks were admitted to the University of Alabama until June 1963, when state officials finally gave in to court-ordered desegregation.

McKISSICK, FLOYD B(IXLER)
b. March 9, 1922; Asheville, N.C.
National Director, Congress of Racial Equality, 1966-67.

The son of a hotel employe, McKissick grew up in Asheville. After military service during World War II, he attended North Carolina College and studied law at the University of North Carolina; in 1952 he became the first black in the school's history to receive an LL.B. McKissick opened a law practice in Durham, N.C.

An ambitious lawyer, McKissick resented racial discrimination in the North Carolina bar. During the 1950s he served as youth chairman of the North Carolina NAACP, and in 1960 he became legal counsel for the Congress of Racial Equality (CORE), a more militant civil rights organization. Much of McKissick's work during the early 1960s consisted of defending CORE demonstrators arrested while protesting segregation at public facilities in Southern cities. McKissick also helped expand the network of CORE chapters in North Carolina. In 1962 he left the NAACP, which had fallen into a dispute with the North Carolina CORE over the planning and leadership of desegregation marches.

Beginning in 1963 McKissick's role in CORE was determined by the growing militance developing in the civil rights movement. Black activists were proud of their earlier struggles, but many were also impatient with the pace of civil rights progress and disappointed by the continued economic misery of American blacks. This unrest gave rise to a desire for greater black self-reliance and independence from white liberal supporters of civil rights. CORE responded to this sentiment by choosing McKissick, known as "a down-home black lawyer," to be national chairman in June 1963; the unpaid position had earlier been held by whites.

McKissick himself was affected by the new currents in the civil rights movement and increasingly stressed the importance of black self-help and control over decision-making in CORE. Speaking at the 1963 CORE convention, he claimed that civil rights litigation had gone as far as possible in the courts, leaving direct action as the only avenue of black advancement. In 1965 McKissick attempted to shift the organization's funding base from middle-class whites to blacks. He also invited Black Muslims to speak for the first time at a CORE national convention in January 1966, dramatizing his commitment to separate black cultural development. The same convention elected McKissick CORE's national director after James Farmer [q.v.] announced his departure from the organization.

Under McKissick's leadership CORE remained on the militant side of the civil rights spectrum. McKissick followed civil rights leader Stokely Carmichael [q.v.] in adopting the rhetoric of black power, calling blacks "a nation within a nation." The greatest support for black separatism came from CORE chapters in Northern cities, and McKissick shifted the organization toward a stronger focus on urban poverty problems. He tried repeatedly to attract federal and foundation money for voter education, job training and aid to black businesses in the ghetto. In a symbolic action McKissick moved CORE's national headquarters to Harlem in August 1966. He also became one of the strongest critics among black leaders of the Vietnam war.

Despite McKissick's policies, many CORE members were not satisfied with his leadership. Much of the tension within the organization resulted from its growing financial difficulties. The rise of black power sentiment had alienated many white financial supporters, and McKissick could not find adequate replacement funding in the black community. To avoid bankruptcy he was forced in January 1967 to curtail a number of CORE projects. This caused resentment in local chapters whose projects were affected and increased competition for remaining funds. According to historians August Meier and Elliot Rudwick, militant CORE staffers also viewed McKissick as a follower rather than a leader of black power, and there were complaints that his Southern background prevented him from relating to blacks in the Northern ghettos. In September 1967 McKissick took a leave of absence from CORE. He resigned as national director in 1968.

After leaving CORE McKissick established his own consulting firm, which dealt with poverty problems.

MADDOX, LESTER G(ARFIELD)
b. Sept. 30, 1915; Atlanta, Ga.
Governor, Ga., 1967-71.

After holding a variety of jobs, Maddox opened a drive-in restaurant called the Pickrick in Atlanta, Ga., in 1947. The restaurant, which refused service to blacks, expanded nine times over the next 15 years. As it prospered Maddox took an increasing interest in politics. He ran as a segregationist candidate for mayor of Atlanta in 1957 and 1961 and for lieutenant governor in 1962. Although he lost all three elections, his campaign for lieutenant governor made him well-known throughout the state of Georgia.

Maddox received national attention in the summer of 1964, when he defied the provision in the newly adopted Civil Rights Act prohibiting racial segregation in public accommodations. When three black ministerial students tried to enter the Pickrick on July 3, they were chased away by Maddox, who brandished a gun, and by his white patrons, who carried ax handles. Similar incidents occurred when other blacks tried to enter Maddox's restaurant in July and August. The three ministerial students sued Maddox in federal court, and in what proved to be the first court test of the 1964 Civil Rights Act, a three-judge federal panel in Atlanta upheld the public accommodations law on July 22. The court ordered Maddox to desegregate his restaurant within 20 days. After this order was affirmed by Supreme Court Justice Hugo Black [q.v.] on Aug. 10, Maddox decided to close his restaurant rather than open it to blacks.

Maddox announced his candidacy for the Democratic nomination for governor of Georgia in October 1965. He spent most of the next year conducting a vigorous grassroots campaign on a platform of support for segregation and opposition to alleged federal encroachment on state and individual rights. Maddox placed second in a field of five candidates in the Sept. 14, 1966 Democratic primary. He then defeated former Gov. Ellis G. Arnall [q.v.] in the Sept. 28 runoff even though Arnall, a racial moderate, had the support of most Georgia newspapers and the state's Democratic hierarchy. In the November election neither Maddox nor his Republican opponent, Rep. Howard H. Callaway (R, Ga.) [q.v.], received a majority of the popular vote. Georgia law required the state legislature to choose the governor in this situation. Even though Callaway had received about 3,000 more popular votes than Maddox, the legislature selected Maddox as governor by a vote of 182 to 66 on Jan. 10, 1967.

Sworn in as governor the same day, Maddox delivered a moderate inaugural address. He promised not to close any schools to prevent desegregation and said no "extremist organization or group" would have "any voice or influence in any state program." He urged respect for federal authority, declared there was "no necessity" for any federal-state conflict and said any disagreements should be solved "under the framework of the Constitution."

Considered a buffoon by many of his critics and a populist hero by his supporters, Maddox surprised most observers with his inaugural and with his actions during his first years in office. He quickly invited Alabama's former Gov. George C. Wallace [q.v.] to address the state legislature, but he also met with President Johnson early in 1967, declaring afterwards that he was "pleasantly surprised" to find Johnson "so knowledgeable." Maddox appointed blacks to local draft boards, to the Georgia Bureau of Investigation and to various special commissions and interim legislative committees. He ordered an investigation of conditions in state prisons after four escaped black prisoners surrendered to him at the governor's mansion to tell him of penal conditions.

Maddox also accepted antipoverty funds from the federal government but denounced federal guidelines on school desegregation and praised a local school board when it again segregated black and white teachers despite the potential loss of federal funds. He criticized President Johnson's formation of a federal commission to investigate the cause of urban riots in 1967, saying government officials knew that the violence was "Communist inspired and directed." Maddox also challenged the need for greater federal spending to cure the country's urban problems and said the country should instead "start instilling" in the urban poor the spirit of initiative "that made this country great."

On August 17, 1968 Maddox announced his candidacy for the Democratic presidential nomination, declaring he represented the "conservative element of American society." He labeled the major aspirants for the nomination "socialists" and, in a nationally televised address, emphasized the need for a stronger American commitment to fight world Communism and for greater law and order at home. His candidacy was generally considered inconsequential, however, and Maddox withdrew his name from consideration shortly before the balloting began at the August 1968 Democratic National Convention.

Meanwhile, in accordance with long practice in Georgia, Maddox and the state Democratic Party chairman personally selected the 107 members of Georgia's delegation to the National Convention. They chose only six blacks and a few moderate or liberal whites. As a consequence, a coalition of blacks and white liberals organized a challenge delegation headed by State Rep. Julian Bond [q.v.]. The Convention Credentials Committee suggested two different compromises between the regular and the challenge delegations, but Maddox rejected both and then resigned as a delegate.

During the remainder of his term, Maddox denounced federal school desegregation suits and met with several other Southern governors to devise means to stop busing for school desegregation. He also urged a full American military victory in Vietnam and continued to warn against socialism and communism within the U.S. While in Washington in February 1970 to testify at Senate hearings on a voting rights bill, Maddox created a furor by passing out his souvenir ax handles at the House restaurant. The state constitution barred Maddox from a second consecutive term as governor. After he lost a court suit to overturn this provision, Maddox ran for lieutenant governor in 1970. He defeated three opponents, including the incumbent, in the September Democratic primary and then won the November election.

MALCOLM X
b. May 19, 1925; Omaha, Neb.
d. Feb. 21, 1965; New York, N.Y.
Black Muslim leader.

Malcom X was born Malcolm Little in Omaha, Neb., where his father was a Baptist minister and an organizer for Marcus Garvey's United Negro Improvement Association. Raised primarily in Michigan,

Little moved to Boston to live with a half-sister after his father died. He developed a reputation in the black ghettos of Boston and New York City as a "hustler" and was sentenced to prison for burglary in February 1946. In jail he discovered the teachings of Black Muslim leader Elijah Muhammad and changed his name to Malcom X. Released from prison in August 1952, Malcolm settled in Detroit where he was appointed assistant minister of Muslim Temple No. 1. He was placed in charge of the Muslims' New York temple in 1954 and in 1963 became the Muslims' first "national minister."

During the early 1960s Malcom X's forceful indictment of white society and the civil rights movement created an unprecedented amount of public interest in the Black Muslims. Regarded by many as a proponent of "racism in reverse," Malcolm was a controversial figure among white and black people alike during this period.

Malcolm X replaced the ailing Elijah Muhammad as the main speaker at the Muslims' national convention in 1963. In his speech he repeated the traditional Black Muslim demands for "everything we need to start our own independent civilization." For the first time he also appealed for unity in the fight for civil rights and for cooperation between the Muslims, the NAACP and the Congress of Racial Equality. Historian William O'Neil maintained that Malcolm's increasing desire for a "popular front" contributed to the split between Malcolm X and Elijah Muhammad.

The first public indication of trouble between Elijah Muhammad and Malcolm X occurred in December 1963, when Muhammad silenced Malcolm for 90 days because Malcolm described President Kennedy's death as a case of "chickens coming home to roost." A rumor that Malcolm was suspended indefinitely from his leadership functions spread throughout the Muslim organization. On February 26, 1964 Malcolm telephoned Muhammad and asked for a clarification of his status.

Muhammad's reply did not satisfy Malcolm, and on March 8, 1964 he announced that he was leaving the Muslims to form an organization that would stress "black nationalism as a political concept and form of social action against the oppressors." A

month later he embarked on a five week pilgrimage to Mecca and Africa, returning again to Africa later the same year. During his first trip abroad he wrote the well-publicized *Letter from Mecca* describing experiences with Caucasian Muslims that caused him to favorably re-evaluate the role which white people in America might play in the struggle against racism. He also adopted the Arabic name El-Hajj Malik El-Shabazz.

According to Alex Haley, Malcolm's trips abroad "sorely tested the morale of even his key members" in his newly formed Organization of Afro-American Unity. Upon returning from his second trip abroad in September 1964, Malcolm sought to solve the financial problems of both his new organization and his family by accepting numerous speaking engagements. He also sought to establish a cooperative relationship with the civil rights movement. On February 3, 1965, he visited Selma, Ala., during the voter registration drive there and, according to Martin Luther King's [q.v.] biographer, David Lewis, confided to Coretta King [q.v.] that he counted on his own militant reputation to "scare" white people to her husband's cause. In public he stopped labeling black integrationists "Uncle Toms."

The relationship between Malcolm X and the Black Muslims continued to deteriorate, and in early 1965 Malcolm reported several death threats. On February 14 Malcolm's home was firebombed. One week later, as he addressed a rally at the Audubon Ballroom in New York City, he was assassinated by men thought to be linked to the Black muslims.

MARSHALL, BURKE
b. Oct. 1, 1922; Plainfield, N.J.
U.S. Assistant Attorney General in charge of the Civil Rights Division, February 1961-December 1964.

A 1943 graduate of Yale University, Marshall was a Japanese language expert for the Army in World War II. After receiving a degree from Yale Law School in 1951, he became a member of a Washington law firm where he specialized in antitrust work. An attorney with an excellent reputation, he was named assistant attorney general in charge of the Justice Department's Civil Rights Division on Feb. 2, 1961.

Marshall, a quiet and cool-headed man and a skillful negotiator, was a key figure in the development of the Kennedy Administration's civil rights policies and its handling of racial crises in the South. He viewed the right to vote as the key to securing other civil rights and significantly stepped up the voting rights work of the Justice Department. While only 10 voter discrimination suits were filed by the Eisenhower Administration, Marshall's division had filed 42 such cases by mid-1963. Marshall also urged the leaders of civil rights organizations to undertake a voter registration campaign in the South in 1961. His proposals helped lead to a foundation-financed Voter Education Project, which began in April 1962.

When the freedom riders—protesters challenging segregated transportation—were attacked by mobs in Anniston and Birmingham, Ala. on May 14, 1961, Marshall joined with other Administration officials in working out means to protect the riders from further violence and to end segregated travel facilities. He personally reached an agreement in October 1961 with three railroads for desegregation of their Southern terminals. Marshall also followed James Meredith's [q.v.] court suit seeking integration of the University of Mississippi from its start. When state officials attempted to block Meredith's court-ordered admission to the school in the fall of 1962, Marshall participated in negotiations with Gov. Ross Barnett [q.v.] to try to secure Meredith's peaceful enrollment and helped to coordinate the federal government's activities during the crisis from Washington.

In April 1963 Martin Luther King [q.v.] began leading civil rights demonstrations in Birmingham, Ala. The historic protest escalated in May and was met with increasing police repression. Marshall arrived in Birmingham on May 4 as President Kennedy's personal representative and began mediating behind the scenes, trying to get city officials, white businessmen and black leaders to confer. His negotiating efforts ultimately led to a May 10 desegregation agreement between white and black leaders. In the summer of 1963, Marshall also helped to arrange a desegregation agreement ending some four months of demonstrations in Cambridge, Md. In addition he worked to forestall crises by quietly touring Southern cities and conferring with local officials to help prepare for peaceful school desegregation. Marshall also aided in drafting the Kennedy civil rights bill introduced in Congress in June 1963 and worked to secure its passage.

According to journalist Benjamin Muse, Marshall was an "official of quiet tact and effectiveness, who enjoyed to a rare degree the respect of all parties to civil rights disputes." Both he and the Administration, however, were often criticized for their policies. The voting rights suits, for example, were labeled "ineffective in ending voting discrimination" by Howard Zinn, and Marshall himself admitted in 1964 that the federal government had not yet succeeded "in making the right to vote real" for blacks in Mississippi and in large parts of Alabama and Louisiana. Some rights workers also charged that the mediation efforts of Marshall and his colleagues in racial disputes were aimed more at restoring order and tranquility than at advancing black civil rights.

The greatest criticism centered on the federal government's failure to protect civil rights workers and local blacks in the South from both private and official harassment and assault. Many of those who participated in the voter registration campaign encouraged by Marshall were especially bitter about the Justice Department's inaction. Marshall countered with the argument that under a federal system of government, many of the assaults on rights workers were outside the reach of the national government. He insisted that the Constitution afforded no basis for sending special federal agents throughout the deep South as some urged. Legal experts were divided on the validity of this view, but Marshall adhered to it, even though he recognized that it caused great frustration and resentment against the government among civil rights workers.

Marshall also helped draft the Kennedy civil rights bill submitted to Congress in June 1963 and negotiated with members of

Congress on a compromise measure in October 1963. He worked for passage of the measure, which was signed into law on July 4, 1964, and then oversaw the Justice Department's efforts to ensure enforcement of the statute.

Marshall resigned his post on Dec. 18, 1964, saying it "would not be wise" for the same person to have his job for more than one presidential term. He then spent several months aiding Vice President Hubert H. Humphrey in his capacity as coordinator of the federal government's policies and programs in civil rights. Although he formally returned to private law practice in January 1965, Marshall joined top Justice Department officials in March of that year to oversee the federal government's activities during the protest march from Selma to Montgomery, Ala., led by Martin Luther King [q.v.]. In February 1966 Marshall was appointed to a 28-member presidential council that prepared a special report and recommendations for the June 1966 White House Conference on Civil Rights.

In June 1965 Marshall joined the International Business Machines Corp. (IBM) as vice president and general counsel. He was named a senior vice president in 1969.

For further information:
Burke Marshall, *Federalism and Civil Rights* (New York, 1964).

MARSHALL, THURGOOD

b. July 2, 1908: Baltimore, Md.
Director-Counsel, NAACP Legal Defense and Educational Fund, 1940-61.
U.S. Circuit Judge, Second Circuit Court of Appeals, 1961-65; U.S. Solicitor General, 1965-67; Associate Justice, U.S. Supreme Court, 1967- .

Marshall's father was a steward at an exclusive Chesapeake Bay Club, and his mother taught school in Baltimore. Marshall graduated from Lincoln University in 1930 and from Howard University Law School in 1933. After practicing law in Baltimore he joined the NAACP as assistant special counsel in 1936. He was named special counsel two years later. When the NAACP Legal Defense and Educational Fund was established in 1940, Marshall was appointed director and counsel. As head of the Fund, he led the legal battle against racial discrimination for three decades. He gained attention as one of the nation's foremost civil rights attorney. Marshall personally argued cases before the Supreme Court on 16 occasions, losing only three times. He participated in almost every major civil rights case in the second half of the century.

Marshall directed a broad attack on segregation during the Truman years, winning victories in suits challenging segregated housing and transportation as well as discrimination in voting and jury selection. He was known for his conversational approach, avoiding legal jargon and presenting his case with "great courtesy and deference." His arguments were tightly reasoned, backed by intense research. In 1944, in *Smith v. Allwright*, he successfully argued that the "white primary" of the Democratic Party in Texas, which excluded blacks, was unconstitutional. Two years later, in *Morgan v. Virginia*, he persuaded the Supreme Court to invalidate segregated interstate bus travel under the commerce clause of the Constitution. The decision in *Shelley v. Kraemer* (1948) struck down state court enforcement of racially restrictive real estate covenants. In 1950 he attacked the doctrine of "separate but equal" in graduate education in *Sweatt v. Painter* and *McLaurin v. Oklahoma State Regents*. Marshall argued that white education was superior to black, even with physical equality, because of "intangible" qualities. The Supreme Court agreed, unanimously ruling that blacks had not had "substantial equality in educational opportunities."

Marshall did not confine his advocacy of civil rights to the courtroom. While he opposed a "disobedience movement" by Southern blacks, claiming in 1946 that such a campaign would result "in wholesale slaughter with no good achieved," he forcefully spoke out against racial discrimination. Concerned with other areas of civil liberties law, he was critical of the decision to intern Japanese-Americans during World War II and attacked the House Un-American Activities Committee. In 1947 he sent a telegram to New York members of Congress calling on them to vote against contempt citations for the Hollywood Ten. He denounced Truman's federal loyalty program in 1949 as "blatantly unconstitutional."

In 1951 Marshall went to Japan and Korea to investigate charges that black soldiers convicted by Army courts had received unfair trials. He discovered that few of those convicted had been treated impartially, and he was disturbed by the harsh sentences blacks received. Marshall, in arguing appeals for black servicemen, had sentences reduced for 22. In his final report to the Army's Far East Command, he criticized Gen. Douglas MacArthur for permitting segregated facilities.

In perhaps the most significant court battle of his career, Marshall supervised the preparation of five cases challenging the validity of racial segregation in public schools. He personally represented the black plaintiffs from Clarendon Co., S.C., in one of the suits, and during oral arguments before the Supreme Court in December 1952 and December 1953, Marshall contended that state-enforced segregation violated the 14th Amendment. On May 17, 1954 the Supreme Court ruled unanimously in *Brown v. Board of Education* that segregation in public education was unconstitutional. During argument in April 1955 on how the decision should be carried out, Marshall urged the Court to order complete desegregation of public schools no later than the fall term of 1956. The Court, however, announced a far more flexible standard in May 1955 and ordered school desegregation "with all deliberate speed." Over the next several years Marshall and the NAACP led a massive program of litigation to enforce the *Brown* decision.

Along with several other NAACP lawyers, Marshall also represented Autherine Lucy [*q.v.*] in her suit to enter the University of Alabama and won a Supreme Court decision in October 1955 ordering her enrollment. Marshall was with Lucy on Feb. 6, 1956, when she was attacked by a mob on the University's campus. After the University's trustees suspended Lucy the next day, Marshall secured a federal court order for her reinstatement. The trustees then expelled Lucy, and she withdrew from the case shortly afterwards.

Marshall was also counsel for the black students who desegregated Central High School in Little Rock, Ark., in the fall of 1957. When Gov. Orval Faubus [*q.v.*] tried to thwart integration of the high school in September 1957, Marshall got an injunction barring the Governor from further interference with the school's desegregation plan. Later in the school year the local school board sought to postpone its desegregation program for two-and-a-half years. In a special Supreme Court term in September 1958, Marshall argued against this delay and won a unanimous decision from the Court ordering continuance of school integration plans.

Marshall also handled cases extending the *Brown* principle to such areas as public recreation and public transit. He participated in the suit growing out of the Montgomery, Ala., bus boycott, which resulted in a November 1956 Supreme Court ruling that segregation in local transportation was unconstitutional. In his last oral argument before the Supreme Court in October 1960, Marshall successfully contended that segregation in restaurants at interstate bus terminals violated federal law.

In his final years with the NAACP, Marshall aided the defense of hundreds of students arrested during the sit-ins, the Freedom Rides and similar nonviolent protests. He helped prepare the December 1961 case in which the Court reversed the convictions of blacks arrested for peaceful lunch counter sit-ins.

President Kennedy nominated Marshall for a judgeship on the Second Circuit Court of Appeals on Sept. 23, 1961, and Marshall began serving in October under a recess appointment. Under the chairmanship of Sen. James O. Eastland (D, Miss.) [q.v.], who opposed Marshall's appointment, the Senate Judiciary Committee delayed hearings on the nomination for nearly eight months and then held six days of hearings stretched out over four months. The Committee finally approved his appointment on Sept. 7, 1962 by an 11-4 vote, and the full Senate confirmed the nomination on Sept. 11 by a vote of 54 to 16. All of the opposition came from Southern Democrats.

As a new judge, Marshall had little opportunity to write majority opinions in significant civil or individual rights cases, and most of his written decisions concerned such areas as federal tort claims, admiralty law or patent and trademark cases. However, his votes on the Court and the opinions he did write identified him as a liberal jurist who usually granted the government broad powers in economic matters but barred it from infringing on the constitutional rights of the individual.

President Johnson appointed Marshall U.S. Solicitor General in July 1965. The first black to serve in that post, Marshall's chief areas of concern were civil rights and eavesdropping by government agencies. He won Supreme Court approval of the 1965 Voting Rights Act, persuaded the Court to reinstate indictments in two cases against defendants charged with conspiracy to murder civil rights workers and joined in a suit that successfully overturned a California constitutional amendment prohibiting open housing legislation. Convinced that all electronic eavesdropping that involved an illegal trespass was unconstitutional, Marshall voluntarily informed the Supreme Court in two cases that the government had used electronic devices to collect information on suspects charged with violation of federal laws. He had no similar qualms about the use of government informers, however, and he successfully argued in the Supreme Court that the government's use of an informer did not invalidate the convictions of James Hoffa and three other Teamster union officials for jury tampering. Marshall argued 19 cases for the government before the Supreme Court, winning all but five.

On June 13, 1967 President Johnson nominated Marshall as an associate justice of the U.S. Supreme Court to fill the vacancy created by the retirement of Justice Tom C. Clark. Once again Marshall was the first black appointed to this position. In announcing Marshall's nomination Johnson declared that this was "the right thing to do, the right time to do it, the right man and the right place." The Senate confirmed the nomination on Aug. 30 by a 69-11 vote, with all of the opposition coming from Southern senators.

From the start Marshall was a liberal and activist jurist who voted most often with Chief Justice Earl Warren and Justice William Brennan [q.v.]. He played a subordinate role in his first years on the bench, writing few majority opinions and rarely dissenting. As the Court became more conservative in the 1970s, however, Marshall became increasingly outspoken. The number of his dissents rose sharply, and he was identified as part of the left wing of the Burger Court.

In racial discrimination cases Marshall almost always voted to expand the civil rights of blacks. He supported school desegregation orders and dissented sharply in July 1974 when the Court upset an interdistrict busing plan to remedy school segregation in Detroit. Marshall also objected to a June 1971 decision sanctioning the closing of public swimming pools in Jackson, Miss., to avoid desegregation and to a ruling a year later allowing private clubs with state liquor licenses to exclude blacks. Although he generally voted in favor of blacks in employment discrimination cases, Marshall wrote the majority opinion in a February 1975 case holding that an employer could fire employes who bypassed their union's effort to resolve a dispute over racial discrimination and picketed on their own.

In other equal protection cases, Marshall urged the Court to adopt a variable standard of review that would take into account the nature of the classification and of the interests involved in each case. Even under the accepted approach to equal protection claims, however, the Justice took a strong stand against all forms of discrimination. He favored making sex a suspect classification that would be subject to strict judicial scrutiny and voted in almost every instance to overturn differences in treatment between men and women. Marshall also opposed government distinctions between legitimate and illegitimate children and between citizens and aliens. However he did rule in a November 1973 majority opinion that the 1964 Civil Rights Act had not outlawed employment discrimination against aliens. He opposed discrimination against the poor and voted in March 1973 to invalidate public school financing systems based on local property taxes.

Justice Marshall supported expansions of the right to vote. His opinion in a June 1970 case held that residents of a federal enclave in Maryland could vote in state and local elections. In a March 1972 majority opinion, Marshall overturned state residency requirements for voting of three months or more. He opposed laws restricting voting on bond issues to property owners and favored a federal law lowering the voting age to 18. Marshall generally supported a strict one-man, one-vote standard of apportionment and dissented in cases which relaxed that standard at the state level.

Marshall spoke for a six man majority in June 1969 to hold the Fifth Amendment's provision against double jeopardy applicable to the states. In other criminal cases the Justice generally favored strong protection of the guarantees afforded by the Bill of Rights. He usually opposed searches without warrants and believed a warrant necessary for electronic eavesdropping. Marshall insisted that a waiver of rights was legitimate only if a defendant was fully informed and uncoerced. As Solicitor General he had argued against the *Miranda* ruling, requiring the police to inform suspects of their rights. But as a justice, Marshall opposed most attempts to cut back that decision. He dissented from rulings authorizing non-unanimous jury verdicts and juries of less than 12 members in state and federal courts and

voted in several cases to expand the right to counsel. Marshall took a broad view of the Fifth Amendment's privilege against self-incrimination, and he voted in June 1972 and July 1976 to hold the death penalty totally unconstitutional as a violation of the Eighth Amendment's ban on cruel and unusual punishment.

Marshall took a liberal stance in most First Amendment cases. In a May 1968 opinion for the Court, he held peaceful labor picketing within a suburban shopping center protected by the Amendment. He dissented vigorously when the Court narrowed this ruling in June 1972 and then overturned it in March 1976. Marshall voted against prior restraints on the press. However he did favor narrowing the protection against libel suits enjoyed by the press when the case involved a private citizen rather than a public figure. In an April 1969 decision, his opinion for the Court held that the private possession of obscene materials within one's own home could not be made a crime. He also joined in a dissenting opinion in several June 1973 cases urging the Court to ban all government suppression of allegedly obscene material for consenting adults.

In March 1971, however, Marshall spoke for an eight man majority to rule that Congress could deny conscientious objector status to draft registrants who opposed only the Vietnam war, not all wars, without violating the First Amendment's guarantee of freedom of religion. In August 1973, while the Court was in recess, Marshall upheld a Second Circuit Court order allowing U.S. bombing of Cambodia to continue while the constitutionality of the action was being litigated. When Justice William O. Douglas [*q.v.*] intervened in the case several days later to order a halt in the bombing, Marshall immediately contacted the other members of the Court and issued an order with their support overriding Douglas's action.

Even before joining the Court, Thurgood Marshall had won a place in history because of his pathbreaking legal work for the NAACP. He stood as a symbol of the fight for black equality through legal action, and in both his NAACP post and later federal appointments, as a symbol of black achievement. As a justice, he was not highly creative or outstanding, but over the years, he became an increasingly articulate advocate of a liberal judicial position. In steadfastly opposing all forms of discrimination and supporting the protection of individual rights, Marshall maintained the Warren Court's tradition of libertarian activism.

Marshall was not actively engaged in the civil rights movement after 1961 because of the government positions he held, but his career exemplified that segment of the movement that relied primarily on the judicial process to win political and social advancement for blacks. In a May 1969 speech at Dillard University in New Orleans, Marshall criticized those blacks who advocated violence saying, "Anarchy is anarchy, and it makes no difference who practices it, it is bad; it is punishable, and it should be punished." Younger black militants, in turn, criticized Marshall's and the NAACP's legal approach during the 1960s as ineffective "gradualism." However, Marshall remained a symbol of black achievement for his work in the NAACP and for the recognition he won in his various federal appointments.

For further information:
Randall W. Bland, *Private Pressure on Public Law: The Legal Career of Justice Thurgood Marshall* (Port Washington, 1973).

MEREDITH, JAMES H(OWARD)
b. June 25, 1933; Kosciusko, Miss.
Civil rights activist.

Meredith grew up on a Mississippi farm and, after graduating from high school in 1951, spent nine years in the Air Force. He returned to Mississippi in August 1960 and enrolled that fall at all-black Jackson State College to complete the college studies he had begun while in the military. Sometime during the semester Meredith decided to

try to enter the all-white University of Mississippi at Oxford, the state's best public college. In his account of this effort, *Three Years in Mississippi*, published in 1966, Meredith wrote that he believed he had a "divine responsibility," a "mission," to help "break the system of 'White Supremacy'" in Mississippi and direct "civilization toward a destiny of humaneness." He sent his application for admission to Oxford in January 1961, intiating a 17-month fight to desegregate the University of Mississippi.

After months of correspondence the University denied admission to Meredith in May 1961. With the aid of Constance Baker Motley and Jack Greenberg [*q.v.*], attorneys for the NAACP Legal Defense Fund, Meredith brought suit against University officials in federal district court, charging the denial was because of his race. Judge Sidney C. Mize turned down Meredith's request for a preliminary injunction in December 1961. After a trial on the merits, Mize ruled on Feb. 3, 1962 that the University was "not a racially segregated institution" and that Meredith had not been refused admission because of his race. The Fifth Circuit Court in New Orleans reversed this decision on June 25, ordering Meredith admitted to the school. U.S. District Judge Ben Cameron, sitting in Mississippi, stayed this order four times during the summer. The Fifth Circuit Court vacated three of the stays, and on Sept. 10, 1962, Supreme Court Justice Hugo Black nullified the fourth and ordered the University to admit Meredith.

Meredith wired the University's registrar on Sept. 11 that he would enroll on Sept. 20. On the night of Sept. 13, in a statewide television and radio address, Mississippi Gov. Ross Barnett [*q.v.*] promised to oppose Meredith's entrance to the University and began a series of state efforts to block implementation of the federal court orders. On Sept. 19 a Mississippi state court issued an injunction barring Meredith from the University. The same day the state legislature passed a law that no one convicted of a crime could attend a state university. The next day a justice of the peace in Jackson convicted Meredith in absentia on a charge of false voter registration and ordered him arrested. The U.S. Justice Department, which had formally entered Meredith's case on Sept. 18, got federal court orders on the 20th voiding the state court injunction and the conviction. Late that afternoon Meredith made his first attempt to register in Oxford and was met by Gov. Barnett, who had been appointed special registrar for Meredith by the University's board of trustees. Barnett read Meredith and accompanying federal officials a state proclamation refusing him admission to the University. The Justice Department then moved for contempt citations against the University's trustees and top officials. At a hearing before the Fifth Circuit Court on Sept. 24, the trustees agreed to enroll Meredith the next day. On the 25th the Fifth Circuit enjoined Barnett from blocking Meredith's admission, but when Meredith tried to register that day, this time at the trustees' office in Jackson, Barnett refused to accept copies of the Circuit Court's injunction and again denied Meredith admission to the University. The Justice Department applied to the Circuit Court for a contempt citation against Barnett.

While this action was pending Meredith made two more unsuccessful attempts to register in Oxford. A Sept. 26 try was blocked by Lt. Gov. Paul B. Johnson [q.v.], and the Justice Department called off another effort on Sept. 27 because of possible violence at the University.

The Fifth Circuit Court found Barnett guilty of civil contempt on Sept. 28 and directed him to comply with earlier court orders by Oct. 2 or be fined $10,000 a day. Behind the scenes the Justice Department had been negotiating with Barnett in an effort to find a peaceful and safe way to enroll Meredith. President Kennedy entered these negotiations on Sept. 29 with three phone calls to the Governor. Kennedy also federalized Mississippi's National Guard, ordered Army units to Memphis in case more forces were needed to protect Meredith and issued a proclamation to the government and people of Mississippi calling on them to cease all obstruction to the federal court orders.

Meredith flew from Memphis to Oxford on Sept. 30 and was taken to his dormitory room around 6 p.m. Barnett made a statement at 9 p.m., indicating that his resistance to Meredith's admission was over. That night a 24-man guard protected Meredith in his room, and 300 federal marshals and a force of Mississippi state troopers were on the University campus. President Kennedy addressed the nation on television at 10 p.m. and appealed to the University's students to preserve both the law and the peace. However, a riot on the campus had already erupted around 8 p.m. Before it was over early the next morning, Kennedy had called in both the National Guard and the Army. Two men died in the rioting; over 350 were injured. At 8 a.m. on Oct. 1, Meredith was escorted to the registrar's office by federal officials and finally enrolled. The crisis at "Ole Miss" posed the most serious state challenge to federal authority since the events in Little Rock in 1957. Although Kennedy regretted having to use troops, his actions upheld the supremacy of the federal courts and the Constitution over state power. They also represented a victory for the civil rights movement because the Kennedy Administration had acted decisively to protect the constitutional rights of a black citizen.

Throughout the crisis Meredith, a quiet and introspective person, had remained controlled and composed. Justice Department attorney John Doar [q.v.], who accompanied Meredith on four of his five registration attempts, said later that Meredith took everything "calmly and coolly." Meredith displayed the same quiet courage throughout the semester as he underwent harassment, threats and ostracism. He announced on Jan. 7, 1963 that he would not return for the spring semester at the University unless "very definite and positive changes" were made to make his situation more conducive to learning. On Jan. 30 Meredith said he had decided to enroll for a second term, and he registered the next day without incident. Protected throughout his months at the University by federal marshals, Meredith completed his studies during the summer term and graduated on

Aug. 18, 1963 with a B.A. in political science.

Although Meredith was widely acclaimed for his entry into "Ole Miss," he was publicly rebuked for the views he expressed at the convention of the NAACP in Chicago in July 1963. Speaking at the organization's Youth Freedom Fund banquet, Meredith critized "the low quality and ineffectiveness of our Negro youth leaders" and reportedly told his audience that "anyone of you burr-heads out there" could be successful in business or politics "if you only believe." The head of the NAACP's college division immediately attacked Meredith for these statements and won a standing ovation from the assembly.

Meredith left Mississippi following his graduation but returned briefly in June 1966 for a pilgrimage from Memphis, Tenn., to Jackson, Miss. Then a second-year student at Columbia University Law School, Meredith said on May 31 that his march was intended to encourage voter registration among Mississippi's blacks and to "challenge the all-pervasive and overriding fear that dominates the day-to-day life of the Negro in the United States—especially in the South and particularly in Mississippi." He began his walk on June 5 accompanied by a few friends. The next day, about 10 miles over the Mississippi border, Meredith was shot from ambush along U.S. Highway 51. He suffered over 60 superficial wounds in the head, back and legs and was taken to a Memphis hospital for emergency surgery. On June 7 civil rights leaders Martin Luther King [q.v.], Floyd McKissick [q.v.] and Stokely Carmichael [q.v.] retraced Meredith's route. On their return to Memphis that evening, they vowed to carry on his march all the way to Jackson. The march was resumed on June 8. During its three-week course divisions among the leadership became increasingly apparent. While King continued to speak of interracial cooperation and nonviolence, Carmichael raised the cry of black power and urged self-defense rather than nonviolence when attacked.

Meredith himself returned to New York City on June 8 to recuperate. There he occasionally expressed some criticism of the

way the march was run, but he rejoined the march on June 24 at Canton, Miss., and spoke at a final rally in Jackson on June 26. By the end of the march, however, Meredith's original protest had been overshadowed by indications of a schism among the major civil rights leaders.

Meredith, who was considered a loner and an individualist within the civil rights movement, expressed support for Carmichael and the black power concept in a television interview in August 1966. He asserted that America was "a military-minded nation" and that nonviolence was "incompatible with American ideas." In the same interview Meredith said he "fully" supported the war in Vietnam and considered it "one of the best things happening to the Negro."

After Harlem Congressman Adam Clayton Powell (D, N.Y.) [q.v.] was excluded from the House of Representatives on March 1, 1967, Meredith announced that he would run on the Republican ticket in a special election for Powell's seat scheduled for April. Meredith said he was acting in accordance with his "divine responsibility," but local black leaders almost unanimously opposed his candidacy. On March 13, after meeting with Floyd McKissick of the Congress of Racial Equality and Mississippi rights leader Charles Evers [q.v.], Meredith withdrew from the race. He went back to Mississippi on June 24, 1967 to complete the march against fear he had initiated the year before. Meredith walked from the place where he had been shot to Canton, Miss., the town where he had rejoined the 1966 march.

Following his graduation from law school, Meredith became a businessman in New York City. In July 1969 he staged a walk from Chicago to New York to "promote Negro pride and positive goals in the black community." Meredith announced in June 1971 that he was moving back to Mississippi. He said that the racial atmosphere in the South had improved greatly and that on a "day-to-day basis," it was a "more liveable place for blacks." In February 1972 he entered the race for the Republican Senate nomination in Mississippi but lost in the July primary election.

MITCHELL, CLARENCE, M., JR.
b. March 8, 1911; Baltimore, Md.
Director, Washington Bureau, NAACP, 1950- .

An attorney educated at Lincoln University and the University of Maryland, Mitchell served on the Fair Employment Practices Commission and the War Manpower Commission during World War II. He headed the NAACP labor department after the War and became director of the Washington bureau of the NAACP in 1950. In this post Mitchell served as a lobbyist, brought the NAACP point of view to the public in the *Crisis,* the NAACP magazine, and worked with the executive branch to promote enforcement of civil rights.

Mitchell was an important force in shaping and articulating NAACP ideas and goals during the 1950s. His basic philosophy was that change would be brought about through legislation, sympathetic moves by whites, and public relations rather than by organized efforts and protests by blacks. In the early-1950s the main thrust of the NAACP was for peaceful desegregation through executive and legislative action. The military was one of the prime targets because by 1953 the Supreme Court had made segregation illegal in government jobs and because an executive order could force immediate desegregation of the Armed Services. In 1953 Mitchell maintained that under Eisenhower desegregation of military bases was lagging and urged it be carried out quickly. He also charged that local opposition was blocking school desegregation on military posts.

Mitchell opposed the congressional seniority system because it often placed Southern Democrats at the head of important committees, where they could block civil rights bills. He singled out Sen. James O. Eastland (D, Miss.) [*q.v.*], chairman of the Senate Judiciary Committee, for particular criticism, calling him a "stinking albatross" around the neck of the Democratic Party. He threatened that blacks would vote Republican if Democrats did not support civil rights demands.

One means Mitchell advocated for pushing desegregation was withholding federal funds from segregated areas. In 1955 he supported Rep. Adam Clayton Powell's (D, N.Y.) [*q.v.*] amendments to Administration school construction and military reserve bills providing that no aid be given to areas practicing segregation. Mitchell believed that such action would result in compliance with the Supreme Court's 1954 decision outlawing segregated schools without provoking violence. That same year he demanded that the government refuse to pay the expenses of the South Carolina delegation to the first White House Conference on Education because of the state's resistance to school desegregation.

Mitchell focused his attention on the protection and extension of voting rights, believing that increased black suffrage would result in civil rights gains in other fields. In 1956 he urged the NAACP to give top priority to a bill that would "protect the right to vote and . . . protect individuals against violence." Mitchell was dissatisfied with the Civil Rights Act of 1957, maintaining that it contained ineffective provisions for enforcement. He also denounced the violence that followed its passage.

The NAACP and other civil rights groups were dissatisfied with the Kennedy Administration's failure to introduce significant civil rights legislation during the early 1960s. In July 1961 Mitchell denounced the President for ignoring the civil rights pledges of the 1960 Democratic national platform, and he repeated his criticism at the NAACP's annual membership meeting in January 1962. The only difference between the Democratic and Republican Parties in the area of civil rights, he charged at the meeting, was that "the Democrats have more Negroes who can explain why we don't need such rights."

In November 1962 the President issued an executive order barring discrimination in federally aided housing. But the following April Mitchell charged that the order was not being enforced, and he placed the blame on the President himself, asserting, "The tempo is always taken by the President. . . . I have been in Washington a long time, and I know this is true under any Administration, under any program. If the President wants it to move, it will move."

Meanwhile, in 1962 and early 1963 Mitchell, who met frequently with liberal congressmen and senators to map civil rights strategy, appeared before the House Education and Labor Committee and other congressional panels in support of measures to combat racial discrimination. His proposals included anti-bias riders added to federal school-aid bills and a national fair employment practices law. However, the Administration did not support these proposals, and they were not passed by Congress.

Southern civil rights protests in the early 1960s and the violent white reaction to them enlarged the national constituency for anti-discrimination laws, and in June 1963 President Kennedy sent a civil rights bill to Congress. The major sections of the bill provided for the desegregation of public accommodations, the withholding of federal aid from all programs and activities in which racial discrimination was practiced and federal initiation of public school desegregation suits.

A House Judiciary Committee subcommittee strengthened the bill, but the Administration felt that the added provisions would deprive the measure of the Republican votes needed for passage. In October 1963 Attorney General Robert F. Kennedy urged the subcommittee to delete sections that expanded the President's definition of public accommodations and that permitted the Justice Department to seek injunctions against local police authorities that employed violent tactics against civil rights demonstrators.

Mitchell asserted, as he had on earlier occasions, that the difficulty in securing passage of effective civil rights laws was not a lack of support for such measures but the unwillingness of President Kennedy to vigorously press for them. He denounced the Attorney General's suggestions and said, "There is no reason for this kind of sellout. . . . The Administration should be in there fighting for the subcommittee bill."

President Lyndon B. Johnson's strong efforts on behalf of civil rights legislation, however, were welcomed and supported by Mitchell and most other rights leaders. On Capitol Hill Mitchell lobbied intensively on behalf of the Civil Rights Act of 1964 and the Voting Rights Act of 1965. In March 1968 he worked closely with House Democratic leaders in an effort to overcome Southern Democratic and Republican resistance to the Administration's open housing bill, covering four-fifths of the nation's housing, which had already been passed by the Senate. Rep. Gerald R. Ford (R, Mich.), the minority leader, wanted a House-Senate conference committee to modify the bill, which was stalled in the House Rules Committee. But Democratic managers of the bill, after meeting with Mitchell, decided to press for the Administration verstion. The assassination of Martin Luther King [q.v.] on April 4 helped generate the additional support needed to bring the bill out of the Rules Committee and pass it on the House floor.

Mitchell was a staunch defender of the Administration's antipoverty program. Many Republicans charged that the black urban riots of the summer of 1967 demonstrated the failure of the program and sought to reduce its budget. Mitchell denounced the attacks on the program as political opportunism and, contending that the riots stemmed from injustice, urged an increase in antipoverty funds.

Although some blacks regarded President Johnson's civil rights record as inadequate, Mitchell defended it in a speech to the NAACP Southeast Regional Conference in April 1968. He praised the President's contributions to the welfare of blacks, citing the civil rights acts of 1964, 1965 and 1968, the antipoverty program and the appointment of two blacks, Robert C. Weaver and Thurgood Marshall [q.v.], as Secretary of Housing and Urban Development and Supreme Court Justice, respectively. President Johnson, he asserted, "has given more successful leadership on civil rights than any other President of the United States."

Mitchell, supporting the Johnson Administration and unsympathetic to the peace movement, backed Vice President Hubert H. Humphrey's bid for the

Democratic presidential nomination in 1968. In December 1968 he criticized President-elect Richard M. Nixon's plan to promote black-owned businesses. Some civil rights leaders, influenced by black nationalist ideology, supported the program. But Mitchell feared it represented "a desire on the part of some to shift away the government assistance to the private enterprise approach" under which the benefits would "trickle down" from wealthy entrepreneurs to the poor.

During the Nixon years Mitchell led the fight against the appointment of conservative judges Clement F. Haynsworth [q.v.] and G. Harrold Carswell [q.v.] to the Supreme Court. Mitchell then directed his efforts in 1970 to gaining congressional extension of the 1965 Voting Rights Act's ban on literacy tests. Despite Nixon's attempt to weaken some of the Act's provisions such as the 18 year old vote amendment, the extension and provisions were signed into law.

With the confirmation of conservative Republican William H. Rehniquist [q.v.] to the Supreme Court in 1971, Mitchell lashed out at the Nixon Administration for its systematic efforts to undermine the achievements of the civil rights movement. When the President vetoed an extension of the anti-poverty program the same year, Mitchell decried the action as yet another example of the Administration's neglect of minority problems. Nixon's announcement in 1972 of his protracted approach to desegregation in public schools prompted Mitchell to condemn the President for his "cruel and savage attempts to use the power of federal government to bludgeon the courts into a surrender to mob rule."

Mitchell once again fought for extension of the Voting Rights Act which was approved in 1975. The following year Congress passed a resolution honoring Mitchell for "his contributions to the enhancement of life in America." Ford also commended the lobbyist extraordinaire for his efforts to eliminate injustices and institutional racism. Mitchell retired from the directorship of the NAACP in 1978.

MOSES, ROBERT P(ARRIS)
b. Jan. 23, 1935; New York, N.Y.
Field Secretary, Mississippi Student Nonviolent Coordinating Committee, 1961-65; Director, Mississippi Council of Federated Organizations, 1962-65.

Born and raised in Harlem, Moses graduated from New York's Stuyvesant High School in 1952 and from Hamilton College in 1956. He received a master's degree in philosophy from Harvard University the next year and then taught mathematics at Horace Mann, an elite private school in New York City. Intrigued by the Southern student sit-ins from the time they began in February 1960, Moses went to Atlanta that summer as a volunteer for the recently organized Student Nonviolent Coordinating Committee (SNCC). Late in the summer he traveled through Alabama and Mississippi recruiting for SNCC. In Cleveland, Miss., he met Amzie Moore, head of the local chapter of the NAACP. Moore convinced Moses that he should return to Mississippi the next summer to launch a voter registration campaign. In July 1961 Moses, by then a fulltime SNCC worker, moved into Amite and Pike Counties in southwestern Mississippi to start registration drives.

Alone at the outset, Moses was the first member of SNCC to undertake civil rights work in a deep South black community on a long-term basis. He opened voter registration schools in the two counties in August 1961 and began accompanying small groups of local blacks to voting registrars' offices. Along with other SNCC workers and local blacks who associated with them, Moses was repeatedly harassed, beaten and jailed. In late October 1961 Moses was found guilty of disturbing the peace after leading a protest march in McComb, Miss. In jail until Dec. 6, Moses found on his release that the violence and intimidation had deterred nearly all the blacks in Amite and Pike Counties from joining the registration drive. Early in 1962 Moses left the region and moved to Jackson, Miss., where SNCC set up its state headquarters.

In the spring of 1962 SNCC joined several other civil rights organizations in Mississippi in a Council of Federated Organizations (COFO). Established to conduct a unified voter registration project in the state, COFO was staffed mainly by SNCC workers. Moses was named project director. From the COFO office in Jackson, Moses drew up the plans for voter registration projects in various parts of the state and served as unofficial campaign manager for the Rev. R. L. Smith, a black Jackson minister who ran unsuccessfully for Congress in the June 1962 Democratic primary. Moses spent most of the summer doing registration work in Cleveland, Miss. but moved the center of COFO activity to Greenwood the following spring after a shooting incident outside that Mississippi delta town seriously wounded a black civil rights worker. (Moses was almost killed in the same nightrider assault.)

Moses was also a key organizer of the November 1963 Freedom Ballot, a mock election sponsored by COFO and open to all blacks over 21. The COFO election was designed to demonstrate the magnitude of the denial of black voting rights in Mississippi and to prove that large numbers of blacks in the state did want to vote. Moses served as campaign manager for Aaron Henry [q.v.] and Rev. Ed King, the Freedom candidates for governor and lieutenant governor, and directed the black and white student volunteers from Northern universities who canvassed throughout the state. Some 80,000 votes were cast in the Freedom Ballot, held simultaneously with the regular state elections.

Following the Freedom Ballot Moses urged COFO and SNCC to make a major voter registration effort in Mississippi during the summer of 1964. According to former SNCC Executive Secretary James Forman [q.v.], Moses argued that a concentrated civil rights drive, especially when aided by white student volunteers, would capture national attention and force the federal government to intervene in Mississippi to uphold blacks' civil and political rights. Moses also wanted to begin building viable community institutions among the state's blacks. His advocacy was in large part responsible for the organization of the 1964 Mississippi Freedom Summer Project. Moses served as director of the effort, which brought over 1,000 volunteers into the state to set up community centers, teach in "freedom schools" and work on voter registration.

Violence flared repeatedly throughout the summer. Three civil rights workers were murdered near Philadelphia, Miss., in June, and in October COFO reported that there had been at least 35 shootings, 80 beatings and assaults, over 1,000 arrests and over 60 churches and homes burned or bombed. Very few blacks were actually registered to vote, and only half of the nearly 100 freedom schools and community centers established during the project continued after the summer. Although the immediate tangible results appeared limited, the project directed national attention to the plight of Mississippi blacks and greatly diminished their isolation from the rest of the civil rights movement. "The Mississippi Summer", wrote historian Howard Zinn, "had an effect impossible to calculate on young Negroes in the state."

The summer project was also the vehicle for organizing the Mississippi Freedom Democratic Party (MFDP). Founded in the spring of 1964, the MFDP was open to all citizens and was intended as an alternative to Mississippi's segregationist regular Democratic Party. Moses helped organize the Party and the "Freedom Registration" drive, which enrolled over 60,000 people as MFDP members during the summer. In August the MFDP held county and district conventions and then a state convention in Jackson where delegates for the August Democratic National Convention were elected.

Moses accompanied the MFDP delegates to Atlantic City, where they challenged the seating of Mississippi's regular delegation at the Convention. When the Convention voted a compromise in which two MFDP members would be seated as at-large delegates and the regular Mississippi delegates would be seated if they took a Party loyalty oath, Moses counseled the MFDP against acceptance. The delegates rejected the compromise by a vote of 60 to 4, and at Moses's suggestion, they staged a sit-in on the Convention floor on the night of Aug. 25.

By the end of the summer, Moses had become uneasy about his role in the civil rights movement. As director of COFO and the 1964 Summer Project, Moses was often forced to make key decisions on policy and strategy. Always reluctant to exercise such leadership, he shared with many others in SNCC a strongly democratic, anti-leadership philosophy. SNCC, Moses once explained, was "in revolt not only against segregation but also against the type of leadership where you have had a select few to speak for the Negro people." He saw his goal as simply helping local people organize so they would be able "to speak for themselves." In addition, Moses's courage, ability and hard work had made him an extremely respected figure among many SNCC members and Mississippi blacks by 1964. Quiet and reflective, Moses feared that a cult was growing around his name. To halt this development he changed his name to Robert Parris in February 1965 and shortly afterwards left both Mississippi and SNCC. He was active in the peace movement for a time, but by 1966 Moses had dropped from public view. In August 1973 the *New York Times* reported that Moses was teaching school in Tanzania.

NEWTON, HUEY P(ERCY)
b. Feb. 17, 1942; New Orleans, La.
Minister of Defense, Black Panther Party, 1966-   .

The son of a sharecropper and Baptist preacher, Newton grew up in Oakland, Calif. He attended high school in Oakland and graduated from Merritt College, a two-year institution, in 1965. He also took courses at the University of San Francisco Law School. Newton's education was interrupted in 1964 by a six-month prison term, which resulted from a political argument in which he threatened an adversary with a knife. While attending Merritt Newton met Bobby Seale [q.v.], a fellow student who shared Newton's interest in black nationalism and the problems of the ghetto. Inspired by the ideas of Malcolm X [q.v.], the two founded the Black Panther Party in October 1966, with Seale as chairman and Newton as minister of defense.

Initiated as a grass-roots organization in Oakland, the Panthers sought to protect ghetto residents against what they considered police harassment and other forms of government oppression. Taking advantage of a California law that permitted bearing arms in public, Black Panthers with weapons appeared as "observers" in police-citizen encounters. The Party was generally unknown outside the Bay Area until May 2, 1967, when 30 armed Panthers marched into the California State Assembly to protest a gun-control measure then under consideration. The national attention that this action received stimulated the growth of the Panthers, who reached the apex of their membership at about 2,000 in the late 1960s, with chapters in most major cities of the North and West.

The growth of heavily armed Panther groups also drew the attention of the police and the Federal Bureau of Investigation. According to the American Civil Liberties Union, police killed or wounded at least 24 Panthers in shootouts between 1967 and 1969. During this period the Black Panthers developed from a militant "self-defense" organization into an openly revolutionary group, with an emphasis on guerrilla tactics and urban warfare. In 1968 the Panther established close contact with a number of white radical groups, joining them to form the Peace and Freedom Party.

One of the first casualties of police-Panther animosity was Newton himself; he was wounded in Oakland on Oct. 28, 1967 in a shootout that left one policeman dead and another wounded. Put on trial for first-degree murder in July 1968, Newton won the support of black and white radicals throughout the country, who considered him a political prisoner. Demonstrators crying "Free Huey" repeatedly converged on the Oakland courthouse, where the trial was held. Newton, who claimed that he was unconscious as a result of a previous gunshot wound during the gun battle, was convicted of voluntary manslaughter. He spent two years in prison before his conviction was overturned by the California Court of Appeals, which found that the judge in the first trial had "omitted instructions" to the jury concerning Newton's claim of unconsciousness.

Released from prison in August 1970, Newton found the Panthers in disarray. Membership had dropped to less than 1,000 due to police harassment and factional quarrels, both within the Panthers and between them and other militant groups. It was later revealed that some of this strife resulted from letters forged by the FBI and accusations spread by infiltrators. Newton attempted to pull the Party together by de-emphasizing violence and anti-police activity. He involved the Panthers in a number of community action programs, including free breakfasts for school children and health clinics for ghetto residents. The Panthers also supported the United Black Fund, a church organization that subsidized social services in ghettos.

Newton's turn to social action brought him into conflict with Panther Education Minister Eldridge Cleaver [*q.v.*], who had fled to Algeria in 1968 to escape imprisonment for a parole violation. Cleaver believed the Panthers should remain an openly revolutionary organization with continued emphasis on armed resistance. In 1972 he withdrew from the Party, taking much of the East Coast membership with him. Senate investigations of U.S. intelligence activities later revealed that this conflict was also exacerbated by threats and accusations planted by the FBI. Newton and Seale remained in control of the Panthers on the West Coast, where they continued their policy of community involvement.

Newton wrote *Revolutionary Suicide*, published in 1973. He also published a collection of interviews and speeches entitled *To Die for the People* (1972).

For further information:
Gilbert Moore, *A Special Rage* (New York, 1971).
"Huey P. Newton," *Current Biography Yearbook, 1973* (New York, 1974), pp. 307-310.

PARKS, ROSA (McCAULEY)
b. Feb. 4, 1913: Tuskegee, Ala.
d. March 14, 1977; Mound Bayou, Miss.
Civil rights activist.

Rosa McCauley attended local black schools in Tuskegee and Montgomery, Ala. She married Raymond Parks when she was 19 and held several different jobs in Montgomery. Rosa Parks was active in black community affairs and worked for her church, for the Montgomery Voters League and for the NAACP, serving for a time as secretary of the local branch.

On Dec. 1, 1955 Parks boarded a city bus in downtown Montgomery to return home from her job as a seamstress at the Montgomery Fair department store. Shortly after she sat down, the driver ordered Parks to give up her seat on the racially segregated bus to a white person. Since the bus was already full, that meant she would have to stand. Parks quietly refused to move, and the driver called the police who arrested and jailed her. She was soon released on bail but ordered to stand trial on Dec. 5.

By the time of this incident, Montgomery's bus system had become a particularly sore spot within the black community. The bus drivers, all of whom were white, were often abusive toward black passengers and on occasion, assaulted them. Blacks had to pay their fare at the front door but then get off the bus and board through the rear door. Drivers would sometimes drive off after a black had paid but before he had reached the rear entry. The first four rows of seats on each bus were reserved exclusively for whites, and even when no white passenger was present a black could not sit there. Blacks also had to give up their seats in the unreserved section if more seats were needed for whites. In the year before Parks's arrest, three other black women had refused to give up their seats and had been arrested, and there had been talk of a protest. Following one of these incidents, blacks did organize a citizens' committee to negotiate with the bus company management for improved treatment for blacks, but no results came from their meeting.

The arrest of Rosa Parks, a gentle and dignified woman who was highly respected in the black community, proved to be the catalyst for a boycott of the bus system by Montgomery's 50,000 blacks. The protest began on Dec. 5, the day of Parks's trial, in which she was found guilty of violating the bus segregation law and fined $10. The boycott continued for 381 days and resulted in a Supreme Court decision holding segregation in local transit facilities unconstitutional. The Montgomery boycott catapulted its leader, Martin Luther King, Jr. [q.v.], to national prominence and inaugurated an era of nonviolent protest against racial segregation and discrimination.

Parks's refusal to give up her bus seat in December 1955 was wholly unprompted and unplanned. She had no idea, she later declared, that it would cause the reaction it did. Parks explained that she had been tired after a long day of work and considered it an imposition to have to move. Her refusal to move back, as Martin Luther King, Jr., later asserted, was also an "intrepid affirmation that she had had enough." Parks had long believed that segregation was unjust. She decided that day, she later said, that she would be pushed no further.

During the boycott, Parks served on the program committee and the executive board of the Montgomery Improvement Association (MIA), the organization set up to supervise the protest. She occasionally traveled to other parts of the country to help raise funds for the MIA. In January 1956 she was fired from her job at the Montgomery Fair and had to take in sewing at home. She also received many threatening and harassing phone calls, and her husband encountered some pressures at his job as a barber.

In August 1957, eight months after the boycott ended, the Parks moved to Detroit where Rosa's brother lived. She worked as a dressmaker for several years and then as a receptionist and staff assistant in the office of Detroit Rep. John Conyers, Jr. (D, Mich.). Although she did not have a major role in the civil rights movement of the 1960s, Parks joined King's Southern Christ-

ian Leadership Conference, remained a member of the NAACP, and participated in several protests such as the 1965 march from Selma to Montgomery. For the part she played in touching off the Montgomery bus boycott, Parks has been called "the mother of the civil rights movement." She was frequently honored by civil rights organizations in later years for her act of civil disobedience.

PATTERSON, JOHN (MALCOLM)
b. Sept. 27, 1921: Goldville, Ala.
Attorney General, Ala., 1955-59;
Governor, Ala., 1959-63.

After his discharge from the Army at the end of World War II, Patterson studied law at the University of Alabama and received his LL.B. degree in 1949. He then practiced law with his father, Albert Patterson, in Phenix City, Ala. Albert Patterson led the opposition to the racketeers who controlled the town, and in 1954 he ran for state attorney general with a pledge to rid Phenix City of gangsters. The elder Patterson won the nomination but was assassinated shortly afterward. John Patterson ran in his father's place and was elected attorney general in 1955.

During Patterson's four-year term he devoted most of his efforts to combating organized crime. Patterson was also a strenuous opponent of integration and achieved prominence for his efforts to stop the operations of the NAACP in Alabama. In 1956 he brought suit against the Association for failing to register as a foreign corporation and for supporting the Montgomery bus boycott, which he termed illegal. As a result a state circuit judge issued a restraining order prohibiting the group from operating in the state. At the end of the decade, litigation was still being carried on over the issue, and the NAACP was unable to conduct business in Alabama.

Patterson ran for governor of Alabama in 1958. During the campaign he solicited the backing of individuals associated with the Ku Klux Klan. Several Klan officers also campaigned for him. He defeated George C. Wallace in the June runoff Democratic primary by 315,000 to 250,000 and easily defeated his Republican opponent in November.

In his inaugural address Patterson reiterated his adamant opposition to integration. He warned that if pressure for desegregation continued, Alabama's schools might be closed and "not be reopened in your lifetime or mine." In October 1959 Patterson urged state officials to refuse cooperation with the Federal Civil Rights Commission, which was investigating black voter registration complaints. The following month he signed legislation permitting voter registration boards to limit their registration activities to predominantly white precincts.

Despite his opposition to integration, Patterson opposed a break with the national Democratic Party. At the Southern Governors Conference in October 1959, he joined Govs. Leroy Collins of Florida and Luther Hodges of North Carolina in opposing a Southern bolt from the Party in 1960 over the issue. The following month he endorsed Sen. John F. Kennedy (D, Mass.) for President.

In May 1961 the Congress of Racial Equality launched a series of Freedom Rides in an effort to integrate interstate bus facilities. The first group of riders reached Anniston, Ala., on May 14, where a mob attacked them and fire-bombed one of the two buses on which they were traveling. Later the same day the freedom riders were again attacked and beaten by a crowd of whites in Birmingham. Following these incidents both the President and Attorney General Robert F. Kennedy tried to secure assurances from Patterson that the riders would be protected in Alabama, but he refused to speak with them and released a statement saying he would not guarantee the riders "safe passage" in the state. Justice Department aide John Seigenthaler, sent to Montgomery on May 19 as President Kennedy's personal representative, finally won from Patterson a promise of protection for the riders when they continued their journey. When the riders entered Montgomery on May 20, however, no police were present and a mob of 200, which eventually grew to about 1,000

people, assaulted the riders. Police arrived 10 minutes later, but it took over an hour to end the riot. The Kennedys then ordered 400 federal marshals into Montgomery under the direction of Deputy Attorney General Byron R. White. In a telegram to the Attorney General, which did not take note of any of the disturbances in Alabama, Patterson protested this action saying the state did "not need" and did "not want" the help of federal marshals.

The next evening Martin Luther King [q.v.] addressed a mass metting in support of the freedom riders at Montgomery's First Baptist Church while federal marshals stood outside. A crowd of about 1,000 whites assembled outside the church, apparently intending to attack the congregation, and at 10 p.m. White notified Attorney General Kennedy that more men were needed. Kennedy called the Governor and, with a second riot threatening, Patterson finally declared martial law and called out the National Guard. The 800 Guardsmen sent into Montgomery that night helped protect the church, but the congregation inside was not able to leave safely until 6 the next morning. When the Freedom Rides resumed on May 24, the Alabama National Guard commander rode on their bus, and other Guardsmen and state police supplied an escort until the riders reached the Mississippi line. As more riders entered the city, the Guardsmen remained on duty in Montgomery until Patterson ended martial law on May 29.

In September 1962 Patterson publicly supported Mississippi Gov. Ross Barnett's [q.v.] efforts to block the court-ordered enrollment of James Meredith [q.v.] at the University of Mississippi. Throughout his term Patterson had pending a million-dollar libel suit against the *New York Times* and four black ministers. Filed in May 1960, his suit charged that a March 1960 advertisement in the *Times*, which criticized Alabama officials and sought to raise funds for civil rights causes, contained "false and defamatory" information. The case was eventually dismissed after the Supreme Court in March 1964 reversed the libel judgment in a companion case brought by another Alabama official. Patterson's term ended in January 1963, and he was succeeded in office by George C. Wallace. Patterson ran again for governor in 1966 but polled only about 4% of the vote in the May Democratic primary.

PEREZ, LEANDER H(ENRY)

b. 1891; Plaquemines Parish, La.
d. March 19, 1969; Plaquemines Parish, La.
President, Plaquemines Parish Commission Council, 1961-67.

Perez graduated from Tulane Law School in 1914 and five years later became a district judge in his native Plaquemines Parish, La., a swampy area along the Mississippi River between New Orleans and the Gulf of Mexico. In 1924 Perez was elected district attorney for Plaquemines and St. Bernard Parishes, a post he held for the next 36 years. He used this position as a power base to become the almost undisputed political boss of Plaquemines and a major influence in Louisiana politics, within both the state Democratic Party and the state legislature.

Perez's friend and political ally, U.S. Rep. Edward Hebert (D, La.), described him as a "benevolent dictator." His biographer, James Conaway, wrote, "Louisiana politics is traditionally ruthless and highly professional . . . but he brought to it a particularly aggressive style, unhampered by either subjective or purely moral considerations."

Perez resisted any outside encroachment upon his parish authority. When in 1943 the state's governor appointed a sheriff not to Perez's liking, he set up a flaming blockade to prevent the appointee from entering the parish. Thirteen years later, when Gov. Earl Long appointed a ward official of whom Perez disapproved, he abolished the ward. His local opponents were suppressed through harassment and intimidation and frequently driven out of the parish.

An unabashed racist, Perez helped to organize the States' Rights Party in 1948 and the White Citizens Councils in 1954. As national pressure for racial integration increased in the late 1950s, he became progressively more vitriolic in his public statements, charging that Communists and "Zionist Jews" were behind the desegregation movement.

In 1960 Perez resigned his post as district attorney but retained his preeminent position within the parish. He was succeeded by his son Leander, Jr., and in 1961 Perez himself became president of the Plaquemines Parish commission council, the newly created governing body of the district.

In 1961 he urged Louisiana citizens not to cooperate with FBI agents entering the parish to investigate voting discrimination against blacks, who composed about 25% of the region's population. Perez also began, during the same year, to sanction the use of force in resisting integration. In February 1961 he spoke before a segregationist rally in Atlanta, Ga. "The national government is the enemy of the people," Perez stated, asserting that Southerners had no choice "but to rise up in physical opposition."

In March 1962 Archbishop Joseph Rummel, whose New Orleans diocese included Plaquemines Parish, ordered the desegregation of diocesan schools. The following month he excommunicated Perez for his adamant opposition to integration. Perez commented to an associate, "I had trouble with my Archbishop. I said, 'If you think you can send me to hell, I'll ask you to go to hell.' " New Orleans's Catholic schools were desegregated, but an explosion damaged one of the parochial schools in Plaquemines after a series of inflammatory speeches by Perez, and the integration effort was abandoned in the parish. Meanwhile, in the early 1960s the state legislature, under pressure from Perez, was passing a series of bills to delay court-ordered integration of public schools. Many of the bills were written by Perez himself.

In the summer of 1963 Perez denounced Defense Secretary Robert S. McNamara's order authorizing military commanders to declare segregated facilities near bases off limits. In retaliation, the parish council, at Perez's behest, approved an ordinance prohibiting bars from admitting or serving military personnel from the nearby Belle Chase naval base.

Early in 1964 Perez denounced President Lyndon B. Johnson for his support of civil rights legislation. He led the conservative faction of the Democratic state central committee in an effort to exclude Johnson from the Louisiana ballot in favor of an independent slate of electors sympathetic to Alabama Gov. George C. Wallace [q.v.]. Ultimately he backed the Republican nominee, Sen. Barry M. Goldwater (R, Ariz.)

In the summer of 1964 Perez announced that he had prepared an isolated 18th-century Spanish fort on the Mississippi River for the incarceration of any civil rights workers who might enter the parish. He asserted, "We're not near ready to surrender our peaceful, beautiful parish to the Communists. And if Martin Luther King [q.v.] comes in, we'll guarantee his transportation across the river—part way, that is."

In 1965 Perez testified against the Johnson Administration's voting rights bill before the Senate Judiciary Committee. His charge that the measure was Communist-inspired amused many of the panel members, and Sen. Everett M. Dirksen (R, Ill.) called the claim "as stupid a statement as I've ever heard."

Shortly after the passage of the Voting Rights Act, federal registrars entered Plaquemines, where only 96 of the parish's 6,500 blacks had been registered as of February 1964. Despite harassment by Perez and his supporters, the registrars enrolled about 2,000 additional blacks. In 1966 a federal district court ordered the desegregation of the parish's public schools. Perez, unable to block integration, established a private school system, which about half of the district's white students attended.

The following year Perez resigned the presidency of the Parish Commission Council and was succeeded by his son, Chalin. In 1968 he enthusiastically backed the Wallace presidential campaign. Perez died on March 19, 1969. Shortly after his death a spokesman for the Roman Catholic Church in New Orleans announced that Perez's ex-communication had been lifted a year earlier, after he had made a conciliatory speech.

For further information:
James Conaway, *Judge: The Life and Times of Leander Perez* (New York, 1973).

POWELL, ADAM CLAYTON, JR.
b. Nov. 29, 1908, New Haven, Conn.
d. April 4, 1972, Miami, Fla.
Democratic Representative, N.Y., 1945-67, 1969; Chairman, Education and Labor Committee, 1961-67.

Adam Clayton Powell's father was pastor of the Abyssinian Baptist Church, whose 12,000 members constituted the largest Protestant congregation in the country at that time. His mother was the illegitimate heiress to the Shaefer brewing fortune. Born into comfortable surroundings, Powell graduated from Colgate University in 1930 and then obtained an M.A. from Columbia in 1932. In his last year at Colgate, Powell decided to become a minister; at the age of 29 he succeeded his ailing father as pastor of Abyssinian Baptist. Powell used his pulpit to plead for civil rights and social advances for blacks. The church opened a soup kitchen for the needy and organized boycotts of unions and companies practicing discrimination. In 1941 Powell became the first black to be elected to the New York City Council. Four years later, in a special election, he won a Democratic House seat representing Harlem.

When Powell took office in 1945 there was only one other Negro congressman, William L. Dawson (D, Ill) of Chicago. The discreet and tactful Dawson, attentive to his congressional business got on well with the House "Establishment," even the segregationists. Powell, in sharp contrast, considered himself the "first bad nigger in Congress" and forced his way into formerly segregated restaurants, baths, showers and barber shops. More troubling to his liberal supporters was Powell's attendance record, among the worst in Congress, and his penchant for congressionally financed vacations. "As a member of Congress," Powell once said, "I have done nothing more than any other member, and by the grace of God, I intend to do not one bit less."

During the 1950s Powell emerged as a leading spokesman for civil rights in the House. In the early months of the Eisenhower Administration, he accused Secretary of the Navy Robert Anderson of undermining the President's orders to desegregate military facilities. The bases were quietly integrated during the year.

Powell attempted to further integration by attaching a number of controversial anti-discrimination amendments to various appropriations bills: public housing, school construction and national reserve measures. These amendments stipulated that federal funds would be denied areas practicing segregation. His most controversial move came in 1956, when he attempted to attach the rider to a school construction bill. Although a coalition of northern Democrats and Republicans passed the amendment, they criticized the proposal. Such liberals as Eleanor Roosevelt and Adlai Stevenson felt that Powell's action would stall school funds needed during the critical classroom shortage of the period. When the House voted on the whole construction bill, Republicans joined Southern Democrats to kill the measure.

During the early years of the Eisenhower Administration, Powell publicly praised the President for aiding the cause of desegregation, but as the 1956 election approached, he condemned Eisenhower for not doing enough on civil rights. On Oct. 11 Powell again reversed himself by endorsing Eisenhower for reelection. In explaining his stand, he said that Eisenhower had a laudible civil rights record and a good image abroad. He also said that Democratic candidate Adlai Stevenson had snubbed him. Local Democrats condemned him, insinuating that Powell had come out for Eisenhower to obtain Administration help with his legal problems.

Powell's endorsement of the President

angered New York City Democratic boss Carmine DeSapio who, with Harlem district leaders, decided to challenge Powell in the 1958 Democratic primary. Powell campaigned hard. In one speech he told DeSapio and Hulan Jack, the black borough president of Manhattan, to avoid walking the streets of Harlem. He warned, "We won't do what the Communists did to the Nixons in South America [Communists had stoned Nixon's car] but we will make it mighty uncomfortable." The NAACP and other leading civil rights groups deplored this statement. Powell retracted it, won the primary, and then went on to make peace with De Sapio.

Powell's flamboyant personality, his poor attendance record and his questionable financial and personal activities compromised his effectiveness as a civil rights leader. During the 1950s he and several staff members were involved in a number of legal problems. Several people in his office, as well as leading officials of the Abyssinian Baptist Church, were found guilty of financial irregularities. Powell fought a 1951 charge of preparing fraudulent income tax returns for his wife. He was finally acquitted in 1960.

Shortly before Powell became chairman of the House Committee on Education and Labor in 1961, the New York Times wrote that his "miserable record as a legislator and his extreme absenteeism all tend to disqualify him as a reasonable and effective chairman." During his six years as chairman, however, he headed a remarkably productive committee. Powell had supported Lyndon B. Johnson's presidential candidacy in 1960, but his relations with the Kennedy Administration were generally cordial. During a House-Senate conference in 1961, Powell rescued the minimum wage bill and helped secure its enactment for the Administration. In 1961 Powell also prodded the Administration into supporting legislation, passed a year later, granting the Secretary of Labor increased power to investigate the management of workers' pension and trust funds.

At the very moment when as a committee chairman Powell held greater power than any other elected Negro official, he became entangled in the difficulties that ultimately wrecked his political career. During a March 6, 1960 television show, Powell off-handedly referred to Mrs. Esther James as a "bag-woman," or graft collector, for the New York City police. Mrs. James sued Powell for defamation and in April 1963 won a $211,500 judgment against him, which he refused to pay. He was held in contempt of court and escaped punishment only by absenting himself from New York.

While the James case was in the courts, newspapers revealed that in the summer of 1962 Powell, accompanied by two young women from his staff, had taken a six-week European vacation paid for with Committee funds.

In the mid-1960s Powell aligned himself with Stokely Carmichael [q.v.] and others in the black power movement. As early as March 1963 Powell had demanded that blacks boycott all civil rights organizations (including the NAACP) "not totally controlled by us." Powell refused to vote for the 1965 Voting Rights Act or the 1966 open housing bill, which he charged was "a phony carrot" for the Negro Middle classes.

In January 1967, at the beginning of the 90th Congress, Powell was ousted from his Committee chairmanship and barred from taking his seat pending an investigation of his fitness to hold office. With the support of House Majority Leader Carl Albert (D, Okla.), Rep. Morris Udall (D, Ariz.) moved to seat Powell pending the outcome of the investigation. The motion was defeated by an overwhelming majority, with many Northern liberals voting with Republicans and Southern Democrats against the Harlem Congressman.

On Feb. 23, 1967 a nine-member select House committee under Rep. Emanuel Celler (D, N.Y.) reported that Powell had "wrongfully and willfully appropriated" public funds and had "improperly maintained his wife" on the congressional payroll. The committee recommended that Powell be censured for "gross misconduct," fined $40,000 and stripped of his seniority.

The House rejected the committee's recommendations on March 1, 1967 and—for only the third time in American history and—for the first time in 46 years—voted 307 to 116 to exclude a duly elected representative. Rep. Celler saw "an element of racism in the vote . . . accompanied by the hysteria that had resulted from the climate of opinion due to Mr. Powell's antics and peculiarities and swagger and defiance."

Black leaders from around the country denounced the expulsion. Floyd McKissick [q.v.], national director of the Congress of Racial Equality, called it "a slap in the face of every black in the country," while A. Philip Randolph [q.v.] of the Brotherhood of Sleeping Car Porters said it was "a mockery of democracy without precedent." However, *Congressional Quarterly* reported that "the most notable aspect of the lobby action in the Powell affair was the lack of concerted effort in Powell's behalf by the organized civil rights lobby." Roy Wilkins [q.v.], chairman of the NAACP, explained that "Powell never called on [the] civil rights movement . . . never invited [its] help."

In April 1967 a special election was held to fill Powell's seat; he was reelected by a margin of 7 to 1. The seat remained vacant for two years. In January 1969, after paying a $25,000 fine, Powell was permitted to return to the House, but he was stripped of all seniority. In June the Supreme Court ruled that Powell's expulsion had been unconstitutional. He was stricken with cancer that year, and before he could decide to retire from politics lost his seat to Charles B. Rangel, who narrowly defeated him in a June 1970 primary. Powell died two years later.

Powell was among the most controversial politicians of his time. To journalist Theodore White he was "the most egregious and frightening" exception to the general excellence of black elected officials. To Chuck Stone, Powell's chief congressional assistant, he was "a mercurial personality who wavered erratically between tub-thumping militancy and cowardly silence"—a man so driven by "hedonistic compulsions" that he undermined his role as a black leader. However, Julius Lester, a black author, remembered him as the man who once "gave blacks a national voice" when other were quietly submissive and deferential.

PRICE, CECIL R(AY)
b. 1938(?)
Chief Deputy Sheriff, Neshoba County, Miss., 1964-68.

Price became chief deputy sheriff of Neshoba County, Miss., in January 1964. The following June three civil rights workers—Andrew Goodman and Michael H. Schwerner, whites from New York, and James E. Chaney, a black from Meridian, Miss.—entered the county to investigate the recent burning of a Negro church, which was to have been used as a Freedom School in the Mississippi Summer Project. The three civil rights workers disappeared, and their bodies were discovered in August in a dam near Philadelphia, Miss., the county seat.

Although these events produced a national outcry, Mississippi authorities never brought any charges in connection with the case. In December 1964 FBI agents arrested Price, County Sheriff Lawrence A. Rainey and 19 others. The Justice Department asserted that a plan to kill the three had been arranged by the White Knights of the Ku Klux Klan. Price was accused of detaining the victims in Philadelphia, recapturing them on a highway and then turning them over to a lynch mob of which he was a member.

Price and the others were indicted under an 1870 statute for conspiring to injure citizens in the free exercise of federal rights. The indictment was struck down by Federal District Judge W. Harold Cox [q.v.] in February 1965, but his decision was overturned by a unanimous ruling of the U.S. Supreme Court in March 1966. New indictments were issued a year later, and in October 1967 Price and six other defendants were found guilty in what was believed to be the first conviction in a civil rights slaying in Mississippi. Price received a prison term of six years.

The U.S. Supreme Court upheld the conviction in February 1970, and Price went to jail shortly thereafter. In July 1973 the U.S. Parole Board refused to grant the seven men a pardon and stated that they would have to complete their terms.

For further information:
Adam Clayton Powell, Jr., *Adam by Adam* New York, 1971).
Chuck Stone, *Black Political Power in America* (New York, 1970).

RANDOLPH, A(SA) PHILIP
b. April 15, 1889; Crescent City, Fla
d. May 16, 1979, New York, N.Y.
President, Brotherhood of Sleeping Car Porters, 1929-68.

The son of a Protestant minister, Randolph left his Florida home in 1911 to join the burgeoning prewar migration of Southern blacks to Harlem, where he hoped to become a stage actor. Soon after his arrival he abandoned his show business dreams and turned to socialist politics. In 1917 he helped found the anti-war journal, *The Messenger,* which became a mainstay of Harlem's Negro Renaissance in the early 1920s.

Long a supporter of black trade unionism, Randolph began organizing Pullman Co. porters in 1925. The effort culminated in August 1937, when the Brotherhood of Sleeping Car Porters signed a contract with Pullman, the first such agreement between a black union and a major American company. With this success Randolph became the most widely respected black leader of his time. In June 1941 his threat of a march on Washington by 100,000 blacks prompted President Roosevelt to issue an executive order banning racial discrimination in federal employment and in defense industries.

1947. In early 1948 the Committee became the League for Nonviolent Civil Disobedience Against Military Segregation.

Appearing before the Senate Armed Services Committee in 1948, Randolph stated he would counsel youth to choose imprisonment rather than cooperate with a segregated conscription system. In response to questioning from Sen. Wayne Morse (R, Ore.), he said he would recommend a program of civil disobedience "to make the soul of America democratic." He followed his appearance with a series of streetcorner meetings in which he urged young men to refuse induction in a segregated Army. Randolph continued his campaign by picketing the Democratic National Convention held in Philadelphia during July 1948. His action, combined with the liberal battle for a strong civil rights plank in the Party's platform and Truman's need to win the black vote, prompted the President to sign an executive order calling for an end to discrimination in the military. In response to the order, issued July 26, Randolph called off the civil disobedience campaign, a decision opposed by the more radical branch of the movement.

During the late 1940s Randolph was also active in leading an unsuccessful struggle for a permanent Fair Employment Practices Commission to insure equal rights in the labor market. His campaign died in 1950 when a bill designed to establish such a body was crushed by a coalition of Republicans and Southern Democrats.

When Randolph brought the Brotherhood into the American Federation of Labor (AFL) in 1935, many unions in the federation excluded blacks. Beginning that year Randolph annually introduced a resolution at the AFL convention calling on the group to devote more energy to organizing black workers and asking them to expel member locals who continued to practice discrimination. Randolph's familiar, booming voice failed to sway the convention delegates. His yearly podium appearance was a signal for many delegates to abandon the convention hall. William Green and George Meany, who became president in 1952, defended Samuel Gomper's policy that racial politics were purely a matter for the locals.

When the AFL merged with the Congress of Industrial Organizations (CIO) in 1955 to become the AFL-CIO, the group adopted a constitution containing a strong anti-discrimination provision. Randolph, elected a member of its executive council, demanded immediate enforcement of its pledge. At the executive council meeting in 1956, he moved that the Federation bar the Brotherhood of Locomotive Firemen and Engineers, widely known for discriminating against blacks, from the AFL-CIO until it ended its racist policies. Meany opposed the motion, preferring to work behind the scenes to end discrimination. His position was supported by the executive council, which voted to admit the Brotherhood.

At the 1959 national convention Randolph introduced a resolution to deny the International Longshoremen's Association entry. Meany indignantly asked Randolph why he had never discussed the proposal with the executive council. The president then reprimanded Randolph for not "playing on the team," implying that the issue should never have been presented to the convention floor. Meany advised Randolph to sit "a little closer to the trade union movement and pay a little less attention to outside organizations . . . ."

A few moments later Randolph introduced another resolution calling for the expulsion of two railroad brotherhoods if they did not cease discriminating within six months. Meany, who supported gradual desegregation, opposed the time limit. He warned Randolph that integration might not be achieved in their lifetime. Randolph then introduced his third resolution calling for the expulsion for member unions charged with racism. The resolution would have covered exclusively black unions as well white groups. Meany then exploded, "Who the hell appointed you the guardian of all Negroes!" The astonished Randolph replied, "Brother President, let's not get emotional."

As a consequence of the slow progress made by the AFL-CIO in ending racial discrimination, Randolph joined with other black trade unionists to organize the Negro American Labor Council (NALC) in November 1959. As president of the new organization, Randolph said discrimination had "reached the stage of institutionalization in the labor movement," but he nevertheless sought to work within the AFL-CIO to change these conditions. During his four-year tenure as NALC president, Randolph was challenged by younger militants in the black labor organization who wished to adopt a more combative posture toward the AFL-CIO leadership. As the New York Times put it in October 1961, Randolph was involved in a "two-front battle," fighting to restrain elements within the NALC and obliged, on the other hand, to maintain his pressure against the organized labor movement itself. Meany identified Randolph with what he termed NALC "dual-union" militants. The AFL-CIO executive council censured Randolph in October 1961 after he had again urged the labor federation to take disciplinary action against racially segregated unions. Meany told the press Oct. 12, "We can only get moving on civil rights if he [Randolph] comes to our side and stops throwing bricks at us."

This rebuke to Randolph was strongly denounced by civil rights leaders Roy Wilkins [q.v.] and Martin Luther King [q.v.] and by Daniel Schulder, president of the New York chapter of the Association of Catholic Trade Unionists. Randolph deplored the tendency of AFL-CIO leaders "to equate opposition to trade union policies with opposition to the trade union movement." Meany met for the first time with an NALC delegation at the December 1961 AFL-CIO convention. At the same meeting the Federation effectively rescinded its motion censuring Randolph and passed a civil rights resolution, which Randolph praised as the best adopted in his 35-year association with organized labor. In November 1962 Randolph opposed a NAACP-sponsored campaign to decertify trade union locals that discriminated against minority workers. He reaffirmed his conviction that "we must carry out our fight within the house of labor."

As a socialist and trade unionist, Randolph emphasized an economic solution to America's racial problems. With Bayard Rustin [q.v.], a radical pacifist who had helped organize the 1941 march on Washington movement, Randolph began planning in December 1962 for a new Washington march. The mass protest was designed to link the demand for strong federal civil rights legislation with the labor movement's call for full employment, a higher minimum wage and a guaranteed income. In February 1963 Rustin and Randolph publicly announced plans for a summer march of 100,000 people, whose slogan would be "jobs and freedom now." During the spring of 1963 Randolph recruited an impressive array of liberal, labor, religious and civil rights organizations in support of the march. According to Murray Kempton, the 74-year-old Randolph was uniquely suited for this task because "alone among the leaders [of the civil rights movement] he neither feels hostility for nor excites it in any other of them." When NAACP Executive Secretary Roy Wilkins objected to Rustin's prominent role in organizing the march, Randolph agreed to assume the title national director, with Rustin as his deputy.

After civil rights demonstrations in Birmingham, Ala. sparked a series of often violent clashes across the South, President Kennedy asked black leaders to the White House on June 22. He requested them to call off their march on the grounds that any disorders at the demonstration could stiffen the resistance of congressional conservatives to pending civil rights legislation. "With great dignity," reported Arthur Schlesinger, Jr., Randolph replied to the President, "The Negroes are already in the streets. It is very likely impossible to get them off." He told Kennedy that the only alternative to the current march was a new black leadership which "cares neither about civil rights nor about nonviolence." The march, which Kennedy eventually endorsed, took place as scheduled on Aug. 28, 1963. An estimated 210,000 participated in the orderly and peaceful demonstration. Randolph chaired the march's Lincoln Memorial assemblage and, in the last major speech of his life, emphasized the link between the fulfillment of civil rights demands and the need for fundamental economic and social changes in American society.

As the civil rights movement began to break into factions in the years after the March, Randolph cast his prestige with those advocating legal tactics and integrationist goals. Reconciled by 1964 to what he considered a slow but steady AFL-CIO anti-discrimination effort, Randolph dropped his ties with the increasingly militant Negro American Labor Council (NALC) and gave his blessing to the formation of the A. Philip Randolph Institute. (The NALC soon withered away without Randolph.) Under Bayard Rustin's direction, the Institute worked closely with the AFL-CIO to advance unionism among blacks and build a liberal-labor-black coalition within the Democratic Party, which Rustin and Randolph by then saw as the key to racial and economic progress. Fearful that the series of riots and demonstrations in the summer of 1964 would harm Lyndon Johnson's chances for election, Randolph joined with civil rights leaders Roy Wilkins [q.v.], Martin Luther King [q.v.] and Whitney Young [q.v.] on July 29 to announce a "broad curtailment if not total moratorium" on mass demonstrations. Although not all in the movement accepted the moratorium, few protest demonstrations took place during the presidential campaign itself.

After the Student Non-Violent Coordinating Committee (SNCC) raised the "black power" slogan in June 1966, Randolph criticized the idea as a divisive and racist. He attacked SNCC for sponsoring a picket line at Luci Johnson's August 1966 wedding and in October 1966 joined with seven other moderate black leaders to "repudiate any strategies of violence, reprisal or vigilantism" and to "condemn both rioting and the demagoguery that feeds it . . . ." He again denounced riots in the summer of 1967 and in August joined with Bayard Rustin to reject SNCC's public defense of the Arabs in their June war with Israel. In the fall of 1968 Randolph supported the New York City United Federation of Teachers strike against the Ocean Hill-Brownsville Community School Board, although many in the black community supported the board as an experiment in greater local control of the schools.

Randolph was one of the strongest supporters of Rep. Adam Clayton Powell (D, N.Y.) [q.v.] when the House sought to expel the Harlem congressman in early 1967. Randolph valued Powell for the power he wielded as chairman of the House Education and Labor Committee and organized two important meetings in his defense, the first in December 1966 at the Brotherhood's Harlem headquarters and the second in January 1967 in Washington. The January meeting, called a "Negro Summit Conference," was canceled at the last moment because its organizers claimed "demand for attendance and participation was too great for meaningful and creative discussion."

As part of his general social program, Randolph favored a larger federal role in economic affairs. In the fall of 1966 Randolph helped sponsor proposals for a $186-billion "Freedom Budget" designed to eliminate poverty in the United States in ten years. Written by a team of economists headed by Leon Keyserling, ex-chairman of the Council of Economic Advisers under President Truman, the budget called for a guaranteed annual income, full employment and greater federal funding of health, housing, welfare and education programs. The budget was to be paid for by the "fiscal dividend" generated by a projected five percent annual rise in the Gross National Product. These budget proposals proved incompatible with the economic demands of the Vietnam war. In December 1966 Randolph attacked cutbacks in President Johnson's antipoverty program as a strategy designed to put the burden of the war on the white and black poor.

In September 1968 Randolph, aged 79 and ailing, resigned as president of the Brotherhood of Sleeping Car Porters, a union reduced by that year to a mere 2,000 members due to the postwar collapse of the railroad passenger industry.

For further information:
Jervis Anderson, *A. Philip Randolph* (New York, 1972).

RAY, JAMES EARL
b. March 10, 1928; Alton, Ill.
Convicted assassin of Martin Luther King, Jr.

James Earl Ray, one of eight children, was raised in St. Louis and Ewing, Mo. His father, an unemployed laborer, was frequently away from home; his mother was an alcoholic. Ray left school in the eighth grade. At 16 he went to work in a tannery in Hartford, Ill. Two years later he enlisted in the Army. He served with the military police in Germany but was given a general discharge in December 1948 because of "ineptness and lack of adaptability to military service."

Over the next decade Ray drifted back and forth between Chicago and the West Coast. He was arrested several times and charged with vagrancy, burglary and armed robbery. In 1955 he was found guilty of forging a Post Office money order and served three years in Leavenworth federal penitentiary. In October 1959 he was arrested for armed robbery in connection with a St. Louis supermarket holdup and was sentenced to 20 years at the Missouri State Penitentiary at Jefferson City. In April 1967 he concealed himself in a large breadbox being sent from the prison bakery and made a successful escape.

According to the FBI, on April 4, 1968, Ray, alias "John Willard," registered at a rooming house across from the Lorraine Motel in Memphis, Tenn., where Martin Luther King [q.v.] was staying. Around 6:00 p.m. Ray shot the civil rights leader, as King was leaning over the second floor balcony railing of his motel room. King was rushed to the hospital and pronounced dead at 7:05. It was later reported that Ray fled the murder scene in a white Mustang. On April 20 Ray was placed on the FBIs 10 most wanted list.

On April 8 Ray had entered Canada, and on the 24th he obtained a Canadian passport. He flew from Toronto to London on May 6 and then, a day later, on to Lisbon. He returned to London May 17. On June 8 Scotland Yard detectives seized Ray at Heathrow Airport in London. In July he was extradited and returned to Memphis, where he was charged with murder.

In August Ray's attorney, Arthur J. Hanes, asked the court to dismiss charges because widespread publicity had made it impossible for his client to receive a fair trial. Judge W. Preston Battle rejected the request. In November Ray dismissed Hanes and hired Percy Foreman, a celebrated trial lawyer, to represent him.

On March 10, 1969 Ray pleaded guilty to murdering King and was sentenced to serve 99 years in prison. Within 24 hours, however, Ray attempted to reverse his plea. Ray stated that he had sold the rights to his life story to journalist William Bradford Huie to raise money for his legal defense. He charged that Huie, Hanes and Foreman had all pressured him to plead guilty. According to Ray, Huie had told him that a book about a man who did not kill King would not sell. Ray also stated that Foreman had promised that he would be pardoned after John Jay Hooker, Jr., son of a Foreman law associate, was elected governor of Tennessee. Ray later told one reporter that he had been "browbeaten, badgered and bribed into pleading guilty."

Foreman denied that Ray had been coerced into pleading guilty. He also suggested that Ray, a racial bigot, had slain Dr. King because "he wanted recognition and praise from his old inmates back at Jefferson City [site of the Missouri State Penitentiary]." Ray dismissed Foreman, but his new defense team was unable to win a new trial on appeal.

Some commentators suggested that Ray might have been given financial and other aid to help him flee the country. Ray himself protested that he was innocent. He claimed that in the summer of 1967 he had become involved with a mysterious French-Canadian named Raoul who in April 1968 sent him to Memphis to aid in a gun-smuggling operation. Ray stated that he knew nothing of the assassination, that Raoul was responsible and that Raoul had framed him. The FBI and Attorney General Ramsey Clark, however, concluded that Ray alone had murdered King. In the absence of sufficient evidence to reopen the case, Ray remained confined to a maximum security prison near Petros, Tenn.

In 1978 the House Assassinations Committee held hearings on the death of Martin Luther King. In its final report, the committee suggested that there was a "likelihood" of a conspiracy in the killing, apparently based on theories that Ray's family had aided him in the assassination. There was also testimony that Ray had acted in the hope of collecting a $50,000 bounty offered by two St. Louis businessmen for King's death. The panel dismissed allegations that the FBI had been involved in the assassination. However, it sharply criticized the Bureau for a "gross" abuse of its legal authority in a surveillance campaign of King.

RICHARDSON, GLORIA (HAYS)
b. May 6, 1922; Baltimore, Md.
Civil rights leader.

The daughter of a prosperous druggist and a graduate of all-black Howard University, Richardson grew up in Cambridge, Md. The town of 14,000 was on Maryland's Eastern Shore, a region that was historically more Southern in outlook than the rest of the state.

Cambridge's blacks, who constituted one-fourth of the population, had the vote by the early 1960s. But the town's public facilities were still segregated. In 1962 Richardson joined the Cambridge Nonviolent Action Committee (CNAC), a civil rights group. Several months later she became president of the organization, becoming the only woman in the country to head a local black protest movement.

During the spring of 1963 Richardson began leading demonstrations to integrate public accommodations. The protests led to violence in early July, culminating on July 12 when, after whites had thrown eggs at the demonstrators, blacks and whites exchanged gunshots. Six whites were injured. The violence in Cambridge represented one of the first instances in which Southern blacks employed force against whites in connection with civil rights activities.

After the shootings Richardson and white officials met with Attorney General Robert F. Kennedy. They agreed to a halt in demonstrations, desegregation of public facilities and a referendum on a local ordinance to outlaw segregation. Shortly before the Oct. 1 vote, however, Richardson reversed her position on the referendum and urged blacks to boycott it. She said it was "wrong to put our constitutional rights to the vote of a white majority." The desegregation ordinance was defeated, 1,720 to 1,994, with only 40% of the registered blacks voting.

Richardson seemed uncertain of her strategy on a number of occasions during the integration struggle. Some observers attributed her indecisiveness to behind-the-scenes influence by male black leaders in Cambridge. Richardson herself, speaking of the rallies in which she participated, said, "When I get on the platform . . . and the men are all there, I just feel there is nothing more to say."

In August 1964 Richardson married and resigned from CNAC.

RUSSELL, RICHARD B(REVARD)
b. Nov. 2, 1897; Winder, Ga.
d. Jan. 21, 1971; Washington, D.C.
Democratic Senator, Ga., 1933-71;
Chairman, Armed Services
Committee, 1951-53, 1955-69.

Russell received a law degree from the University of Georgia at Athens in 1918. Three years later he was elected to the state Assembly and in 1927 became its speaker. In 1930 Russell was elected governor of Georgia on an economy platform. While in office he drastically reduced the number of executive departments and commissions in an effort to reduce the state budget.

In 1932 Russell won an election to fill a vacant U.S. Senate seat. He was a supporter of most New Deal programs, helping to pass bills creating the Rural Electrification Administration and the Farmers Home Administration. Russell also drew up the legislation establishing the first nationwide school lunch program. As a Senate authority on national security affairs, he helped bring many military installations to Georgia. After World War II, however, he became an opponent of social welfare programs, explaining later, "I'm a reactionary when times are good. . . .In a depression, I'm a liberal.

Throughout his Senate career Russell was an unrelenting foe of civil rights measures. In 1935 and 1937 he led filibusters against anti-lynching bills, and in 1942 he was one of four Southern senators who filibustered to save the poll tax. By the late 1940s Russell was solidly established as the leader of the Southern bloc in the upper house of Congress, and at the 1948 Democratic National Convention he was put forward as his region's candidate for the Party's presidential nomination. However, he refused to join the Dixiecrat bolt from the national Party after the nomination of President Harry S Truman.

Despite Russell's strong identification with the dissident Southern wing of the Democratic Party, he was highly respected by almost all senators. A member of a patrician family, he was known for his dignified bearing and courteousness as well as for his formidable intelligence, and he was widely regarded as the embodiment of the best traditions of the upper house. Aided by this reputation and a single-minded dedication to his work (he never married), an intimate knowledge of parliamentary procedure and his leadership of the powerful Southern senatorial caucus, Russell became one of the most influential members of Congress in the 1940s and 1950s.

Russell's leadership of the Southern bloc was most apparent in his role in the fight against integration and civil rights measures. In his capacity as a defender of the Southern system of race relations, he fought vigorously against all federal efforts to intrude upon Southern society. Yet in the 1950s Russell was prepared to make strategic compromises rather than take hopeless, diehard stands.

In 1956 Sen. Strom Thurmond (D, S.C.) drafted a Declaration of Constitutional Principles, popularly known as the "Southern Manifesto," that endorsed the doctrine of state interposition and declared the Supreme Court's 1954 school desegregation decision unconstitutional and illegal. But when a number of moderate Southern congressmen refused to sign the Manifesto, a committee headed by Russell wrote a new draft that excluded those clauses.

The following year, before the Senate considered an Administration civil rights bill aimed particularly at enabling blacks to vote, Russell warned that the measure would be "vigorously resisted by a resolute group of senators." He and his allies succeeded in eliminating clauses giving the President power to use troops to enforce existing civil rights laws and permitting the Attorney General to institute civil action for preventive relief in civil rights cases. They also added a clause guaranteeing a jury trial in contempt cases against persons interfering with the exercise of the right to vote.

On August 24 Russell declared that Southern leaders were still "unalterably opposed" to the bill. Reflecting a recognition that the compromise was the best the Southerners could hope to obtain, he added, however, that "there was no collective agreement that we would undertake to talk the proposition to death." On Aug. 28 Thurmond conducted a record 24-hour filibuster against the bill. Russell said that this action could have created an "unparalleled disaster" by beginning a move to restore provisions that had been eliminated by the Southerners. He denounced Thurmond, asserting that "if I had undertaken a filibuster for personal political aggrandizement, I would have forever reproached myself for being guilty of a form of treason against the people of the South."

In 1960 Russell and 17 other members of the Southern bloc succeeded, with the aid of the filibuster, in weakening Administration proposals to strengthen the 1957 Civil Rights Act. A plan for court-appointed referees to help blacks register and vote was amended to reduce the power of the referees. A provision enabling the federal government to pay half the costs incurred by local schools for desegregation was killed, as was an amendment strengthening anti-job discrimination provisions applying to companies with federal contracts. As in

1957 Russell denounced the final version of the civil rights bill but did not attempt to block its passage.

In 1956 Russell, who had a close political and personal relationship with Sen. Johnson, backed Johnson's bid for the Democratic presidential nomination. Four years later a rift developed between them over Johnson's efforts, as majority leader, to pass the 1960 civil rights bill. The rift widened when Johnson accepted the Democratic vice presidential nomination after the Party's National Convention had adopted a strong civil rights platform that included implied support for peaceful sit-in demonstrations against segregated lunch counters. Russell initially declined to back the national ticket but gave his endorsement after receiving a personal appeal from Johnson.

Russell continued to lead the Southern opposition to civil rights measures during the early 1960s. In 1962 he directed a successful filibuster against a bill to bar the arbitrary use of literacy tests against persons seeking to register to vote in federal elections. Defending the filibuster during a debate over cloture, he asserted, "The Founding Fathers intended . . . that the Senate should remain the one bulwark of our government against precipitate actions of the mob. . . ."

When President Kennedy introduced a public accommodations civil rights bill in June 1963, Russell declared that he believed in equality before the law for all Americans but that the Administration measure would use federal power "to compel the mingling of the races in social activities to achieve the nebulous aim of social equality." Such compulsion, he asserted, "would amount to a complete denial of the inalienable rights of the individual to choose or select his associates."

In 1964 Congress considered the public accommodations bill originally proposed by President Kennedy; it was the most far-reaching anti-discrimination measure since Reconstruction. When the bill was received by the Senate in February after House passage, Russell directed the Southern forces in a debate that involved some of the most complex parliamentary maneuvering in the history of the Senate. His goal was to delay passage of the bill until the summer, believing that the Administration would then drop it to avoid the spectacle of an intra-party dispute during the Democratic National Convention.

However, President Johnson indicated to the Senate leadership that he was prepared to sacrifice all other legislation rather than abandon the bill in the face of a Southern filibuster. Meanwhile, public sentiment in favor of legislation promoting racial equality was steadily mounting. On June 10 the Senate voted to close off debate on an anti-civil rights filibuster for the first time in its history. Angry over his defeat Russell shouted on the Senate floor, "We're confronted here not only with the spirit of the mob but of the lynch mob." Some observers believed that Russell had made a strategic error by his refusal to accept a compromise bill.

Russell was hospitalized for emphysema in 1965 and could not lead the fight against the voting rights bill. In the remaining years of the Johnson Administration, he suffered additional defeats in the area of civil rights. Despite these setbacks and the growing size of the black electorate in Georgia, he refused to modify his views.

Although Russell voted for President Johnson's mass transit and Appalachia aid bills, he generally opposed Great Society programs. In 1964 he refused to campaign for Johnson or even to endorse him by name. But the two men had developed a close friendship during their years in the Senate, and the President discussed political strategy with Russell even concerning matters on which they disagreed.

In 1969 Russell stepped down as chairman of the Armed Services Committee to head the Appropriations Committee. During the same year he became President Pro Tempore of the Senate. In 1970 a United Press International poll found that Russell was one of three Democratic senators supporting President Nixon's decision to send U.S. troops into Cambodia. On Jan. 21, 1971, while still a senator, he died of respiratory insufficiency after six weeks of hospitalization.

RUSTIN, BAYARD
b. March 17, 1910; West Chester, Pa.
Civil rights leader.

One of 12 children, Rustin was raised in poverty by his grandparents in West Chester, Pa. He was early influenced toward pacifism by his grandmother, who belonged to the Society of Friends. Rustin's decision to combat segregation originated when he was physically ejected from a restaurant because of his race.

In 1936 Rustin joined the Young Communist League (YCL), believing it to be an organization committed to pacifist ideals and equal rights for blacks. He moved to New York City two years later and began organizing for the League. At the same time he attended City College at night and sang in nightclubs with Josh White and Leadbelly to earn money. Rustin left the League in 1941 when, after the Nazi invasion of the Soviet Union, the YCL subordinated its commitment to social protest to the cause of defeating Germany.

Soon after departing Rustin joined the Fellowship of Reconciliation (FOR), a pacifist nondenominational religious organization opposed to racial injustice. He subsequently organized the New York chapter of the Congress of Racial Equality (CORE), a secular offshoot of FOR. In 1941 he joined with A. Philip Randolph [q.v.], president of the Brotherhood of Sleeping Car Porters, in organizing a March on Washington for improved job opportunities for blacks. When President Roosevelt issued an executive order banning racial discrimination in defense industries, the march was cancelled. In 1942 Rustin traveled to California to aid Japanese-Americans whose property was jeopardized after they were placed in work camps. Imprisoned as a conscientious objector during World War II, Rustin served more than two years in jail.

To test a Supreme Court decision banning segregation on interstate bus travel, Rustin helped plan and then participated in the 1947 Journey of Reconciliation. The protest served as a model for the Freedom Rides of 1961, the Montgomery bus boycott of 1955-56 and the student sit-ins of the 1960s. Rustin was arrested in North Carolina when he refused to move to the back of a Trailways bus. He subsequently served 22 days on a chain gang. (His account of this experience led to the abolition of chain gangs in the state.)

In 1948 Rustin joined Randolph in the League for Nonviolent Civil Disobedience Against Military Segregation. As executive secretary of the League, Rustin led a successful campaign that persuaded President Truman to issue his July 1948 executive order calling for an end to discrimination in the military. After this victory Randolph wanted to disband the League. Rustin opposed the action, contending that it would be unfair to blacks still serving prison sentences for refusal to cooperate with the conscription system. In spite of Rustin's position, Randolph withdrew. Without his influence the League collapsed in November of that year.

Rustin resigned his post with FOR in 1953 to become executive director of the pacifist War Resisters League. Five years later he traveled to England to help the Campaign for Nuclear Disarmament organize its first Aldermaston to London "ban the bomb" peace march, which took place in 1959. In 1960 Rustin was arrested in France for protesting atomic tests in the Sahara.

From 1955 to 1964 Rustin served as chief tactician of the civil rights movement. In 1955 he helped Martin Luther King, Jr., [q.v.] organize the Montgomery, Ala., bus boycott, and he played a significant role in the formation of King's philosophy of nonviolence. Rustin stressed the political advantages of peaceful direct action. In October 1956 he wrote that "insofar as the Negro retains the nonviolent approach, he will be able to win white sympathy and frustrate the aims of the White Citizens Council [white supremacists]. . . ." If white racists succeeded in provoking blacks to violence, Rustin contended, "Negroes will lose their moral initiative, liberals will become even more frightened and inactive and a deeper wedge will be driven between white and black workers." He also asserted that ongoing nonviolent direct action would exert immediate economic and social pressure on the South and was more important than "a one-shot performance at the polls in November."

In 1957, at King's request, Rustin drew up plans for the organization of Southern Christian Leadership Conference, which advocated racial equality through nonviolent means. That year he also wrote a series of statements used by King and the Rev. Ralph Abernathy [q.v.] at a meeting with **Vice President Richard M. Nixon.** They included the assertions that federal action would be needed to end racial discrimination and that neither political party had been sufficiently active in promoting civil rights. They also demanded that President Eisenhower make an appeal to the nation on behalf of racial equality; and that Nixon make a trip to the South and "speak out in moral terms" for civil rights in general and voting rights in particular.

In June 1960 Rustin drafted a letter which King sent to both national parties proposing action on civil rights. It called for them to repudiate the segregationists within their ranks; to reduce, in accordance with the 14th Amendment, the congressional representation of areas denying blacks the right to vote; to explicitly endorse the Supreme Court's 1954 school desegregation decision as both morally correct and the law of the land; and to oppose colonialism in Africa. The letter also urged Congress to include in the civil rights bill then under consideration a section empowering the federal government to bring suits on behalf of blacks denied civil rights and to frame the bill so as to place responsibility for the protection of black voting rights in the hands of the President rather than the Southern courts.

In 1960 Rustin, acting on behalf of King and Randolph, organized civil rights demonstrations at the Democratic and Republican national conventions. Because Rep. Adam Clayton Powell, Jr., (D, N.Y.) [q.v.] informed King that he would publicly denounce Rustin for his radical background and alleged homosexuality unless King fired him, Rustin agreed to leave the project in the interest of harmony. For the next two years rumors circulated that Rustin was a "draft-dodging Communist." Randolph, with whom he had established a close working relationship over the previous two decades, was the only leader who kept up his ties with Rustin.

During the winter of 1962-63 Randolph asked Rustin to draw up plans for a mass march on Washington. Believing that blacks could overcome their second-class citizenship only through basic economic and social reforms, Rustin contended that the demonstration should concentrate on demands for federal action in the areas of jobs, housing and education. The Birmingham demonstrations of April and May 1963 further convinced him that such demands were the order of the day. In June Rustin contended that those protests represented a watershed for the civil rights movement because they were the first to involve masses of black workers who, not satisfied with token integration of public accommodations, insisted upon equal opportunity and full employment.

The original plans for the march reflected Rustin's views. But during the two months preceding the demonstration, march leaders shifted its emphasis from economic and social reforms to traditional civil rights objectives in order to secure the support of moderate blacks such as Roy Wilkins [q.v.], executive director of the NAACP.

Randolph had planned to make Rustin the director of the march, but Wilkins felt that Rustin's radical background might expose the project to unnecessary attack. In the spring of 1963 Randolph agreed to be the official director of the march, but he appointed Rustin to serve as his deputy, and the latter was the actual organizer of the demonstration.

Rustin was successful in gaining the support of approximately 100 civil rights, religious and labor organizations for the march, although the AFL-CIO, fearing possible disorders, declined to endorse the demonstration. On Aug. 28 an unprecedented 200,000 to 250,000 persons participated in a well-ordered and peaceful March on Washington for Jobs and Freedom.

During the mid-1960s Rustin elaborated upon the strategy he had proposed during the early planning phase of the March on Washington. His program was presented most comprehensively in "From Protest to Politics: The Future of the Civil Rights Movement," an influential article that appeared in the February 1965 issue of *Commentary*. Rustin contended that the legal basis of American racism had been destroyed during the decade between the Supreme Court's school desegregation decision of 1954 and the Civil Rights Act of 1964 but that the desegregation of public accommodations was "relatively peripheral . . . to the fundamental conditions of life of the Negro people."

To effect basic change in the lives of blacks, Rustin continued, the civil rights movement had to extend its concern beyond race relations to fundamental economic problems. The private sector of the economy, he argued, could not fulfill the aspirations of blacks because it was not producing enough jobs. Furthermore, Rustin wrote, technology was eliminating unskilled jobs while creating positions that required professional training. The result, he said, was that the individual no longer could work his way up from the bottom of the economic ladder on personal initiative alone. He concluded that it was essential for blacks to promote federal programs for full employment, the abolition of slums and the reconstruction of the educational system. To win such programs, Rustin said, blacks should place less stress upon protest demonstrations and devote more attention to electoral politics.

Rustin argued that the great majority of blacks had more in common with white workers than with Negro businessmen and that his proposals for federal action represented a program around which a majority coalition could be formed within the Democratic Party. The organized labor movement, Rustin asserted, was the major natural ally of the mass of poor blacks. He urged black organizations to work with the established AFL-CIO leadership to create such a coalition. Black separatism, he argued in a September 1966 *Commentary* article, was not a viable alternative because it would merely solidify the black bourgeoise's control of Negro communities, isolate blacks politically and foster anti-black sentiments.

In the mid-1960s Rustin, who had previously devoted most of his attention to behind-the-scenes organizing of civil rights protests, began to appear frequently before black, union and liberal organizations to promote his political perspective. A tall, grey-haired figure with the appearance of both urbanity and athletic prowess, Rustin, who had cultivated a British accent in the radical, anti-American days of his youth, was an imposing figure and a forceful speaker. Late in 1964 he became executive director of the newly created A. Philip Randolph Institute, an AFL-CIO-supported organization which attempted to place young blacks in union apprenticeship training programs and promote political proposals for the labor-liberal-black coalition, which Rustin thought Lyndon Johnson's landslide 1964 election victory had inaugurated.

Though Rustin generally supported the policies of President Johnson, he frequently criticized the Administration's antipoverty program as inadequate. With other civil rights leaders and liberal economists, Rustin advocated a 10-year, $185 billion "freedom budget" by which the federal government could put all employable persons to work rebuilding ghettoes, constructing hospitals and schools and aiding other socially useful projects.

In 1968 Rustin strongly endorsed the presidential candidacy of Vice President Hubert H. Humphrey. Noting the seating of Julian Bond [q.v.] and of the integrated Mississippi delegation at the Democratic National Convention, Rustin wrote in the Sept. 21 New York *Amsterdam News* that "the Negro-labor-liberal forces are clearly on top in the Democratic Party." He praised Humphrey as having an outstanding record in the area of civil rights and on matters pertaining to the welfare of workers. Rustin noted "the divisions among the progressive forces over Vietnam," but he attempted to minimize that issue, stating that the progressive coalition should not allow itself to become divided over the war because it "will end before long, but our problems at home will haunt us for generations if we do not act now."

Rustin's close relationship with the AFL-CIO, his support of coalition politics and his allegiance to integration increasingly isolated him within the ranks of black leadership in the late 1960s. In February 1964 he had organized a one-day New York City school boycott for integration led by Rev. Milton A. Galamison [q.v.], a strike that was supported by most black leaders. But by 1968 many blacks had lost hope in the possibility of integration and were supporting the decentralization of the New York school system and black control of local school boards. During that year the United Federation of Teachers (UFT) went on strike when the black-controlled governing board of the Ocean Hill-Brownsville demonstration school district ordered 13 tenured teachers transferred out of the district. Rustin, who still staunchly supported integration and a black-trade union alliance, was one of the few prominent blacks who backed the UFT. A large number of blacks felt that the UFT and its president, Albert Shanker [q.v.], were hostile to their aspirations, and Rustin was widely denounced within the Negro community for his support of the union.

Rustin was one of the major critics of the Nixon Administration's civil rights policies. In 1970 he joined other blacks in denouncing a memo by Daniel P. Moynihan [q.v.], a domestic adviser to President Nixon, which claimed that blacks had made great strides in the past 20 years and called for a period of "benign neglect" on the race issue. The next year Rustin attacked the Administration's housing policy. Nixon, in a major policy statement, had differentiated between "racial" and "economic" forms of discrimination, saying the latter was outside the government's domain. Rustin considered the distinction racist in effect and the whole policy "chaotic" and "a disaster."

In a May 1971 article for *Harper's Magazine,* Rustin criticized the President's Philadelphia Plan, ostensibly designed to increase the number of construction jobs available to blacks, as illusionary since it would merely shift black workers from one site to another. Nixon's suspension of the 1931 Davis-Bacon Act, allowing non-union labor to be hired at less than union rates, was denounced by Rustin as an anti-union device with the effect of pitting black worker against white and placing deflationary pressure on wages. Rustin charged in the same article that near the end of Nixon's first term in office, the Administration had "engaged in an assault on the advances of the past decade" with the "intent of building a political majority on the basis of white hostility to blacks."

In the late 1960s and early 1970s, Rustin continued to oppose separatist tendencies. In 1969 he denounced college officials for capitulating to black student demands for "soul courses," contending that black studies would not provide blacks with economically usable skills. In 1972 Rustin became cochairman of the newly merged Socialist Party-Democratic Socialist Federation (later Social Democrats U.S.A.), a group dominated by trade union leaders and others who favored the type of black-labor-union coalition he advocated. The Federation had endorsed Democratic presidential nominee George McGovern [q.v.], but it criticized both his foreign and domestic policy proposals as "casual" and "vague."

In the mid-1970s Rustin turned his attention to what he considered to be the errors of white liberals. He argued, in his *Strategies for Freedom: The Changing Patterns of Black Protest* (1976), that during the past decade the civil rights movement had failed to shift from social to economic issues in part because of liberals preoccupation with the Vietnam war, political corruption, the environment and feminism. In a May 1976 article in the *New York Times Magazine,* he called the "anti-growth" ideas of the environmentalist movement a middle-class elitist tendency that would stunt the economic gains necessary for black equality.

For further information:
Thomas R. Brooks, "A Strategist Without a

Movement," *The New York Times Magazine* (Feb. 16, 1969), pp. 24+.
Bayard Rustin, *Down the Line: The Collected Writings of Bayard Rustin* (Chicago, 1971).

SEALE, BOBBY
b. Oct. 22, 1937; Dallas, Tex.
Chairman, Black Panther Party,
1966-

The son of a laborer, Seale grew up in Dallas and Oakland, Calif. He dropped out of high school to enlist in the Air Force but was given a dishonorable discharge after becoming involved in a fight with an officer. Returning to Oakland, Seale finished high school at night and enrolled in Merritt College, a two-year institution. There he met Huey Newton [*q.v.*], another black student deeply interested, like Seale, in black problems. The two studied the ideas of Malcolm X [*q.v.*] and other angry black authors and in October 1966 founded the Black Panther Party. Seale was chairman and Newton was minister of defense of the new organization.

The primary stated concern of the heavily armed Panthers was to protect ghetto residents from police violence, which Newton and Seale viewed as the most obvious form of external control over the black community. In May 1967 Seale led a demonstration of armed Panthers in the California State Assembly, which was considering gun control legislation opposed by the Panthers. The incident won the Panthers national attention and helped increase their membership to about 2,000 during the late 1960s. Though an all-black organization, the Panthers welcomed cooperation with white radicals. Seale was official leader of the Party but at first had less to do with internal Panther affairs than Newton. Instead, he sought to establish contacts with other radicals in the peace and black movements. In 1968 the Panthers joined several white radical groups to form the Peace and Freedom Party.

Seale went to Chicago in August 1968 to participate in demonstrations at the Democratic National Convention; he later became one of the famous "Chicago Eight" who were indicted for violating the anti-riot provision of the new Civil Rights Act. The trial, which began in March 1969, became a radical cause celebre. For his repeated outbursts against the judge, Seale was at one point ordered gagged and bound to his chair. On Nov. 5 Seale was sentenced to four years in prison for contempt of court, and his case was severed from that of the others. The government later requested, however, that the charges against him be dropped.

With Newton in jail from 1968 to 1970 for the shooting of a policeman, Seale took a greater part in internal Panther affairs. In early 1969 he announced a drive to rid the Panthers of "provocateur agents, kooks and avaricious fools" seeking to use the organization for their own purposes. (It was later revealed that the Federal Bureau of Investigation had, in fact, placed agents in the Panthers in an attempt to disrupt the organization.) In 1971 Seale went on trial in New Haven, Conn., on charges of ordering the 1969 execution of a Panther member suspected of being a government informer. The trial began in March and again aroused the anger of many radicals, who accused the government of trying to "get Bobby." When the jury failed to reach a verdict in May, the judge dismissed the charges against Seale, claiming that "massive publicity" made a new trial impossible.

Free from legal entanglements, Seale returned to Oakland and leadership of the Panthers. He cooperated with Newton in reorienting the Party from "armed defense" to community action projects, such as health clinics for ghetto residents and a free breakfast program for school children. In 1973 Seale ran for mayor of Oakland as a Democrat, finishing second among nine candidates with 43,710 votes. Although he lost the race, Seale's surprisingly strong showing indicated to some observers that the "new" Panthers had shifted their strategy to organizing ghetto residents, with the aim of gaining political power and community self-control.

SHUTTLESWORTH, FRED L(EE)

b. March 18, 1922; Mugler, Ala.
President, Alabama Christian Movement for Human Rights, 1956-70;
Secretary, Southern Christian Leadership Conference, 1957-70.

Shuttlesworth grew up near Birmingham, Ala., and received a B.A. from Selma College and a B.S. from Alabama State College. A Baptist minister, he began preaching in 1948 at two rural churches near Selma. In March 1953 he became pastor of Birmingham's Bethel Baptist Church. There Shuttlesworth began to involve himself in civil rights causes, participating, for example, in an unsuccessful attempt in 1955 to get blacks placed on the local police force. He joined the NAACP, and when the organization was outlawed in Alabama in 1956, he helped establish the Alabama Christian Movement for Human Rights (ACMHR) to continue the fight for black equality in Birmingham. Shuttlesworth was elected its first president.

Called the "Johannesburg of America" by some blacks, Birmingham was governed in the late-1950s by officials who firmly opposed any attempts at desegregation. As the leader of the integration movement in the city, Shuttlesworth headed many attempts to end segregation in local public facilities. On Dec. 20, 1956, shortly after the Supreme Court had declared segregation on local transportation illegal, Shuttlesworth called on the city commissioners to end segregated seating on Birmingham's buses. His home was destroyed by dynamite on Christmas night, but Shuttlesworth still led more than 20 blacks the next day onto local buses, where they sat in the seats reserved for whites. Following the arrest of 22 blacks, Shuttlesworth called off any more demonstrations until the segregation law could be tested in the courts. In October 1958, just before a federal court hearing on the law was to be held, the city commission repealed the statute and passed a new one authorizing the bus company to establish its own segregation rules. Shuttlesworth then helped organize a test of this new ordinance. Thirteen blacks were arrested on

Oct. 20 for sitting in seats reserved for whites, and Shuttlesworth himself was arrested the next day for having "incited" the protest. A legal challenge to the new law was started the next month, but not until November 1961 did a federal district court finally order an end to segregation on Birmingham's city buses.

Shuttlesworth also tried to desegregate the waiting rooms at Birmingham's railroad terminal in March 1957. That September he tried to enroll four black children, two of them his own, at a white high school. He was beaten by a mob outside the building, and the children were refused admittance. Shuttlesworth filed a court suit challenging the 1957 Alabama pupil placement law, which was intended to forestall school desegregation. However he lost the case in November 1958 when the U.S. Supreme Court ruled that the statute was not unconstitutional on its face. In June 1958 an attempt was made to dynamite Shuttlesworth's church. It failed only because a volunteer guarding the church removed the explosives before they went off. During the spring of 1960, Shuttlesworth aided student sit-ins in Birmingham and was arrested for his participation.

A believer in the philosophy of nonviolent direct action espoused by Martin Luther King, Jr. [q.v.], Shuttlesworth helped organize the Southern Christian Leadership Conference (SCLC) in 1957. He was elected its secretary and became one of King's top aides in the SCLC. He spoke at the May 1957 Prayer Pilgrimage in Washington, D.C.

In 1960 Shuttlesworth became pastor of the Revelation Baptist Church in Cincinnati, Ohio, but he remained active in Birmingham and was a key aide to King. When the first of the Freedom Rides ended in violence at Anniston and Birmingham, Ala. on May 14, 1961, Shuttlesworth helped arrange for the riders' safe passage out of Alabama. When the rides, which were aimed at desegregating interstate transportation facilities, were continued, Shuttlesworth joined them and was arrested on

May 17 in Birmingham and on May 25 in Montgomery, Ala. He headed an SCLC nonviolent training center in Birmingham during the early 1960s and backed student-led sit-ins and boycotts there in 1960 and 1962.

At a May 1962 board meeting of the SCLC, Shuttlesworth proposed that the SCLC join with his ACMHR in an anti-segregation campaign in Birmingham. The suggestion led to the dramatic Birmingham demonstrations, which began on April 3, 1963 and were led by King and Shuttlesworth. Once described as "one of the most articulate and fastest-talking leaders of the Negro drive for equality in the South," Shuttlesworth addressed daily mass meetings in Birmingham, led demonstrations and marches, and was arrested on April 6 and again on April 12. He was also injured in a May 7 demonstration when police turned fire hoses on the crowd and a stream of water hit Shuttlesworth, lifting him up and throwing him against the side of a building. Despite his injuries Shuttlesworth participated in the negotiations between Birmingham's black and white leadership, and on May 10 he announced the terms of the agreement they had reached.

Following the Sept. 15 bombing of a black church in Birmingham which killed four young girls, Shuttlesworth organized protests in the city, met in Washington with President Kennedy on Sept. 19 and, after two more bombings in Birmingham, called for federal troops to be sent into the city. The historic events in Birmingham contributed to President Kennedy's decision to seek strong civil rights legislation and created support for the passage of a new federal law. The spring demonstrations also increased the momentum of the civil rights movement. During the summer of 1963, desegregation drives emerged in numerous Southern cities, including Danville, Va., where Shuttlesworth helped lead the campaign.

Charging that Birmingham's white leaders had not lived up to the desegregation agreement reached in 1963, Shuttlesworth led more demonstrations in the city during the spring of 1964. He joined in an SCLC integration campaign in St. Augustine, Fla. that summer and was arrested in demonstrations at a segregated motel on June 18. Shuttlesworth helped organize the march from Selma to Montgomery, Ala., in March 1965 to protest voting discrimination in the state. He also led demonstrations against voting discrimination in Birmingham in January 1966.

In August 1965 a dispute over Shuttlesworth's leadership developed within the congregation at his Cincinnati church. When Shuttlesworth's opponents accused him of being dictatorial and misusing church funds, he denied the charges and alleged that the opposition to him was part of an effort to discredit him within the civil rights movement. The controversy ended in January 1966 when several hundred of his supporters formed a new church in Cincinnati, and Shuttlesworth accepted their invitation to become its pastor. During riots in Cincinnati in June 1967, Shuttlesworth met with city officials in an effort to reach an agreement on black demands and prevent further violence.

Between 1958 and 1969 Shuttlesworth was a party in 10 Supreme Court cases involving civil rights. Altogether the Court overturned six of Shuttlesworth's convictions resulting from his role in the 1961 Freedom Rides and in various Birmingham demonstrations. In New York Times v. Sullivan, decided in March 1964, the Supreme Court also reversed a $500,000 libel judgment against Shuttlesworth, three other black ministers and the New York Times. The suit had resulted from a March 1960 advertisement in the Times that criticized Alabama officials and sought to raise funds for civil rights causes. However, in June 1967 the Court upheld contempt-of-court convictions stemming from the 1963 Birmingham demonstrations against Shuttlesworth and King. Shuttlesworth served a five-day sentence in Alabama in October 1967.

THURMOND, STROM
b. Dec. 5, 1902; Edgefield, S.C.
Democratic Senator, S.C., 1955-56,
1956-64; Republican Senator, S.C.,
1964-.

The son of a South Carolina politician, Thurmond received a B.S. degree from Clemson College in 1923 and worked as a high school teacher for the next six years. He was admitted to the South Carolina bar and joined his father's law firm in 1930. Three years later Thurmond won election to the state Senate. While in the legislature he supported a number of social welfare programs, including the state's first bill providing aid to the aged, to the blind, and to needy children. In 1938 Thurmond became a circuit judge. He enlisted in the Army shortly after American entry into World War II.

Thurmond resumed his judgeship after being discharged from the service in 1946, but in May he resigned his post to run for governor. His conservative opponents in the Democratic primary charged him with being a New Dealer and hinted that he was receiving money from the Congress of Industrial Organizations. Nevertheless, he won his Party's nomination, which was equivalent to election in South Carolina. As governor, Thurmond increased appropriations for education and health care facilities, led a successful drive to repeal the poll tax and backed a minimum wage and maximum hour bill. He made a strong but unsuccessful effort to convict a white mob charged with lynching a black and appointed the state's first black to the state board of medical examiners.

Although Thurmond was regarded as a moderate by his state's black leaders, he was a segregationist and a states' rights advocate. In October 1947 he criticized the recommendation of President Truman's Committee on Civil Rights, which had called for federal legislation to protect black and other minority rights in voting, housing and employment. Thurmond believed that such measures would be unconstitutional, an encroachment on states' rights. He also opposed federal control of oil rich tidelands claimed by certain states. In 1948 he backed Mississippi Gov. Fielding Wright's call for Southern Democrats to break with Truman and the national party if they continued pressing for civil rights. In February 1948, following the presentation of Truman's civil rights program to Congress, the Southern Governors' Conference appointed Thurmond to head a delegation to call on Democratic National Chairman J. Howard McGrath. The delegation asked him to have Truman withdraw the offending legislation in return for Southern support in the 1948 presidential election. The Chairman flatly refused. The Southern governors then recommended that the states choose delegates to the Democratic National Convention opposed to Truman and pick presidential electors who would refuse to vote for any candidate favoring civil rights. The governors hoped to deny either of the two major party candidates an electoral majority and throw the election into the House of Representatives, where either a Southern President would be chosen or a compromise candidate found.

In May Democrats from Mississippi and Alabama held a conference in Jackson, Miss., to solidify plans for the Democratic National Convention. Thurmond delivered a keynote address laden with anti-civil rights emotionalism. He exaggerated Truman's civil rights stance and declared that "all the laws of Washington, and all the bayonets of the Army cannot force the Negroes into Southerners' homes, schools, churches . . . and places of amusement." Thurmond suggested that the Democratic National Committee be notified that Southern delegates would not support civil rights nominees so that they could not be accused of "bolting or breaking faith with the party." The Jackson conference planned to reconvene at Birmingham, Ala., following the National Convention if a strong civil rights stand was not repudiated.

At the Convention members of several Southern delegations refused to accept the platform committee's moderate civil rights plank. They moved that the Convention adopt the Southern view, reject civil rights and replace Truman at the head of the ticket. When the deadlocked meeting offered to restate the tepid civil rights endorsement of 1944, they refused the compromise. The Southern delegations were divided between those who would take their fight outside the party and those who would not. Perhaps moved by Southern intransigence, the Convention then adopted the strong civil right plank pushed by Hubert Humphrey [q.v.] and the liberal Democrats. It even added a commendation for the President's personal role.

At that point Mississippi and half the Alabama delegation walked out. At the subsequent Dixie caucus Thurmond shouted, "We have been betrayed and the guilty shall not go unpunished!" While the Thurmond-Wright dissidents cast about for a viable third party candidate, the rest of the South satisfied itself with uniting behind the candidacy of Sen. Richard B. Russell (D, Ga.) [q.v.], who refused any third-party role. Russell delivered a ringing speech in defense of the South. He received 263 votes to Truman's 947, and the President was nominated.

The dissidents reconvened in Birmingham on July 17. With the exception of Mississippi's congressional delegation accompanied by Wright, Southerners in Congress refused to actively support a third party move. Present were state officials, extreme segregationists, anti-New Deal Democrats, and representatives of corporate interests and the petroleum industry in the South. They adopted a "declaration of principle" that supported segregation and called on "any other loyal Americans" to join in defeating "Harry Truman and Thomas E. Dewey and every candidate for public office who would establish a police state" in America. The conference nominated Thurmond for President and Wright for vice president and formally adopted the name of

States' Rights Democrats. They were quickly dubbed "Dixiecrats" by the press. In accepting the nomination Thurmond denounced the federal anti-lynching bill and endorsed racial segregation. He rejected the "white supremacy" mantle, however, saying he would campaign as an "open progressive" on the states' rights platform. Thurmond also refused the support of Gerald L. K. Smith, whom he denounced as a "rabble rouser."

The roots of the Dixiecrat rebellion lay in those one-party states of the Deep South that faced no Republican challenge and so could afford division. The rebels were not primarily motivated by racism but by fear that the Southern economic system would be overturned by racial equality. Segregationists with New Deal inclinations, such as Sen. Olin D. Johnston (D, S.C.), and followers of the late Mississippi Sen. Theodore G. Bilbo [q.v.] did not support the movement. Dixiecrat leaders such as Thurmond and Wright were state officials who feared their powers and prerogatives would slowly slip away to Washington. In North Carolina, Virginia and Tennessee—Southern states with a rudimentary Republican threat—local Democrats did not back Thurmond. Florida, Texas and Arkansas had few Republicans but fewer blacks than Mississippi and South Carolina and a weaker tradition of white supremacy. Here, too, the Dixiecrats did not take hold. Louisiana was a unique case. The Long and anti-Long factions practically formed two parties under the Democratic umbrella. Only by first manipulating the state ballot to exclude Truman's name entirely and then permitting Thurmond to run under the traditional Democratic emblem did the Dixiecrats succeed there.

Thurmond opened his campaign in North Carolina in late July. Refused support by Gov. Cameron Morrison, he denounced the three other presidential nominees for supporting civil rights. Thurmond continued his campaign through Texas and Maryland, where the States' Rights ticket had a chance. He did speak in New York, but his campaign was primarily a struggle for control of party machinery between conservatives and progressives in the South. Although they were on the ballot in 13 states and polled 1.2 million votes, the Thurmond-Wright ticket ultimately carried only Mississippi, South Carolina, Alabama and Louisiana, where they were the official Democratic Party nominees. They won 38 electoral votes from these states, plus one from Tennessee, while Truman won 88 electoral votes in the mid and upper South.

Following Truman's victory, the States' Rights protest lost much of its popular support and financial backing. In July 1950 Thurmond lost a bitter primary battle to Olin Johnston on the issues of party loyalty and Thurmond's comparatively liberal record as governor. Both campaigned against Truman's civil rights program, but Thurmond favored resolving the dispute outside the Democratic Party and Johnston within it. Supreme Court decisions in the *Sweatt*, *Henderson*, and *McLaurin* cases handed down in June 1950 struck at the heart of institutionalized white supremacy. They, together with the final banning of school segregation by the Court in 1954, made white Southern voters feel abandoned by the Democratic Party. When South Carolina's Democratic machine kept Thurmond's name off the Senate primary ballot in 1954, he won election as a write-in candidate, the first person in the state to do so.

Thurmond was one of Congress's most aggressive opponents of integration and civil rights legislation. In 1956 he initiated a movement among Southern members of Congress to issue a Declaration of Constitutional Principles as a challenge to the Supreme Court's 1954 opinion in *Brown v. Board of Education* outlawing segregation in public schools. Thurmond wrote the initial draft, which contained sections endorsing the doctrine of interposition and declaring the Court's decision to be unconstitutional and illegal. He and Sen. Harry F. Byrd (D, Va.) circulated the draft among Southern members, but moderates would not sign it until these clauses were removed. As modified by Sen. Richard B. Russell (D, Ga.) [*q.v.*] and others, the Declaration,

popularly known as the "Southern Manifesto," was presented to Congress on March 12, 1956 with the signatures of 101 Southerners. It described the school desegregation opinion as "a clear abuse of judicial power" and urged the states "to resist forced integration by any lawful means."

In 1957 Thurmond conducted a record-breaking filibuster against a civil rights measure aimed primarily at protecting voting rights. The bill initially proposed by the Administration was weakened by the deletion of provisions authorizing the President to use troops to enforce existing civil rights laws and permitting the Attorney General to institute civil action for preventive relief in civil rights cases. It was further diluted by the addition of an amendment permitting jury trials in criminal contempt cases against those obstructing voters. Most Southern congressmen believed that the final version of the bill did not pose a serious threat to their region's racial practices and that it was the most favorable measure they could obtain. On Aug. 28, Sen. Sam Ervin (D, N.C.), speaking on behalf of senior Southern senators, said there would be no filibuster against it. Later in the day, however, Thurmond began a one-man filibuster lasting 24 hours and 18 minutes, the longest in Senate history. Many of his fellow Southerners believed that Thurmond's action could have created a backlash leading to a strengthening of the bill. Agreeing with Sen. Herman Talmadge's (D, Ga.) description of the filibuster as a "grandstand" performance, they branded Thurmond an opportunist who would seek to advance his political career even at the expense of the Southern cause.

During the early 1960s Thurmond opposed civil rights bills and social welfare legislation while favoring a militantly anti-Communst foreign policy and large defense appropriations. According to *Congressional Quarterly*, he was the most frequent Senate Democratic opponent of major Kennedy-backed measures in 1961, 1962 and 1963 and was the leading Southern Democratic senatorial supporter of the upper house's conservative coalition in 1961 and 1962.

In May 1961 the Senate rejected a Thurmond amendment to an aid-to-education bill that would have prohibited the withholding of school aid funds from states or school districts maintaining segregated schools. During July 1963 he warned that the Kennedy Administration's civil rights bill would destroy property rights. The following month Thurmond denounced Bayard Rustin [q.v.], organizer of the civil rights March on Washington for Jobs and Freedom, charging, among other things, that Rustin was a former Communist and had been arrested for "sex perversion" and "vagrancy and lewdness."

Thurmond transferred his allegiance from the Democratic to the Republican Party in September 1964 so that he could work openly for the presidential candidacy of conservative Sen. Barry M. Goldwater (R, Ariz.). During each. of the remaining four years of the Johnson presidency, Thurmond was among the five leading Republican supporters of the Senate's conservative coalition.

A foe of all of the Johnson Administration's civil rights proposals, he asserted that the voting rights bill of 1965 would usurp the constitutional authority of the states to establish voter qualifications and would create a "totalitarian" federal government. He denounced a 1967 measure to protect civil rights workers from harassment, stating that it would give "added protection to roving fomenters of violence, such as Stokely Carmichael [q.v.] and H. Rap Brown [q.v.]." Equally opposed to most Great Society programs, Thurmond attacked such measures as the 1965 housing bill and the 1967 elementary school aid bill as promoting dangerous expansion of federal power.

In 1968 Thurmond backed Richard M. Nixon for the Republican presidential nomination and was credited with convincing most Southern Republican delegates to the Party's National Convention to vote for Nixon instead of right-wing Gov. Ronald Reagan of California. Many observers believed that the formulation of Nixon's "Southern strategy" originally was based on an agreement between the candidate and the South Carolinian in which Nixon, in exchange for Thurmond's support, pledged to oppose school busing, appoint "strict constructionists" to the Supreme Court, reduce federal spending and promote a strong military establishment.

Thurmond wielded considerable influence in the White House during the Nixon Administration. Harry Dent, his former aide, was a political adviser to the President, and about 20 other friends and associates of the Senator received significant administrative jobs.

In the early 1970s Thurmond continued to vote against social welfare programs, but he began to make serious attempts to secure federal housing and welfare funds for South Carolina. A major reason for his efforts was the Senator's desire to win the votes of the growing black electorate in the state.

TILL, EMMETT L(OUIS)
b. July 25, 1941; Chicago, Ill.
d. Aug. 28, (?) 1955; Money, Miss.
Lynching victim.

In the summer of 1955 Emmett Till, a 14-year-old black from Chicago, went to visit his uncle in LeFlore Co., Miss., near the town of Money. Sometime around Aug. 28 Till was murdered; his body was pulled from the Tallahatchie River on Aug. 31. Till arrived in Mississippi when racial tension was at its peak. The White Citizens Council had publicly defended segregation and had called for armed resistance to the Supreme Court's school desegregation decision of 1954. Several blacks had been murdered throughout the South in reprisal for black voter registration. In LeFlore Co. threats and intimidation had stopped blacks from voting in the August 1955 primary.

Till's uncle named Roy Bryant and J. W. Milam as the men who had kidnapped Till. The two men were tried for murder. They admitted abducting the boy to question him about having whistled at and insulted Mrs. Bryant in a store in Money. An all-white jury acquitted Bryant and Milam on the grounds that the body was too decomposed to identified. A grand jury later refused to indict them for kidnapping. Despite requests from the NAACP and other organizations, the Administration refused to enter this sensitive case. Presidential advisers deliberated suggesting that Congress probe the matter, hoping that it could put the onus of delay on Southern Democrats. However, the plan was never accepted, and the Justice Department announced it did not have the authority to enter the case.

The verdict aroused a storm of protest throughout the world and increased efforts to win strong government support for civil rights.

As a result of the growing demand for federal action on civil rights and the Administration's fear of losing black votes during the 1956 election, Attorney General Herbert Brownell began to draft legislation designed to protect voting rights and create a civil rights commission to investigate rights problems. The bill made little progress on Capitol Hill during 1956 but became the basis for the Civil Rights Act of 1957.

WALKER, WYATT TEE
b. Aug. 15, 1929; Brockton, Mass.
Executive Director, Southern Christian Leadership Conference, 1960-64.

A Baptist minister who received his divinity degree from Virginia Union University, Walker was pastor of a Petersburg, Va., church and president of the NAACP in Virginia before joining the Southern Christian Leadership Conference (SCLC) as executive director in 1960. In that post Walker became one of the chief aides to SCLC President Martin Luther King [q.v.] with much of the responsibility for raising funds and for organizing SCLC direct action campaigns.

Walker joined the 1961 Freedom Rides, which challenged segregation in interstate transportation facilities, and was a member of the Freedom Rides Coordinating Committee organized in May. He was arrested twice during the rides—on May 25 in Montgomery, Ala., and on June 21 in Jackson, Miss.,—for entering the white section of Trailways bus terminals. Walker also helped direct an anti-segregation campaign in Albany, Ga., which began in November 1961 and which the SCLC joined in mid-December. The protests in Albany continued into 1962 and were intensified in July when King was jailed for violating a public assembly ordinance. Walker opened and ran an SCLC office in Albany and led many of the July demonstrations. Although the Albany movement was judged a failure by most observers, Walker later hailed it as "a mile-post in the early stage of the non-violent revolution" and "a big beginning in the Deep South."

Walker played a key role in the planning and organization of the SCLC's desegregation drive in Birmingham, Ala., in the spring of 1963. With King and Ralph Abernathy [q.v.], Walker met with black leaders in the city to build unity and support for the campaign. Walker also did reconnaissance work in Birmingham before the demonstrations started to determine priority targets and map out routes for marches. Late in 1963 Walker also devised a direct action campaign to challenge segregation in public accommodations in Atlanta, Ga. His plans were adopted by the Negro Leadership Conference, an association of civil rights groups in the city, and were put into effect in January 1964.

Walker resigned as executive director of the SCLC in 1964 to become a vice president of Educational Heritage Inc., a new company created to publish a 24-volume series on the history and culture of black Americans.

WALLACE, GEORGE C(ORLEY)
b. Aug. 25, 1919; Clio, Ala.
Governor, Ala., 1963-67, 1970- ; Independent candidate for President, 1968.

Wallace was born and raised in southeastern Alabama and worked his way through the University of Alabama, receiving a law degree in 1942. He served as an assistant state attorney general in 1946 and in the state House of Representatives from 1947 to 1952. A protege of the state's neo-populist governor, "Big Jim" Folson, Wallace established a liberal record in the legislature. He sponsored bills to provide scholarships to the dependents of deceased or disabled veterans, to increase old age pensions and to construct state vocational schools. Wallace then won election as judge of Alabama's third judicial circuit in 1952.

With other Southerners Wallace fought the adoption of a strong civil rights plank at the 1948 Democratic National Convention. As Alabama's delegate on the 1956 Democratic Convention Platform Committee, he helped secure a civil rights compromise acceptable to Southern Democrats. In 1958 Wallace entered the Democratic gubernatorial primary where he qualified for the runoff against state Attorney General John Patterson [q.v.]. During the campaign Patterson took a strong segregationist position, receiving the backing of the Ku Klux Klan. Wallace was considered the more moderate candidate, and he lost the June 3 runoff. According to his biographer, Marshall Frady, he said after his defeat that "John Patterson out-nigguhed me," but "I'm not goin' to be out-nigguhed again."

Wallace's term as circuit judge ended in January 1959. He spent the next three years campaigning for the 1962 gubernatorial elections. In his spring 1962 primary campaign, Wallace ran on a militant segregationist platform, promising to resist all efforts "of the federal courts, the Justice Department and the Civil Rights Commission to destroy our social and educational order." He was the front-runner in the May 1 Democratic primary and won the May 29 runoff primary with the largest popular vote ever received by a gubernatorial candidate in Alabama's history. In his January 1963 inaugural address, Wallace reasserted his segregationist stance. "I draw the line in the dust," he proclaimed, "and toss the gauntlet before the feet of tyranny, and I say: segregation now—segregation tomorrow—and segregation forever."

Wallace devoted much of his first year in office to vain attempts to prevent desegre-gation in Alabama. Shortly before a desegregation agreement was reached in Birmingham, where Martin Luther King [q.v.] led mass demonstrations in the spring of 1963, Wallace announced he would "not be a party to any. . .compromise on the issues of segregation." Rioting erupted in Birmingham on May 11 after the motel where King was staying and the home of King's brother were bombed. President Kennedy ordered federal troops to bases near Birmingham to be used in case more violence developed, and Wallace immediately filed a federal court suit challenging Kennedy's action and asking, among other things, that the 14th Amendment be held unconstitutional. The Supreme Court rejected his appeal in a *per curiam* opinion on May 27.

By 1963 Alabama was the only Southern state without any desegregated schools. During his campaign for governor, Wallace had promised to "resist any illegal federal court orders" for school desegregation "even to the point of standing at the schoolhouse door in person." He fulfilled the pledge on June 11, 1963 at the University of Alabama. On May 21 a federal district court had ordered the enrollment of two black students at the University's main campus in Tuscaloosa, and Wallace immediately announced he would "be present to bar the entrance of any Negro" who attempted to enroll. Hoping to avoid the violence that accompanied James Meredith's [q.v.] entry into the University of Mississippi in September 1962, the Justice Department secured a federal court injunction prohibiting Wallace from interfering with the students' enrollment and sent a team headed by Deputy Attorney General Nicholas Katzenbach to Tuscaloosa to help arrange for the peaceful entry of the students. President Kennedy placed nearby Army troops on alert and issued an executive proclamation ordering Wallace and all others to "cease and desist" from obstructing justice. Despite the court injunction, Wallace stood in the doorway of Foster Auditorium, the University's registration center, on June 11, blocking the entrance of the two students, Katzenbach and other Justice Department officials who accompanied them. Katzenbach read the President's proclamation and demanded that Wallace comply with the federal court orders. Standing before a lectern, Wallace responded with his own proclamation, claiming that the federal government was usurping the state's authority to control its own school system. He was barring the doorway, he said, not "for defiance's sake, but for the purpose of raising basic and fundamental constitutional questions. My action is a call for strict adherence to the Constitution." Katzenbach withdrew, the two students were accompanied to their dormitory rooms. President Kennedy federalized the Alabama National Guard and ordered several units onto the campus. At a second confrontation late in the afternoon, the National Guard commander escorted the two students to the registration center where Wallace was again blocking the doorway. He told the Governor, "It is my sad duty to ask you to step aside, on order of the President of the United States." Wallace stepped aside. The two students registered, and two days later another black student enrolled at the University Center at Huntsville without incident.

Wallace again tried to forestall integration in the fall of 1963. Federal courts had ordered school desegregation at the elementary and secondary levels in Mobile, Tuskegee, Birmingham and Huntsville, and local authorities were prepared to comply when the schools opened in September. On Sept. 2, however, Wallace began eight days of defiance in which he issued executive orders delaying the opening of the schools and sent state troopers to physically keep them closed. On Sept. 9 Wallace opened the schools but used the troopers to keep blacks from entering them in three cities. On the same day all five federal district court judges in Alabama issued injunctions ordering Wallace and the state's forces not to interfere further with desegregation. Wallace replaced the state troopers with National Guardsmen, but on Sept. 10 Kennedy federalized the Guard and ordered all the troops back to their barracks. The black students finally entered the schools. Five days later a black church in Birmingham was bombed, killing four young girls. Wallace declared that the tragedy "saddened all Alabamians" and offered a $5000 reward for information leading to the arrest of the bombers. On Sept. 16, however, President Kennedy issued a statement saying it was "regrettable that public disparagement of law and order had encouraged violence which has fallen on the innocent." The remark was generally considered a reference to Wallace.

Contending that the leadership of both national parties had strayed from "the principles on which this country was founded," Wallace launched a campaign for the presidency in the spring of 1964. Repeatedly denying charges that he was a racist, Wallace campaigned against big government and the federal bureaucracy. He declared that the "federal government in Washington is reaching into every facet of society and encroaching on the rightful powers of the state." He denounced the pending civil rights act as yet another usurpation of individual liberty and local government authority and condemned the federal courts as a "judicial oligarchy," manipulating the American people "as cogs in a gigantic socialist pattern."

Wallace entered three Democratic primaries in April and May, capturing 34.1% of the vote in Wisconsin, 29.9% in Indiana and 42.8% in Maryland. The size and source of the Wallace vote thoroughly impressed political observers. He scored heavily in working-class neighborhoods in Milwaukee and Baltimore and carried every white precinct in the mill town of Gary, Ind. Wallace withdrew from the race on July 19, four days after the Republicans nominated Sen. Barry M. Goldwater (R, Ariz.), declaring that his "mission" of helping "conservatize" the national parties was accomplished.

Wallace continued his segregationist policy as governor over the next two years. Early in 1965 Martin Luther King [q.v.] made Selma the site of a major voter registration drive among blacks. On Feb. 2 King announced plans for a march from Selma to Montgomery to protest the denial of voting rights to Alabama's blacks. Wallace asserted on March 6 that "such a march cannot and will not be tolerated," and the next day state troopers, acting under his orders, broke up the march as it left Selma. A second march attempt was also turned back.by state troopers on March 9.

On March 17 a federal district court gave its approval to the march, enjoined Wallace from interfering with the demonstrators and ordered the Governor to provide police protection for the marchers. Wallace denounced the ruling but said he would "obey, even though it be galling." He notified President Johnson, however, that Alabama could not afford the cost of mobilizing the National Guard to protect the marchers. Johnson federalized the Guard on March 20, and the marchers were protected on their five-day trek to Montgomery. Wallace refused to meet a delegation from the march when it arrived at the state capitol on March 25, but he did meet with the delegation five days later. In April 1966 Wallace ordered the resegregation of state mental hospitals, which had been integrated in March by the State Hospitals Board. In the same month he announced that Alabama would not comply with the school desegregation guidelines recently issued by the federal Office of Education, and in September Wallace won passage of a law declaring those federal guidelines "null and void" in Alabama.

Aside from his efforts to prevent desegregation, Gov. Wallace built 14 new junior colleges and 15 new trade schools in the state, initiated another $100 million school construction program and expanded the state's free textbook system to include all 12 grades. He began the largest highway construction program in the state's history, introduced a clean water act, devised plans for new nursing homes and medical clinics, and encouraged greater industrialization in Alabama. However, his tax program was regressive, consisting of increased sales taxes and higher taxes on beer, cigarettes, gasoline and sports events. Organized labor criticized Wallace's administration, alleging that the state's highway patrolmen were union-busters and that the state's child labor laws were virtually worthless. Alabama had no minimum wage law, and the state ranked near the bottom of all states in welfare payments to depen-

dent children. Although Wallace had promised to increase old age pensions to at least $100 per month, they rose only 36 cents during his term to $69.66 per month. Average unemployment compensation rose slightly to $38 per month.

Because the Alabama constitution barred a governor from serving two consecutive terms, Wallace announced in September 1965 that he would seek a constitutional amendment to change this provision. He called a special session of the state legislature; while the House rapidly passed the succession bill, the Senate voted it down on Oct. 22. Wallace circumvented his possible political eclipse by running his wife, Lurleen Wallace, for governor in 1966. Announcing her candidacy on Feb. 24, Wallace said that if his wife were elected, he would be "by her side" as governor and would "make the policies and decisions affecting the next administration." Lurleen Wallace won 52% of the vote in the May 1966 Democratic primary, defeating nine other candidates, and won the November election by a two-to-one margin. When his wife was sworn in as governor in January 1967, Wallace became her special assistant and did in fact serve as de facto governor, continuing the policies of his own administration, until she died of cancer on May 7, 1968.

Throughout 1966 Wallace indicated he would run again for the presidency in 1968. He began organizing a new campaign in the spring of 1967 and formally announced his third party candidacy on Feb. 8, 1968. In this campaign, Wallace struck many of the same themes he had in 1964. Alleging that "there's not a dime's worth of difference" between national Democratic and Republican leaders, Wallace said the central issue of his campaign was whether the federal government "can take over and destroy the authority of the states." He denounced the growing federal bureaucracy and said the average man—"the steel worker, the paper worker, the rubber worker, the small businessman, the cab driver"—was "sick and tired of theoreticians in both national parties and in some of our colleges and some of our courts telling us how to go to bed at night and get up in the morning." Portraying himself as the defender of the workingman, Wallace promised to end the trend "toward the solution of all problems with more federal force and more takeover of individual liberty and freedom." Wallace again said he was not a racist, but he attacked federal civil rights laws as a denial of property rights and an infringement on states rights and personal liberty. He attacked the national news media and, as a strong "law and order" advocate, blamed the federal courts for an increase in crime. "If you are knocked in the head on a street in a city today," he complained, "the man who knocked you in the head is out of jail before you get to the hospital" because the courts had "made it impossible to convict a criminal."

Wallace's campaign had a major impact on the 1968 elections. His supporters succeeded in getting his name on the ballot, usually as the candidate of the American Independent Party, in all 50 states. Until the mid-summer of 1968 pollsters gave Wallace 10% of the national vote at best, but June polls showed him with 16%, and both Gallup and Harris polls gave Wallace 21% of the vote in late September. At that point many believed that Wallace might well be able to carry enough states to deny either major party candidate an electoral vote majority, throwing the election into the House of Representatives, where Wallace could influence the choice of a president.

Wallace's prospects began to decline in October. Vice President Hubert H. Humphrey, the Democratic candidate, launched a strong attack on Wallace as a racist and anti-unionist, and organized labor undertook a vigorous campaign attacking Wallace's record on labor issues while governor. Wallace's image was also tarnished by the disorders and protests accompanying many of his campaign appearances. On Oct. 3 Wallace announced he was choosing former Air Force Gen. Curtis E. LeMay as his running mate for the vice presidency. LeMay quickly aroused enormous controversy by saying that the U.S. should "bomb the North Vietnamese back to the Stone Age". The General also said he would advocate the use of nuclear weapons

in Vietnam if necessary. Wallace won 13.6% of the national vote in November and carried five states—Arkansas, Louisiana, Mississippi, Alabama and Georgia. Over four million of Wallace's 9.9 million votes came from Northern and Western states, and many analysts believed that only last-minute vote changes kept Wallace from amassing a much larger vote. According to Kevin Phillips, who studied the 1968 election in detail in *The Emerging Republican Majority*, Wallace's candidacy hurt Republican Richard M. Nixon more than it did Humphrey. Wallace drew off many conservative votes that would have gone to Nixon in a straight Nixon-Humphrey race. Wallace came close to defeating Nixon in South Carolina and Tennessee, and in Texas he diverted enough votes from Nixon to give Humphrey a plurality. Wallace supplied his own assessment of the election on Nov. 6. Claiming victory in defeat, he contended that he had been "the bellwether for the two national parties" on campaign issues. He asserted his movement was still alive since President-elect Nixon had said "almost identically" the same things in his campaign that Wallace had.

After the election Wallace supporters took steps to form a national conservative party. In February 1969 Wallace followers met in Dallas and Louisville and in May announced the creation of the American Independent Party. Although it was clearly intended as a vehicle for Wallace, he remained officially aloof from it, wishing to preserve all of his options. He did say, however, that he felt a third party movement was "still necessary," and he continued to address political rallies and speak out on issues.

Wallace quickly became a vocal opponent of the Nixon Administration, posing criticism from the right. In a July 1969 television appearance, he set out guidelines for the President: "Conclude the war honorably, give some tax reduction to the middle class of our country and cut out unnecessary spending, restore law and order and get the government out of the control of local institutions such as schools." In November, Wallace visited

Vietnam and on his return attacked Nixon's policies of troop withdrawal and Vietnamization. Keeping the issue of school desegregation prominent in his speeches, he accused Nixon of breaking his campaign pledge not to bus children to achieve racial balance. In a February 1970 speech in Birmingham, Wallace urged Southern governors to disregard federal court orders to integrate schools and told his audience, "We'll see to it that Mr. Nixon is a one-term President." Shrewdly capitalizing on the Administration's so-called Southern strategy, the effort to win the South over to the Republican Party, Wallace sought to keep pressure on the Administration in the area of school desegregation.

Wallace's wife, Lurleen, had died of cancer in 1968 and was succeeded as governor by Albert Brewer. In February 1970 Wallace announced his candidacy against Brewer in the May gubernatorial primary. The outcome of the race was considered decisive for Wallace's political future and political analysts watched the race closely. Not certain of victory, Wallace turned to explicit racial appeals toward the end of the campaign, charging that Brewer was a favorite of the "bloc vote," a code word in Alabama politics for blacks. Brewer, on the other hand, subtly appealed to blacks by promising to look to the "future" instead of the past. Although Brewer placed first in the voting he failed to achieve a majority and was forced into a runoff. Wallace received the support of the Ku Klux Klan and defeated Brewer in the runoff. Immediately after his victory Wallace called on Nixon to deliver his "two-year-old unfulfilled pledges to stop busings and school closings and to reestablish freedom of choice," and pointedly declared that "the Republican Party knows it cannot win without the South in the next election."

With his eye on the 1972 presidential race, Wallace continued to exploit anti-busing sentiment. In August 1971 he ordered Alabama school boards to disregard court-ordered integration plans and to keep the schools closed if necessary. The following month, however, schools opened quietly and without incident. Wallace's stand did seem to have an effect. In August, Nixon reiterated his opposition to busing and warned federal officials that they risked losing their jobs if they sought to impose busing plans on local school districts. In November the House for the first time overwhelmingly approved an amendment to an education aid bill to prohibit the use of federal money for busing to achieve racial balance.

On Jan. l3, 1972, Wallace formally announced his candidacy for the Democratic presidential nomination. He told a large rally in Tallahassee that he was the only candidate to protest busing and other intrusions of "big government" into their private lives. He also made crime prevention and tax reduction issues in his campaign and claimed to speak for the "little man." Democratic National Chairman Lawrence F. O'Brien [q.v.] immediately disavowed the Wallace candidacy and AFL-CIO president George Meany attacked him as a "bigot" and a "racist" and accused him of being "anti-labor right down to the soles of his feet." Wallace's entry into the Democratic race quickly magnified the importance of the busing issue. On Feb. 14, Nixon promised to take steps soon to limit busing, and Sen. Henry Jackson [q.v.], another presidential aspirant, proposed a constitutional amendment to prohibit busing. A nonbinding referendum on school busing was also placed on the ballot in the Florida primary.

Wallace made the March 14 primary in Florida a test of his viability as a candidate. Although expected to win, he surprised observers by the size of his victory. Capturing 42% of the vote, he had more than double the ballots of second-place finisher Hubert Humphrey. Declaring himself a "serious candidate," Wallace took his campaign North to prove that he had national appeal. In primaries in Wisconsin and Pennsylvania in April, Wallace placed an impressive second, and in Indiana the following month he won over 40% of the vote, with strong support in the suburbs and in blue-collar districts.

He also easily won primaries in Alabama, Tennessee and North Carolina. The strength of his campaign led George McGovern [q.v.] and Hubert Humphrey, the only other serious candidates left, to mount last-minute "stop Wallace" drives in Michigan and Maryland, where primaries were scheduled for May 16.

On May 15 tragedy struck the Wallace campaign. While walking through a crowd of supporters in a shopping center in Laurel, Md., he was shot several times and critically wounded. His assailant, a young drifter named Arthur Bremer who had been following Wallace on the campaign trail, was immediately seized by the Secret Service. Wallace was rushed to a hospital where the bullets were removed, but doctors announced that he would be paralyzed from the waist down. The next day he won easy victories in Michigan and Maryland, but his physical condition considerably diminished the viability of his campaign. After McGovern won the California primary in June, he was virtually assured the nomination. With McGovern's first-ballot victory and the rejection by the Party's Platform Committee of an anti-busing plank, Wallace announced that he would remain neutral in the presidential campaign and barred a third party candidacy for himself.

Wallace's name figured prominently in the Senate Watergate hearings. John Dean [q.v.] revealed that Wallace was on the President's infamous enemies list, and H.R. Haldeman [q.v.] testified that secret campaign funds had been used to aid Wallace's opponents in the 1970 gubernatorial contest. It was also revealed that the Nixon Administration had used the Internal Revenue Service to try to obtain damaging information on Wallace and members of his family.

Wallace ran for reelection in 1974. The campaign, however, was far different from previous ones. The racial issue remained in the background, and Wallace actively courted black votes, declaring that if reelected he would be governor of both "whites and blacks" and promising "opportunities for all." Although national civil rights leaders opposed him, many lo-

cal black politicians endorsed Wallace in recognition of his power to disperse federal and state funds and provide political appointments. Wallace easily defeated his opponents without the need for a runoff, receiving 64% of the vote, including about one-quarter of the black vote.

Wallace came under increasingly heavy criticism during his new term as governor. Opponents attacked his preoccupation with national politics at the expense of Alabama's daily affairs. Critics charged that Alabama was really run by federal Judge Frank M. Johnson who, in the absence of action from Wallace, ordered the desegregation of schools and the state police, the redrawing of the state's political boundaries to insure fair representation, the cleaning up of the state's decrepit prison system and mental hospitals and the reassessment of commercial property for tax purposes. Wallace's claim to represent working people was also challenged. Despite his many years as governor, opponents pointed out that Alabama had no minimum wage law, minimal workmen's and unemployment compensation benefits, the lowest per pupil expenditures on education of any state, and was near the bottom in personal income. Its tax system, moreover, was among the most regressive in the country. There were also charges of rampant corruption, with two major kickback convictions, a major theft conviction and several resignations under fire of top state officials.

Wallace's 1976 race revealed both the limits and extent of his appeal. By toning down his extremism, he failed to attract the sizable number of disenchanted voters who turned to him in the past to register a protest. On the other hand, his new image did not convince those liberal and middle-of-the-road Democrats who remembered his past record. Wallace's campaign received a serious blow from which it never recovered when he lost the March 14 Florida primary to dark horse candidate Jimmy Carter [q.v.]. Wallace had predicted a repeat of his 1972 victory, but the ex-Georgia governor won the votes of Southerners motivated by regional pride but reluctant to support Wallace. Later in

March Carter also defeated Wallace in North Carolina. Wallace called him a "warmed-over McGovern" and warned Carter supporters that "smiling and grinning a lot" would not bring change. But Carter continued to win primaries and amass delegate strength. In May, Wallace announced that he "could support" Carter, and the following month he withdrew from the race and endorsed his opponent.

Although a change in Alabama election law had permitted Wallace to seek a second consecutive term, the law prevented him from running again in 1978. In June 1977 he announced his intention to seek the seat of retiring Sen. John Sparkman [q.v.], but the following year he changed his mind. When Alabama's junior Sen. James Allen [q.v.] died unexpectedly on June 1, 1978, Wallace said that he was giving "serious consideration" to running in the November special election. However when November came, Wallace was not in the race.

Despite the growing disenchantment with his governorship, Wallace, in November 1975, announced his candidacy for the 1976 Democratic presidential nomination. Avoiding for the most part the race issue, he concentrated on crime and high taxes and declared that the main issue in the campaign was whether the middle class could "survive economically." A Gallup poll in December placed him second in popularity among possible candidates, behind Hubert Humphrey, who was not openly campaigning.

For further information:
Philip Crass, *The Wallace Factor* (New York, 1976).
Wayne Greenhaw, *Watch Out for George Wallace* (New Jersey, 1976).

WHITE, WALTER F(RANCIS)
b. July 1, 1893; Atlanta, Ga.
d. March 21, 1955; New York, N.Y.
Executive Secretary, NAACP, 1931-55.

White decided to devote his life to civil rights after his father, an Atlanta mailman, was killed during a race riot. He graduated from Atlanta University in 1916 and briefly sold insurance. In 1918 White joined the NAACP as James Wilbur Johnson's assistant secretary. From 1918 to 1929 he personally investigated 41 lynchings and eight race riots. During the 1920s he gained fame for his novels, one of which, *Rope and Faggot* (1929), was a powerful indictment of lynching. White became executive secretary of the NAACP in march 1931. He served at that post until his death.

As leader of the most prominent civil rights group of that period, White acted as a lobbyist in Washington for anti-lynching, anti-segregation and anti-poll tax laws. During World War II White condemned discrimination against blacks in the armed forces and defense industries. He drafted President Roosevelt's executive order of June 1941 prohibiting racial discrimination in defense industries. From 1943 to 1945 White toured the war theaters as a special *New York Post* correspondent. An outgrowth of his travels was *A Rising Wind* (1945), a book on the treatment of black soldiers.

A moderate, White advocated the use of legislation and particularly the power of the executive to end segregation. He believed that such action would end discrimination more quickly than violence and direct mass action. During the postwar period he urged Truman to establish a permanent fair employment commission, eliminate segregation in Washington D.C, end discrimination in the civil service and abolish "once and for all" segregation in the armed forces. White appeared before the platform committee at the 1948 Democratic National Convention to demand a strong civil rights plank. "The day of reckoning has come," he said, "when the Democratic Party must decide whether it is going to permit bigots to dictate its philosophy and policy or whether the Party can rise to the heights of America which alone can justify its continued existence." He praised the strong civil rights plank pushed through by liberal leaders.

Although he objected to Truman's inclusion of several men whom he considered racist in the cabinet, White generally applauded the President's efforts to end discrimination. He praised Truman's 1947 speech before the NAACP promising to attack racial discrimination, and he supported the executive order of July 1948 barring discrimination in the armed forces and civil service. Despite official NAACP neutrality he vigorously supported Truman during the 1948 presidential campaign. In his syndicated newspaper column White belittled the efforts of Henry Wallace and Thomas E. Dewey on behalf of blacks while praising Truman's frontal attacks on racial and religious discrimination. He condemned Southerners as "morons" and the GOP as "transparently dishonest." White was so pro-Truman that he ousted W. E. B. Dubois from his position as research director of the NAACP because of his support of Wallace.

In 1947 White announced that the NAACP would go to court against segregated school systems in 17 states. Although a federal court in Charleston, S.C., upheld public school segregation in June 1951, White was undeterred, predicting that racial segregation would be abolished within 10 years. Following bloody race riots in Cook Co., Ill., in July 1951, he wrote in the New York *Herald Tribune* that the conflict had resulted from black confinement in Chicago's ghettos and whites' opposition to admitting them to suburbia. He attacked the refusal of real estate associations, mortgage companies and banks to lend money to blacks.

During the 1952 presidential campaign White charged that Dwight D. Eisenhower had advocated racial segregation in the armed forces and opposed admission of black officers since they had received "vastly inferior education" to whites. He also attacked Democratic vice-presidential candidate John Sparkman as a racist. In June 1953 White announced that NAACP policy was no longer "separate but equal facilities" but "total integration. White died in March 1955 at the age of 72.

For further information:
Donald R. McCoy and Richard T. Tuetten, *Quest and Response: Minority Rights and the Truman Administration* (Lawrence, Kan., 1973).
Walter White, *A Man Called White* (New York, 1948).

WILKINS, ROY
b. Aug. 30, 1901; St. Louis, Mo.
Executive Secretary, NAACP, 1955-64;
Executive Director, 1965-77.

Wilkins majored in sociology at the University of Minnesota and was secretary of the St. Paul, Minn., chapter of the NAACP in his senior year. After graduating in 1923 he began working as a reporter for the *Kansas City Call*, a weekly black newspaper, and eventually became its managing editor. In 1930 Wilkins worked against Senate confirmation of Judge John J. Parker, an allegedly racist Supreme Court nominee and the reelection of Kansas Sen. Henry J. Allen (R, Kan.), a segregationist. As a result of this activity, he was offered the post of assistant secretary of the national NAACP in New York City. In his new position he investigated conditions of black workers on the Mississippi levees in December 1931. During and after World War II, he ran the national office in the absence of Walter White, the organization's leader. In 1950 Wilkins organized an Emergency Civil Rights Mobilization in Washington, D.C., to lobby on behalf of civil rights legislation. In 1955 Executive Secretary White retired, and Wilkins replaced him as leader of the 240,000-member organization. The goal of the NAACP was the elimination of racial discrimination; its primary methods were legal suits and legislative lobbying.

Wilkins's major function was formulating the strategy of the NAACP's legal and legislative efforts. He also administered the national office, made speeches throughout the country, wrote pamphlets and raised funds. One of Wilkins's first activities after becoming NAACP executive secretary was to help raise money to support the Montgomery bus boycott led by Martin Luther King, Jr. [q.v.]. However, he focused his primary attention upon attempts to integrate Southern schools. In June 1955 the national office urged NAACP Southern chapters to petition local school boards for implementation of the Supreme Court's 1954 *Brown v. Board of Education* decision outlawing segregation in public schools.

In 1956 Wilkins attacked both major political parties for allegedly taking weak positions on civil rights. He criticized Democratic presidential aspirant Adlai E. Stevenson in February as favoring a go-slow approach in granting blacks their rights as citizens. In August Wilkins unsuccessfully urged the Republican Platform Committee to promise an amendment to Senate rules that would bar filibusters. Subsequently, he criticized both national party platforms as inadequate. Since the NAACP was a nonpartisan organization, Wilkins did not express a preference in the presidential race.

In February 1957 Wilkins, testifying before a subcommittee of the House Judiciary Committee, described the Administration's civil rights bill as "minimum legislation." Before its enactment by Congress, the Senate eliminated the crucial Part III, permitting the Attorney General to obtain court injunctions in all cases of civil rights violations. Nevertheless, Wilkins decided that the bill, which established a civil rights commission and gave blacks some protection in exercising their right to vote, was the best that could be obtained at the mo-

ment. He also concluded that it represented an historic breakthrough that would open the way for more far-reaching legislation in the future. Wilkins convinced the Leadership Conference on Civil Rights, a coalition of groups opposing racial discrimination, to back the measure.

On June 23, 1958 Wilkins, King, A. Philip Randolph [q.v.] and Lester B. Granger met with President Eisenhower to present a nine-point program to further civil rights. The plan included the organization of a White House conference on school desegregation; the granting of funds to officials and community groups seeking to promote the desegregation of schools; the denial of federal funds for segregated institutions; the assurance of federal protection against terrorist bombings in the South; and the enactment of Part III of the original 1957 civil rights bill. They received little more than a polite audience from the President.

Wilkins denounced the 1960 Civil Rights Act which extended the voting rights protection of the 1957 rights legislation. He declared, "The Negro has to pass more check points and more officials than he would if he were trying to get the United States gold reserves in Fort Knox. It's a fraud." In that year he again denounced both parties' civil rights planks as inadequate and participated in picketing the Democratic National Convention. He and other rights leaders believed that, among other things, the major parties should repudiate the segregationists within their ranks and, in accordance with the 14th Amendment, back a reduction of congressional representation in areas where blacks were denied the right to vote.

In 1960 Wilkins endorsed new, direct-action techniques to promote desegregation in the South. He announced in the spring that the NAACP would support student "sit-ins" at lunch counters and that the organization itself would stage "wade-ins" in the summer to integrate swimming facilities.

As a U.S. senator, John F. Kennedy had been regarded by civil rights leaders, in Arthur M. Schlesinger's words, as a "sympathetic. . .but detached" friend of

Negroes. Wilkins had provided Kennedy with a letter during his 1958 reelection campaign, endorsing his record as one of the best in the Senate. In his campaign for the presidency, Kennedy pledged executive action, particularly in the field of housing, to end discrimination "by a stroke of the president's pen." Executive actions were taken soon after his inauguration to end discrimination in federal employment, but they fell short of what civil rights leaders believed Kennedy had promised. There was no stroke of the pen ending discrimination in federally financed housing until Nov. 30, 1962. Wilkins and his colleagues were also disappointed in Kennedy's refusal to back civil rights legislation introduced by congressional liberals to fulfill the 1960 Democratic platform pledges. In July 1961 Wilkins led a delegation of NAACP officials to meet with the President and voice their dismay at "the absence of a clear call" from him for new legislation. Kennedy replied that existing civil rights legislation had not been fully utilized. Furthermore, he said, the Administration lacked the votes to pass significant legislation.

At the President's request, Wilkins submitted a 61-page memorandum in 1961 urging Kennedy to sign an across-the-board executive order—to govern "the whole executive branch of government"—barring employment discrimination throughout the federal government and in all state programs receiving federal aid. Federal expenditures in excess of $1.1 billion, the civil rights leader noted, continued to "require, support or condone" discrimination in 11 Southern states. Sensitive to the political repercussions of cutting off aid to state programs, President Kennedy never issued the sweeping order.

During 1961 the Administration pressed voting rights and school discrimination cases in the courts, used federal marshals to defend freedom riders in Alabama and successfully petitioned the Interstate Commerce Commission to order desegregation of facilities in interstate bus terminals. But the initiative Wilkins hoped for was missing. Addressing the annual meeting of the NAACP in January 1962, Wilkins praised Kennedy for "his personal role in civil rights" but declared his "disappointment with Mr. Kennedy's first year"

because of his failure to issue the housing order and his strategy of "no legislative action on civil rights." When the Administration introduced a measure to bar the arbitrary use of literacy tests in January 1962, Wilkins testified for the bill but also complained that it was "inadequate" and only "a token offering." (Even this limited bill was killed by a Southern filibuster in the Senate.)

The rapid spread in early 1963 of the direct action movement and the repression it met in many Southern communities forced the Administration to revise the "no legislation" strategy. In June President Kennedy sent Congress a draft civil rights act aimed at ending discrimination in public accommodations, permitting federal initiation of school desegregation suits and eliminating racial bias in voter registration. Earlier in the month Wilkins, widely regarded as the most moderate of all the prominent civil rights leaders, had been arrested with the NAACP's Mississippi field secretary, Medgar Evers [q.v.], during a demonstration in Jackson. Evers was shot to death outside his home less than two weeks later.

Civil rights leaders feared that even the momentum generated by events in the South and the Administration's support might prove insufficient to overcome congressional resistance. The idea of a peaceful mass march on Washington began to win support as a dramatic protest against any congressional delay. Initially, Wilkins was skeptical about the march. But the competition from the more direct-action civil rights organizations, the abandonment of plans for civil disobedience by the march organizers and the threat of a Southern filibuster against the bill won him over. Reflecting the mood of militance among delegates to the NAACP's Chicago convention in early July, Wilkins endorsed the march. (One factor contributing to Wilkins's hesitation was the choice of Bayard Rustin [q.v.] to direct the march. He feared Rustin's radical past might discredit the demonstration in the eyes of moderates on Capitol Hill. As a compromise, A. Philip Randolph [q.v.] served as the director with Rustin acting as his deputy.) Addressing the throng of over 200,000 that assembled on Aug. 28 at the Lincoln Memorial, Wilkins demanded not only passage of the Kennedy bill but also the inclusion of a fair employment practices provision. (The legislation was eventually passed in 1964.)

Wilkins's and the NAACP's long preeminence in the struggle for equality was increasingly challenged during the early 1960s by more militant leaders and organizations. Dry and somewhat aloof in manner, Wilkins lacked the evangelical fervor of such Southern leaders as Martin Luther King [q.v.] and rejected the stridency of the student leaders. Under Wilkins's leadership, the NAACP continued to stress legislative and legal action, often being scorned for its moderation and ridiculed as part of the establishment by those seeking a revolutionary confrontation with white society. Despite these attacks, Wilkins remained the leader of the nation's largest and most active civil rights organization with some 500,000 members and 1,600 local chapters. By virtue of its size and stable leadership, the NAACP was a significant factor in the growth of the direct action movement. Wilkins, impatient with those who disparaged the NAACP, once remarked that the more militant organizations tended to garner "the publicity while the NAACP furnishes the manpower and pays the bills."

As the volume of civil rights legislation increased, Wilkins and the NAACP gave more attention to fully implementing existing legal rights. In January 1965 Wilkins announced plans for creation of a national network of "citizenship clinics," intended to acquaint blacks with the provisions of new laws and educate them for "the assumption of full citizenship responsibilities." The NAACP subsequently sponsored voter registration drives in a number of Northern ghettos. Wilkins also participated in several civil rights marches in Mississippi and Alabama during the mid-1960s. The NAACP was not the leader, however, in the direct action movement of this period.

Developments of the mid and late 1960s put the NAACP in the midst of a growing controversy within the civil rights movement. A veteran in the struggle for racial equality, Wilkins was less impatient and frustrated than many blacks over the progress of legislative reform. He therefore reacted strongly against the call for "black power," first raised by civil rights leader Stokely Carmichael [q.v.] in June 1966.

An NAACP convention in July 1966 attacked Carmichael's advocacy of racial separatism and his justification of the use of violence by blacks in self-defense. Wilkins joined other moderate black leaders, including Martin Luther King [q.v.] and Whitney Young [q.v.], in condemning the outbreak of rioting in many Northern ghettos during the summer of 1967; NAACP chapters were put on "red alert" on June 16 and urged to prevent unrest. Wilkins also resisted the growing opposition of many civil rights activists to the Vietnam war, claiming that civil rights and peace issues should be kept separate.

Wilkins's consistently moderate stand drew considerable criticism within the civil rights movement. More militant black leaders identified him with the white establishment and derided the NAACP's reformist strategy as "outmoded." The militant Student Nonviolent Coordinating Committee and the Congress of Racial Equality refused to join the NAACP in supporting the civil rights bill of 1966, which they viewed as a "sham." In 1967 Wilkins was the target of an abortive assassination plot by the Revolutionary Action Movement, a small black terrorist group.

Within the NAACP a group of militants known as the Young Turks sought to reduce Wilkins's influence and change what they viewed as the organization's "middle-class" image. Strongest in the Northern and Western chapters of the NAACP, the Young Turks favored closer ties to the peace movement and a more positive attitude towards black power. They attempted to gain control of the NAACP Board of Directors in 1967 and one year later demanded the right to function as an autonomous group within the organization. Wilkins defeated both challenges to his leadership but at the price of numerous resignations from the NAACP, including the organization's entire legal staff.

Due to internal unrest and competition from more militant civil rights groups, the NAACP grew slowly during the mid-1960s. Wilkins himself blamed this stagnation on "the uncertainty induced by violence, the punitive mood of Congress, the confusing and provocative statements of a wide variety of individuals and organizations and the frustrations induced by the overwhelming problems of the central cities."

With Richard Nixon's succession to the presidency in 1969, the black militant movement, which had become increasingly vocal throughout the 1960s, gained greater momentum. Wilkins' pro-integrationist stance and rejection of black power and black nationalism as a return to "segregation and Jim Crow" made him the target of criticism both within the more dissident ranks of the NAACP and from the new generation of black separatists. Undaunted, Wilkins continued to counsel moderation as the most effective means for gaining widespread support for civil rights issues. With the rise of the Black Panther Party and the organization's subsequent clash with police around the country, Wilkins helped form the Commission of Inquiry into Black Panthers and Law Enforcement Officials in order to explore the reasons for these clashes.

Wilkins led the campaign to extend civil rights laws despite Nixon's informal moratorium on the subject. He successfully opposed Nixon's nomination of civil rights opponent Clement F. Haynesworth [q.v.] to the Supreme Court in 1969 and of conservative G. Harrold Carswell [q.v.] the following year. Frustrated over the Nixon Administration's retreat on civil rights, Wilkins mobilized the Washington based lobbying wing headed by Clarence Mitchell [q.v.] to press for broader legislation and gain extension of the 1965 Voting Rights Act's ban on literacy tests. Although the Administration unsuccessfully attempted to modify provisions of the bill, it was signed into law in 1970.

Wilkins also led the fight against Nixon's anti-busing stance. Together with the legal wing of the NAACP, he sought to challenge the constitutionality of Nixon's position and won an impressive Supreme Court ruling with the case of *Alexander v. the Holmes County (Mississippi) Board of Education* in 1969. The verdict endorsed the implementation of a desegre-

gation program to take effect immediately.

In 1972 Nixon countered by outlining his desegregation program to Congress which imposed severe restrictions on busing and delayed school desegregation until the latter part of 1973. The NAACP denounced the Nixon program, but Congress approved the measure. Despite this setback the NAACP made progress in other areas. It succeeded in gaining passage of the Equal Employment Opportunity Act which broadened the coverage of its predecessor passed in 1964. The law forbade discrimination by federal, state and local agencies and allowed the Equal Employment Agency to go into court to obtain endorsement of the bills provisions.

Under Wilkins' leadership the NAACP expanded its fight for equal opportunity on all fronts. The organization established day care centers for low income working mothers in 1973 and coordinated programs which sponsored housing construction and counseling centers for former prison inmates. Wilkins retired as an NAACP officer in July 1977 at the age of 76.

WILLIAMS, HOSEA
b. Jan. 5, 1926; Attapulgus, Ga.
Project Director, Southern Christian Leadership Conference, 1963-70.

Williams, the son of a black sharecropper, grew up in Attapulgus. He worked as a fruit picker in Florida and served in the Army before studying at Morris Brown College in Atlanta, where he graduated in 1951. After working briefly as a high school teacher, Williams became a research chemist in the Savannah office of the U.S. Department of Agriculture. He also did volunteer work in Savannah for two civil rights organizations, the NAACP and the Southern Christian Leadership Conference (SCLC). In 1963 he left the Department of Agriculture to become a full-time project director for SCLC.

Williams's skill in grass-roots organization soon made him one of the top assistants of SCLC leader Martin Luther King [*q.v.*]. In 1963 he led anti-segregation drives in Savannah and St. Augustine, Fla. He subsequently helped organize other important SCLC projects, including 1965 voter registration campaigns in Selma, Ala., and Americus, Ga. Williams also served as a liaison between the SCLC and leaders of the Student Nonviolent Coordinating Committee (SNCC), a militant civil rights group that joined the SCLC in many demonstrations. As a result of his activities during the mid-1960s, Williams was jailed over 40 times; on one such occasion in 1966 he initiated a suit that resulted in a court order desegregating Alabama prisons.

Williams remained with the SCLC after King's assassination in April 1968. In May he supervised Resurrection City, an encampment of 3,000 poor people and poverty workers brought to Washington by the SCLC to demonstrate for greater federal antipoverty spending. Williams became a regional vice president of the SCLC in 1970 and national program director in 1971. At this time he emerged as the leader of a radical faction within the SCLC. In 1970 he rejected integration as a civil rights goal and espoused "black power," a concept King had criticized. Williams claimed, however, that black power meant self-respect and not violence.

Williams attempted to enter Georgia politics during the late 1960s, running unsuccessfully for state assemblyman and later for president of the Atlanta City Council. In 1974 he gained election to the state Assembly.

WRIGHT, FIELDING L(EWIS)
b. May 16, 1895; Rolling Fork, Miss.
d. May 4, 1956; Jackson, Miss.
Governor, Miss., 1948-52; Vice Presidential Candidate, States' Rights Democrats, 1948.

Fielding Wright was born in the Mississippi delta and received his law degree from the University of Alabama. He then joined his uncle's law firm, where he specialized in corporate law. In 1928 Wright was elected to the Mississippi State Senate. Four years later he won election to the lower chamber and in 1936 was unanimously chosen speaker of the house. Wright was widely considered a business progressive who favored industrial development to supplement Mississippi's overwhelmingly agricultural economy. After briefly retiring from politics, he was elected lieutenant governor in 1943 and succeeded to the governorship three years later upon the death of incumbent Tom Bailey.

Gov. Wright first attracted national attention in March 1947, when he convened a special session of the state legislature after the Supreme Court had ruled that blacks be permitted to vote in primary elections. A few months later Wright and the legislature decreed that such eligibility hinged on voters affirming belief in the segregationist principles of the state Democratic Party. In November Wright won election to a full term as governor. Several days before, the President's Civil Rights Commission had recommended legislation to protect rights in voting, employment and housing.

In his January 1948 inaugural message, Wright attacked Truman's civil rights panel and called for a break with the national Democratic Party. When Truman recommended civil rights legislation to Congress the following month, Wright carried his crusade to the Southern Governors' Conference and called for a March meeting of Southern Democrats in Jackson, Miss. The governors initially demurred. They called upon Democratic National Chairman J. Howard McGrath [*q.v.*] and requested he have Truman withdraw the offending legislation. McGrath refused. It was becoming clear that he and the President intended waging the 1948 campaign on a strong civil rights plank to win big-city black and ethnic voters. Wright, meanwhile, continued crusading for solidarity among Southern Democrats by broadening the states' rights issue. In February he condemned Truman not for favoring civil rights, but for favoring federal ownership of offshore oil lands claimed by Mississippi and other states. The following month the Mississippi Democratic Committee recommended that delegates quit the national convention if not given "proper" assurances on civil rights.

In May party leaders in Mississippi and Arkansas convened the states' rights conference Wright sought. In a radio address aimed at blacks on the eve of the meeting, Wright defended segregation and in measured tones advised blacks opposed to it to leave Mississippi. The meeting was dominated by men from those states with the largest black populations. Wright was elected temporary chairman of the conference, and South Carolina Gov. J. Strom Thurmond [q.v.] delivered the keynote address. The dissidents sought the restoration of the Democratic Party rule requiring that a presidential candidate be nominated by a two-thirds majority, support of state claims to offshore oil and abandonment of all commitments to civil rights. Anticipating defeat at the national level, the conference planned to reconvene in Birmingham, Ala., following the Democratic National Convention.

At the July Convention the Mississippi delegation, which was pledged to support neither Truman nor any civil rights plank, had difficulty getting seated. Later Wright's forces lost the key vote to restore the two-thirds rule by a wide margin. Despite this show of weakness, they were unwilling to compromise and continued their campaign against a strong civil rights platform. When a deadlocked platform committee offered to restate the tepid civil rights endorsement of 1944, they refused the offer. They also rejected a final compromise to eliminate endorsement of federal control of tidelands oils in return for acceptance of a civil rights plank. When the Convention adopted a strong civil rights plank, Wright's delegation walked out along with half of that from Alabama.

The dissident Democrats reconvened at Birmingham. Having refused political compromise, the rebels now sought to deny the Democratic and Republican candidates an electoral majority and so throw the election into the House of Representatives. Wright alone was accompanied and supported by his state's congressional delegation. He was nominated for vice president by the newly-formed States' Rights Democrats while Thurmond was nominated for President. The two ran on a platform stressing states' rights and listing a "long trail of abuses and usurpations of power by unfaithful" Democratic leaders. The platform called the Democratic civil rights plank "this infamous and iniquitous program" and said it would mean a "police state in a totalitarian, centralized, bureaucratic government" if adopted. It declared that if a foreign power attempted to force the program on the people "it would mean war and the entire nation would resist such effort."

Called "Dixiecrat" by the press, the new movement was the expression of a continuing intraparty Democratic feud. "The race problem," according to Wright was only "a side issue" as anti-New Deal Democrats joined with new Southern corporations and oil interests in a campaign for states' rights and laissez-faire economics. However, a large number of Southern conservatives feared a Republican victory more than one by Truman and either remained aloof from the Dixiecrats or opposed them outright.

When, in September, Truman announced his pro-labor Fair Deal and the integration of the Armed Forces, it fanned Dixiecrat fears that the government would overturn the Southern economic order through racial equality. Nevertheless, although the States' Rights Democrats appeared on the ballot in 13 states, the party carried only those where its candidates were the officially-designated Democratic nominees. Mississippi, South Carolina, Louisiana and Alabama combined with one vote from Tennessee to give Thurmond and Wright 39 electoral votes. At the same time Truman won 88 electoral votes throughout the South. The Dixiecrat ticket won 1,169,000 popular votes.

The states' rights protest lost popular support and financial backing following

Truman's election. Despite this decline Wright and other Dixiecrat leaders established a national states' rights committee to propagandize "the Southern way of life" in May 1949. A year later the Supreme Court began striking at the heart of institutionalized white supremacy and the South began the move to massive resistance to school desegregation. In May 1951 Wright declared, "We shall insist upon segregation regardless of consequences" and made Mississippi one of the key states in the massive resistance movement. Following the end of his term in 1952, Wright returned to his private law practice. Three years later he was defeated in the primary gubernatorial. He died of a heart attack in 1956.

WRIGHT, J(AMES) SKELLY
b. Jan. 14, 1911; New Orleans, La.
U.S. District Judge, 1949-62; U.S. Court of Appeals Judge, 1962- .

Wright, a native of New Orleans, graduated from Loyola University in 1931. While working as a high school English teacher, he attended Loyola University law school, from which he received his degree in 1934. After a year as a lecturer at Loyola, Wright became an assistant U.S. attorney for New Orleans; he remained at that post until 1946. Two years later he became U.S. attorney for the eastern district of Louisiana, which included New Orleans. In 1949 Wright became a U.S. district court judge for the eastern district.

During the 1950s Wright was involved in many Louisiana desegregation suits. In 1957 he ruled that laws designed to keep Louisiana State University and other state universities segregated were unconstitutional, and the following year he ordered the desegregation of New Orleans transportation facilities. In 1959 Wright ruled a law banning sports events between whites and blacks unconstitutional, and in 1960 he ordered Washington Parish, La., registrars to restore blacks to the voting rolls.

Wright was deeply involved in the effort to desegregate New Orleans public schools. In 1952 the NAACP filed a suit against the Orleans Parish School Board for the desegregation of the public schools. The suit made no progress until 1956, when the U.S. district court in New Orleans ruled that segregation was unconstitutional under the Supreme Court's 1954 *Brown* decision. Wright then ordered the School Board to make arrangements for integration "with all deliberate speed" but conceded that he did not require it be done "overnight" or "even in a year or more."

A series of appeals delayed action on the case, but in 1959 the NAACP got Wright to order the School Board to submit a desegregation plan by March 1960. When it refused Wright ordered integration to begin in September on a grade-per-year basis. In the face of this decision, Louisiana Gov. Jimmie Davis took control of the schools under a recently enacted statute in an attempt to close them and thus maintain segregation. Wright then issued restraining orders prohibiting the move. Integration was achieved in New Orleans on Nov. 14, when four blacks entered two previously white schools over the protests of taunting white mobs.

In March 1962 Wright barred Tulane University from discriminating against Negro applicants and ordered the University to admit two black students. Wright ruled that Tulane was a "public institution" receiving a "very substantial state subsidy" and thus subject to the 14th Amendment's ban on discrimination.

One month later Wright invalidated Louisiana's pupil placement law and ordered the New Orleans public schools to accept blacks in the first six grades beginning with the fall term of 1962. He ruled that rather than being assigned to a school by the school board, a pupil could choose to attend either the Negro or white school nearest his or her home.

This decision was modified in May by Wright's successor, Frank Ellis, who ruled that only the first grade had to be integrated that September. In December Ellis ruled that, because Tulane was a private institution, it could not be forced to admit blacks.

As U.S. Court of Appeals judge for the District of Columbia during the Johnson Administration, Wright continued to rule on important civil rights cases. In 1967 Wright, trying the case as a district judge, declared de facto segregation of blacks in the District of Columbia's public schools unconstitutional. The next year the Court of Appeals ruled in favor of renters in an opinion declaring that slum landlords had no legal right to evict tenants in retaliation for reporting housing code violations.

During the 1970s Wright handed down several important decisions dealing with the Alaska pipeline, military justice and nuclear reactors. Wright was a member of the court that, in 1973, ordered President Richard Nixon to turn over his Watergate tapes to the U.S. district court.

YOUNG, ANDREW
b. Mar. 12, 1932; New Orleans, La.
Democratic Representative, Ga., 1973-77.

Young, who was born into a middle-class black family, graduated from Howard University in 1951 and the Hartford Theological Seminary in 1955. Ordained as a minister of the United Church of Christ, he served as pastor of churches in Alabama and Georgia. He became involved in the civil rights movement when he helped organize the 1956 Montgomery, Ala. bus boycott led by Rev. Martin Luther King, Jr. [q.v.]. He then served on the staff of the National Council of Churches in New York, but left when King asked him to become his chief aide in the Southern Christian Leadership Conference (SCLC) which led the civil rights movement during the 1960s. Young was often arrested for participating in the many nonviolent protest demonstrations organized by the SCLC in the South to end discrimination against black people.

In 1969, about a year after King's assas-sination, Young, who was executive vice president of the SCLC, announced a shift in the organization's strategy. Instead of backing nationwide civil rights protests, the organization would use most of its funds to register black voters in order to win local elections in the South. The following year Young ran an unsuccessful campaign to unseat Rep. Fletcher Thompson, Jr. (R, Ga.), a conservative elected from an Atlanta-area district. Young won the seat in 1972 when redistricting had consolidated a district that included most of the city of Atlanta with its black majority and some affluent white suburbs. Young won 53% of the vote and became the first black elected to the House from the Deep South since 1898.

During his four years in the House, Young generally opposed the Nixon-Ford legislative programs and regularly voted to override Nixon-Ford vetoes of social welfare legislation. He vigorously supported congressional efforts to legislate an end to the Vietnam war. He compiled a consistently liberal voting record, backing almost every position advocated by the liberal Americans for Democratic Action, the AFL-CIO's Committee on Political Education and consumer groups.

In 1974 Young opposed the Holt Amendment, which sought to prohibit the Department of Health, Education and Welfare from withholding funds from school districts to compel them to assign students and teachers to schools and classes on the basis of race, sex, creed or national origin and to keep records on such factors. Although busing was not mentioned in the Amendment, Holt intended it to be an anti-busing measure. Young argued that the Amendment would increase school busing suits because it closed the door to negotiating settlements of segregation problems. The following year Young vigorously supported extending the Voting Rights Act of 1965, which was due to expire. He pointed out that voter registration of eligible blacks had increased from 29% in 1964 to 56% in 1972 in the states affected by the law. Young also advocated broadening the law to cover discrimination against language minorities. Congress extended the Voting Rights Act for seven years, included language minorities in its coverage and permanently banned the use of literacy tests for voter registration eligibility.

Young was among Jimmy Carter's [q.v.] first supporters for the presidential nomination and actively campaigned for him. The fact that Young, a prominent civil rights leader and Rev. King's former right-hand man, supported the Carter candidacy helped convince many blacks and white liberals that Carter was not a bigot in disguise. Young had an independent power base and was able to give Carter frank and excellent advice during the election campaign. Carter publicly stated that Young was the only man to whom he owed a political debt for his election.

Young was reelected in 1976 but resigned his seat when Carter appointed him U.S. Ambassador to the United Nations in 1977.

YOUNG, WHITNEY M(OORE)
b. July 31, 1921; Lincoln Ridge, Ky.
d. March 11, 1971; Lagos, Nigeria.
Executive Director, National Urban League, August 1961-March 1971.

A graduate of Kentucky State College, Young received an M.A. in social work in 1947 from the University of Minnesota. He worked for the St. Paul Urban League from 1947 to 1950 and then served as executive secretary of the Omaha (Neb.) Urban League. Young was named dean of the School of Social Work at Atlanta University in 1954 and served as vice president of the NAACP in Georgia and as an adviser to the black students who organized the 1960 Atlanta sit-ins. In August 1961 Young was appointed executive director of the National Urban League, then a professional social work agency that provided a variety of social services for urban blacks. Throughout the 1960s the League remained one of the

more conservative groups working for black rights, but the sophisticated and articulate Young broadened the League's programs and supplied it with more aggressive and outspoken leadership. He improved the planning and coordination between local branches and the national office early in his tenure, increased the League's funding, and expanded its staff. In 1963 he launched one of the League's most successful projects, the National Skills Bank, which collected job profiles on skilled blacks and placed them in positions in government and industry.

In line with the League's traditional social work interests, Young emphasized the economic and social needs of urban blacks in the early 1960s. At a September 1962 convention of the Southern Christian Leadership Conference, Young asserted that blacks had made little progress on the "meat, bread and potatoes issues" of integration and noted that the average black family's income was 54% of the average white family's income. At a June 1963 news conference Young presented his proposal for a "domestic Marshall Plan." Warning that racial incidents in the South were "mild in comparison with those on the verge of taking flame in the tinderbox of racial unrest in Northern cities," Young called for a massive aid program to close the economic, social and educational gaps between the races. Young's plan, which he said would indemnify blacks for past discrimination, proposed that $145 billion be spent on job training and apprenticeship programs, health programs and hospital construction, capitalization of cooperative business and industrial enterprises, programs for nursery children and working mothers, and scholarships, book-buying and tutorial programs. Young's widely publicized plan was one of several proposals for aid to the poor which contributed to the Johnson Administration's war on poverty legislation.

Young joined with the leaders of other civil rights organizations in July 1963 to form the Council for United Civil Rights Leadership. He was selected a co-chairman of the Council, which was designed to raise funds for civil rights work and to coordinate long-range planning and strategies among various rights organizations. Young also was a co-sponsor of the August 1963 March on Washington. After meeting with President Kennedy on the day of the march, Young addressed the crowd assembled at the Lincoln Memorial declaring, "Civil rights, which are God-given and constitutionally guaranteed, are not negotiable in 1963."

One of the first civil rights leaders to be consulted by President Johnson in December 1963, Young cooperated closely with the Johnson Administration in the planning and passage of its War on Poverty legislation. Testifying in support of the program at congressional hearings in April 1964, Young asserted, "Negroes today are wary lest they find themselves with a mouthful of civil rights and an empty stomach." Following the passage of the Economic Opportunity Act in August 1964, Young organized a Community Action Assembly in Washington in December. Over 350 black leaders gathered to hear League officials explain in detail the provisions of the 1964 civil rights and antipoverty laws and ways in which local black organizations could implement the legislation and secure antipoverty funds. The League sponsored a series of similar workshops throughout 1965. With its own $8 million contract from the Labor Department, the League developed a major job training program for unemployed blacks.

Young supported Johnson in the 1964 presidential election and called the Republicans' nomination of Sen. Barry Goldwater (R, Ariz.) "an attempt to appeal to all of the fearful, the insecure, prejudiced people in our society." With three other civil rights leaders, Young signed a July 1964 statement urging a "moratorium" on mass civil rights demonstrations during the 1964 campaign.

Young participated in the march from Selma to Montgomery, Ala., organized by Martin Luther King [q.v.] in March 1965. When James Meredith [q.v.] was shot in June 1966 while on a solitary protest march in Mississippi, Young favored continuation of his march by other civil rights leaders. However, Young refused at first to sign a march "manifesto" containing a strong indictment of American society and government. He frowned on the cry of "black power" raised by Stokely Carmichael [q.v.] during the Meredith march. At an Urban League convention in July, Young deprecated black power as meaning "all things to all men." With six other black leaders he signed an October 1966 advertisement in the *New York Times* which repudiated the black power concept and reaffirmed his commitment to nonviolence, integration and the "democratic process" as the major tenets of the civil rights movement. In July 1967 Young also joined in a statement appealing for an end to riots in Northern ghettos. At an Urban League convention the next month, he added that the choice blacks faced was not one of "moderation vs. militancy" but of "militancy vs. extremism."

Young's emphasis on "responsible militancy" presaged a shift in his views on black power. Speaking at the July 1968 convention of the Congress of Racial Equality, Young endorsed a black power concept that emphasized "control of one's destiny and community affairs." He supported "as legitimate and historically consistent a minority's mobilization of its economic and political power to reward its friends and punish its enemies." At an Urban League convention the same month, Young launched a "New Thrust" program of community action in black ghettos. Labeling the program a "constructive black power" effort, Young explained that the League would now provide "technical assistance to the ghetto to help it organize, document its needs, select its own leadership and arrange for creative confrontations with appropriate officials." The "New Thrust" program signaled a major shift for the League from social service work to grass-roots organizing in the ghetto to build black economic, social and political power. Over the next several years, Young directed a major League rehabilitation program among the black poor which spent an average of $25 million per year.

Throughout the Johnson years Young was frequently called to the White House for consultation, and he served on seven presidential commissions including a national advisory council for the antipoverty program. Young went to South Vietnam in July 1966 to investigate the condition of black servicemen. When Martin Luther King made a strong statement in opposition to the Vietnam war in April 1967, Young opposed King's linking of the anti-war and civil rights movements, stating that the "limited resources and personnel" of the civil rights movement "should not be diverted into other channels." Young also joined a delegation of 22 prominent Americans who went to South Vietnam to observe the September 1967 elections there. He later said he was "terribly impressed" with the elections. In 1969, however, Young came out strongly against the Vietnam war, arguing that it divided the nation and used funds which could best be spent in the nation's cities.

During the Nixon years Young criticized the Administration for permitting what he called a "massive national withdrawal" from urban and racial problems. He also opposed an Administration proposal for pre-trial detention of "dangerous" criminals. Young endorsed bills for a national health insurance program and continued to call for greater aid to the poor. In March 1971 Young drowned while swimming in Lagos, Nigeria.

Appendix

Chronology

1941

January 26: NAACP chapters organize protest meetings in 23 states to demand equal participation by blacks in the national mobilization effort.

May 1: A. Phillip Randolph and other black leaders issue a "Call for Negro America to March on Washington for Jobs and Equal Participation in National Defense."

June 25: President Roosevelt issues Executive Order 8802 banning discrimination in defense industries and government employment and setting up a Fair Employment Practices Committee (FEPC) for the duration of the national emergency.

1942

June: The Congress of Racial Equality (CORE) is formed in Chicago. It pledges itself to interracial cooperation and to nonviolent action for social change.

June: The FEPC holds public hearings in Birmingham, Ala., to investigate discrimination against blacks in defense industries.

June 16: 20,000 blacks rally in Madison Square Garden in New York City for jobs, equal rights and equal justice.

1943

June 20: Racial violence erupts in Detroit. During the summer, race riots occur in over 40 cities.

1944

April 3: In *Smith v. Allwright*, the Supreme Court rules that Negroes cannot be barred from voting in the Texas Democratic primaries on the grounds of race and rejects the contention that political parties are private associations.

1945

September 6: Truman delivers a special postwar message to Congress in which he recommends making the wartime FEPC permanent.

1946

February 9: A Senate filibuster kills a bill that would have created a permanent FEPC.

February 24–25: Mob violence erupts in Columbia, Tenn., led by the Ku Klux Klan, which terrorizes black residents.

June 3: In *Morgan v. Commonwealth*, the Supreme Court rules that uniform seating without regard to race must apply on buses engaged in interstate commerce.

June 30: The wartime FEPC expires.

September 19: Civil Rights leaders confer with President Truman and urge action to stem the rise of racially motivated violence.

December 5: Truman issues Executive Order 9808 establishing the President's Committee on Civil Rights.

1947

April 9: Eight blacks and eight whites begin a "Journey of Reconciliation,"

sponsored by CORE, through the upper South to test the Supreme Court's ruling in *Morgan v. Commonwealth.*

October 23: The NAACP submits a petition of grievances on behalf of black Americans to the United Nations.

October 29: The President's Committee on Civil Rights issues its findings in a report entitled "To Secure These Rights." Among the recommendations are creation of special federal and state investigative units for civil rights cases, elimination of poll taxes, and specific laws against bias in housing, education, health and public services.

1948

January 12: In *Sipuel v. Board of Regents of the University of Oklahoma*, the Supreme Court rules that a state may not deny blacks admission to its law school on the basis of race.

February 2: Truman sends a 10-point civil rights program to Congress calling for an end to segregation in public schools and accommodations and reducing discrimination in employment.

May 3: In *Shelley v. Kraemer*, the Supreme Court rules that state courts cannot be used to enforce racially restrictive covenants.

May 10: Southern Democrats, meeting in Jackson, Miss., vow to form a third party if the Democrats include a civil rights plank in the national platform.

July 14: Liberal forces at the Democratic National Convention, led by Hubert Humphrey, win approval of a strong civil rights plank.

July 17: Southern Democrats opposed to the Party's stand on civil rights form the

States Rights Party, which nominates Strom Thurmond for president on a platform calling for strict segregation of the races.

July 26: Truman issues two executive orders calling for equality of treatment and opportunity in the armed forces and prohibiting discrimination in federal employment.

1949

March 17: The Senate adopts a new filibuster rule that strengthens the right to filibuster, thus making the passage of civil rights legislation unlikely.

1950

January 15–17: The NAACP, along with labor, church and civil liberties groups, sponsors an Emergency Civil Rights Mobilization. 4,000 lobby in Washington, D.C. for civil rights legislation.

May 22: The President's Committee on Equality of Treatment and Opportunity in the Armed Forces issues its fact-finding report, "Freedom To Serve," that details substantial progress in eliminating segregation and discrimination in the U.S. military.

June 5: In *McLaurin v. Oklahoma State Regents*, the Supreme Court rules that, having admitted a black to its law school, a state cannot deny him equal use of all facilities.

June 5: In *Sweatt v. Painter*, the Supreme Court holds that a state cannot bar the admission of a black to a state law school on the grounds that there is a black law school available.

1951

June: The NAACP national convention in Atlanta gives top priority to court challenges against segregation in education.

December 25: H.T. Moore, state coordinator of the NAACP in Florida, is killed when a bomb explodes in his home.

1954

May 17: In *Brown v. the Board of Education*, the Supreme Court unanimously rules that segregated schools are "inherently unequal."

June 10: Southern governors, meeting in Richmond, vow not to comply with the *Brown* decision.

July: The first White Citizens Council is founded in Indianola, Miss., by Robert Patterson, a manager of a large cotton plantation.

1955

May 26: James Eastland of Mississippi introduces in the Senate a resolution calling for an investigation into alleged subversive influences upon Supreme Court decisions.

May 31: The Supreme Court implements its earlier school desegregation decision by imposing the guideline of "all deliberate speed" on local school boards.

August 28: Emmett Till, a 15-year-old black, is kidnapped after allegedly propositioning a white woman. Three days later his body is recovered from the Tallahatchie River. An all-white jury later acquits the two white men accused of the murder.

November 25: The Interstate Commerce Commission bans racial segregation on interstate trains and buses.

December 1: Rosa Parks is arrested for refusing to give up her bus seat to a white man in Montgomery, Ala.

December 5: Under the direction of Martin Luther King, Jr., Montgomery, Ala., blacks begin a 54 week boycott of city buses.

1956

January 5: In his state of the union address, Eisenhower makes his first civil rights request, recommending the creation of a bipartisan commission to investigate the denial of voting rights.

January 24: At a conference in Richmond, Va., four Southern governors endorse the doctrine of interposition. They pledge the use of state power to prevent desegregation by placing the sovereignty of the state between local school board officials and federal courts.

January 30: Martin Luther King's home is dynamited in Montgomery, but King and his family escape injury.

February 3: Autherine Lucy attempts to integrate the formerly all-white University of Alabama. She is expelled four days later because her presence "threatens public order."

March 11: 101 Southern Senators and Representatives issue a Declaration of Constitutional Principles, known as the "Southern Manifesto," denouncing the

Supreme Court's desegregation decision and pledging to use all "lawful means" to resist it.

March 22: Martin Luther King, Jr., is convicted by an Alabama court on charges of conspiracy stemming from his leadership of the Montgomery bus boycott.

April: 65 leaders of the massive resistance movement meet in New Orleans and form the Citizens Councils of America to coordinate resistance to desegregation in the South.

July 23: The House passes an Administration civil rights bill focusing on the protection of voting rights. Parliamentary maneuvers prevent the bill from reaching the Senate floor.

August 16: Liberals fail in an attempt to insert a strong civil rights plank in the Democratic National platform.

November 13: The Supreme Court unanimously rules the Montgomery, Ala., city ordinance requiring racial segregation in buses unconstitutional.

December 21: The year-long boycott of buses in Montgomery ends in victory as the city's buses comply with the Supreme Court's desegregation order.

1957

January 10–11: King and 60 other black leaders from 10 Southern states meet in Atlanta to form the Southern Christian Leadership Conference.

May 17: King, Randolph and Roy Wilkins lead a "prayer pilgrimage" in Washington, D.C. to commemorate the *Brown* decision. 37,000 attend the rally.

July 20: The Southern Regional Council reports that in 11 Southern states only 25% of the eligible black voters are registered, compared with 60% of the white voters.

August 28: Senator Strom Thurmond stages a 24-hour 27-minute filibuster in an effort to prevent passage of a civil rights bill.

August 29: The Senate passes a civil rights bill that focuses on voting rights.

September 4: Arkansas Gov. Orval Faubus orders National Guardsmen to bar nine black students from entering Little Rock's Central High School.

September 9: Eisenhower signs the 1957 Civil Rights Act, establishing a six-man bipartisan commission with power to investigate the denial of voting rights and to study all aspects of the matter of "equal protection of the laws under the Constitution." It is the first civil rights act in 82 years.

September 14: Faubus and Eisenhower confer at Newport, R.I., on the question of school integration in Little Rock.

September 20: Faubus orders the removal of National Guardsmen from Central High School in compliance with a federal court injunction.

September 23: Federal officers secretly escort the nine black students into the high school building. With an enraged white mob outside and harassment of the students inside, they are removed after three hours.

September 24: Eisenhower federalizes the Arkansas National Guard and sends federal troops to Little Rock to enforce integration.

1958

May 8: Eisenhower orders the removal of federalized National Guardsmen from Little Rock's Central High School.

June 30: In *NAACP v. Alabama,* the Supreme Court holds that the NAACP has the right, by freedom of association, not to divulge its membership list.

July 29: Orval Faubus wins a 3rd term as governor of Arkansas by a sweeping majority.

September 28: In *Cooper v. Aaron,* the Supreme Court denies a Little Rock, Ark., school board request for additional time to implement its integration plan. Gov. Faubus responds by ordering the closing of all Little Rock high schools for the remainder of the school year.

1959

February 5: In a special message to Congress, Eisenhower submits a seven-point civil rights program that includes support for school integration.

August 12: Four Little Rock public high schools, closed since 1958 to avoid integration, reopen.

September 8: The Civil Rights Commission issues its first report on voting rights. It finds that only 25% of eligible black voters are registered in the South and outlines a dozen specific legislative measures to assure blacks their full voting rights.

1960

February 1: Black students quietly sit in at a segregated lunch counter in Greensboro, N.C.

April 8: The Senate, by a vote of 71–18, passes a civil rights bill that gives increased authority to the federal courts and the Civil Rights Commission to prevent the intimidation of black voters in the South.

April 15–17: SCLC sponsors a conference in Raleigh, N.C., for leaders of the student sit-ins. The meeting leads to the formation of the Student Nonviolent Coordinating Committee.

May 27–29: Over 1,000 black trade unionists, meeting in Detroit, form the Negro American Labor Council to fight racial discrimination in labor unions.

June 20: In *Hannah v. Larche,* the Supreme Court upholds the right of the Civil Rights Commission, under the Civl Rights Act of 1957, to hold hearings in Louisiana and take measures to preserve the anonymity of informants.

July: Both major parties include strong civil rights planks in their national platforms.

September 1: The Supreme Court unanimously denies appeals to delay school integration in Houston, New Orleans and Delaware.

October 17: National variety chains Woolworth, Kresge, W.T. Grant, and McCrory-McLellan announce that lunch counters in their stores have been integrated in more than 100 Southern cities.

October 25: King is arrested and jailed in Georgia for violation of probation. As concern for his safety mounts, Democratic Presidential candidate John F. Kennedy calls King's wife, Coretta Scott King, and exerts his influence to win the release of the jailed civil rights leader.

December 5: In *Boynton v. Virginia,* the Supreme Court rules that racial discrimination in bus terminal facilities serving interstate passengers is a violation of the Interstate Commerce Act.

1961

March 6: Kennedy issues an executive order establishing the Committee on Equal Employment Opportunity.

May 4: CORE launches its first "Freedom Ride" to test the Supreme Court's decision banning segregation of bus terminal facilities.

May 14: A freedom riders' bus is stoned and burned in Anniston, Ala.

May 21: Four hundred U.S. marshals are sent to Alabama after 20 people are hurt in racial violence stemming from the Freedom Rides.

September 11: Congress approves a two-year extension of the Civil Rights Commission.

September 22: The Interstate Commerce Commission issues a regulation banning segregation in bus facilities serving interstate transportation.

December 11: The Supreme Court, in its first decision on sit-in cases, reverses breach-of-the-peace convictions of 16 black students from Baton Rouge, La.

December 12–16: Over 700 blacks, including Martin Luther King, Jr., are arrested in Albany, Ga., in a mass campaign aginst segregation.

1962

February 26: The Supreme Court holds that no state can require racial segregation of interstate or intrastate transportation.

April 1: Major civil rights organizations announce the start of the Voter Registration Project, a coordinated effort to register black voters in the South, financed by private foundations.

May 9: The Senate votes, 43–53, to reject cloture on a bill outlawing literacy tests in federal elections.

July–August: Martin Luther King, Jr., leads a series of unsuccessful demonstrations in Albany, Ga., for the integration of public facilities.

August 27: A constitutional amendment to abolish the poll tax as a requirement for voting in federal elections is approved by Congress and sent to the states for ratification.

September 28: A U.S. Court of Appeals finds Gov. Ross R. Barnett guilty of civil contempt for attempting to block the integration of the University of Mississippi.

October 1: Three thousand troops quell Mississippi rioting and arrest 200 as James Meredith enrolls at the University of Mississippi.

November 20: Kennedy signs an executive order barring racial discrimination in housing built or purchased with federal funds.

1963

February 28: Kennedy sends a civil rights message to Congress that stresses the need to ensure blacks the right to vote.

April 2: Led by Martin Luther King, Jr., the SCLC begins an integration campaign in Birmingham, Ala.

May 2–7: Major civil rights demonstrations take place in Birmingham. Police assaults and arrests lead to black riots.

May 9: Birmingham leaders announce an agreement calling for the phased integration of bus facilities and the establishment of a permanent biracial committee.

May 20: The Supreme Court rules that state and local governments cannot interfere with peaceful sit-in demonstrations for racial integration of public places of business.

May 27: The Supreme Court prohibits an "indefinite delay" in the desegregation of public schools.

May 31: Jackson, Miss., police arrest 600 black children involved in an integration demonstration.

June 3: The Supreme Court rules that desegregation plans permitting pupils to transfer out of schools where their race is a minority are unconstitutional.

June 11: The first blacks enroll at the University of Alabama over the protest of Governor George Wallace.

June 11: In response to events in Alabama, President Kennedy delivers a televised address to the nation on civil rights.

June 12: Mississippi NAACP Field Secretary Medgar W. Evers is murdered following mass demonstrations in Jackson.

June 12: Civil rights activists picket New York City construction sites to protest racial discrimination in hiring.

June 14: The National Guard is mobilized in Cambridge, Md., to maintain order after the outbreak of violent clashes between blacks and whites.

June 19: Kennedy asks Congress to enact extensive civil rights legislation to give all citizens equal opportunity in employment, public accommodations, voting and education.

July 12: Modified martial law is imposed in Cambridge, Md., as racial strife continues.

August 28: Over 200,000 participate in a March on Washington, D.C. and hear King deliver his "I Have a Dream" speech.

September 10: Kennedy federalizes the Alabama National Guard to prevent its use against the desegregation of public schools.

September 15: A bomb blast in a Birmingham, Ala., church kills four black girls.

October 22: Chicago civil rights forces stage a one-day "Freedom Day" boycott of public schools in which about 225,000 pupils stay home to protest de facto segregation in that city.

November 27: Johnson addresses a joint session of Congress and asks for the "earliest possible passage" of a civil rights program.

December: The SCLC launches a major civil rights campaign in Atlanta against discrimination.

1964

January 23: The 24th Amendment barring the use of a poll tax in federal elections is ratified.

February 3: 464,000 New York City public school students boycott classes to protest de facto segregation in the city's school system.

April 7: Alabama Gov. George Wallace receives 34.1% of the Democratic vote in the Wisconsin presidential primary.

May 19: Wallace polls 42.8% of the vote in the Maryland Democratic presidential primary.

June 10: The Senate invokes cloture on the civil rights bill by a vote of 71–29, marking the first time the Senate ever voted to cut off debate on civil rights legislation.

June 14: The United Steelworkers of America and 11 steel companies agree not to practice racial discrimination in the industry.

June 21: Three civil rights workers, partipants in the Mississippi Freedom Summer Project, are murdered in Neshoba County, Miss.

June 22: In *Bell v. Manford*, the Supreme Court reverses the convictions of civil rights activists arrested during sit-ins on charges of trespass.

July 2: Johnson signs a civil rights bill providing for the integration of public accommodations and closing voting rights loopholes in earlier civil rights legislation.

July 18: Racial violence breaks out in Harlem and Brownsville, two predominantly black sections of New York City. During the summer riots break out in Rochester, N.Y., suburban Chicago, Philadelphia, and several other cities.

August 20: Johnson signs the economic opportunity bill of 1964, authorizing 10 separate programs, under the supervision of the director of the Office of Economic Opportunity, designed to make a coordinated attack on the causes of poverty, illiteracy, unemployment and lack of public services.

August 25: Members of the delegation of the Mississippi Freedom Democrats reject the seating compromise offered by national Party leaders and stage a protest demonstration on the convention floor.

October 14: King is awarded the Nobel Peace Prize.

December 14: The Supreme Court unanimously upholds the constitutionality of the public accommodations section of the 1964 Civil Rights Act.

1965

February 21: Former Black Muslim leader Malcolm X is assassinated in New York City as he prepares to address a rally of his supporters.

March 7: About 500 blacks, beginning a protest march from Selma to Montgomery, Ala., are attacked by sheriff's deputies and state troopers.

March 15: In response to events in Selma, Johnson delivers a strong message to Congress urging passage of voting rights legislation.

March 21: The civil rights march from Selma to Montgomery, Ala., begins under the protection of federal troops.

April 11: Johnson signs the elementary and secondary school education bill, granting aid to schools with large concentrations of children from low-income families and providing funds for educational materials and the creation of educational centers.

April 29: U.S. Commissioner of Education Francis Keppel announces that public school districts will be required to desegregate schools by the autumn of 1967.

August 6: Johnson signs the voting rights bill suspending the use of literacy tests and other voter qualification tests.

August 11: Rioting breaks out in the black section of Los Angeles known as Watts. In a five-day period over 30 peo-

ple are killed in the most destructive outbreak of racial violence in decades.

1966

January 7: Martin Luther King announces plans for an "Open City" campaign in Chicago to attack the problems of Northern ghetto residents. It is the SCLC's first civil rights campaign in the North.

January 10: The Georgia House of Representatives votes not to seat State Rep. Julian Bond, a SNCC leader, because of his public opposition to the Vietnam war.

January 13: Johnson appoints Robert C. Weaver Secretary of Housing and Urban Development, making Weaver the first black ever to serve in a cabinet post.

March 7: The Supreme Court upholds the constitutionality of seven major provisions of the 1965 Voting Rights Act.

March 25: The Supreme Court voids the use of poll taxes in state elections.

April 28: Johnson sends Congress a civil rights message proposing legislation to ban discrimination in the sale, rental and financing of all housing.

May 14: SNCC staff members vote to exclude whites from policymaking and from organizing among blacks.

June 1: The White House Conference on Civil Rights opens.

June 6: James Meredith is shot during a solitary protest march in Mississippi.

June 7: Stokely Carmichael, the newly elected chairman of SNCC, raises the cry of "Black Power."

July 1–4: At its national convention in Baltimore, CORE endorses Black Power. The convention also adopts a resolution calling for the withdrawal of U.S. troops from Vietnam.

July 10: The SCLC drive to make Chicago an Open City is launched with a rally of 30,000.

July 12: Racial violence breaks out in Chicago. During the summer of 1966, over 20 cities, including New York, Los Angeles, Atlanta, Omaha and Detroit, experience riots or serious disturbances.

August 26: Civil rights leaders and Chicago officials agree on a program to end housing discrimination in Chicago.

September 19: An administration civil rights bill, including a controversial open housing provision, fails when the Senate refuses to invoke cloture against a filibuster.

October: The Black Panther Party is formed by Huey P. Newton and Bobby Seale in Oakland, Calif.

November 8: Edward W. Brooke is elected U.S. senator from Massachusetts, becoming the first black in the Senate in 85 years.

November 14: By a vote of 5 to 4, the Supreme Court for the first time sustains the state convictions of nonviolent civil rights demonstrators.

December 5: The Supreme Court unanimously reverses the decision of the Georgia House of Representatives to deny a seat to Julian Bond.

1967

January 3: The Equal Employment Opportunity Commission reports that enforcement of the 1964 Civil Rights Act has led to substantial gains in employment for blacks in the Southern textile industry.

February 15: Johnson sends Congress an omnibus civil rights bill. No major part of Johnson's program wins approval in 1967.

March 1: The House of Representatives votes 307–116 to deny Adam Clayton Powell his seat in Congress for improper use of government funds and other misconduct.

April 2: The Southern Education Reporting Service reports that only 16% of black students in the South are attending integrated schools.

April 15: Martin Luther King, Jr., leads a march of over 100,000 in New York City in opposition to the Vietnam war.

May 2: 30 armed members of the Black Panther Party march into the California State Assembly to protest a gun-control measure then under consideration.

May 29: The Supreme Court invalidates a California constitutional amendment that nullified existing municipal and state fair-housing legislation.

June 14: Leaders of nine major civil rights organizations announce that Cleveland will be the target of their combined efforts against racial discrimination in the North during the summer.

June 19: U.S. District Court Judge J. Skelly Wright orders an end to de facto segregation in Washington, D.C. public schools by the opening of the autumn term.

July 12: Rioting breaks out in Newark, N.J. During the "long, hot summer," of 1967 racial violence disrupts 50 American cities.

July 20–23: The largest group of black

American leaders ever assembled meet in Newark for a national conference on Black Power.

July 23: The worst race riot in U.S. history breaks out in Detroit, resulting in 43 dead and 5,000 injuries.

July 25: The National Guard enters Detroit to help curb disorders.

July 27: Johnson appoints a special advisory committee on civil disorders to probe urban race riots.

August 14–17: The SCLC annual convention calls for massive civil disobedience in Northern cities and adopts a resolution repudiating the war in Vietnam.

August 28: Civil rights advocates led by the Rev. James Groppi begin daily demonstrations in Milwaukee in support of open housing.

October 2: Thurgood Marshall is sworn in as the first black Supreme Court justice.

November 7: Black mayors are elected in two Northern cities, Carl B. Stokes in Cleveland and Richard G. Hatcher in Gary, Ind.

1968

February 8: Former Alabama Gov. George Wallace announces that he will enter the presidential race as a third party candidate.

March 2: The National Advisory Commission on Civil Disorders (Kerner Commission) issues its final report, asserting that "white racism" is chiefly responsible for black riots and warning that the U.S. is "moving toward two societies, one black and one white—separate and unequal."

March 18: HEW extends its school desegregation guidelines to Northern schools for the first time.

April 4: Martin Luther King, Jr., is assassinated in Memphis, Tenn. The killing leads to riots in Washington, Chicago and numerous other cities.

April 11: Johnson signs a civil rights bill barring discrimination in the sale or rental of about 80% of the nation's housing. The bill also contains anti-riot and gun-control provisions.

April 23: Black students occupy a campus building at Columbia University to protest the university's construction of a gymnasium in a city-owned park used by Harlem residents.

May 2: The Poor People's March on Washington begins. Later in the month 3,000 marchers camp near the Washington Monument on a site dubbed "Resurrection City."

May 7: In the Alabama Democratic primary, voters elect a delegation to the party's National Convention that includes blacks for the first time.

May 27: In a unanimous decision, the Supreme Court invalidates "freedom of choice" plans for school desegregation.

June 18: The Supreme Court rules that an 1866 civil rights act prohibits racial discrimination in the sale and rental of housing and other property.

June 24: Police clear Resurrection City after the protesters' permit expires.

August 20: The Credentials Committee of the Democratic National Convention votes to unseat the regular Mississippi delegation and seat instead a liberal, biracial challenge delegation.

September 9: 55,000 New York City public school teachers strike in protest against a school decentralization program that gave substantial power over hiring and firing to local school boards elected by ghetto residents.

September 16: CORE adopts a new constitution that bars whites from membership in the organization.

November 6: San Francisco State College students strike for reforms, particularly in the area of black studies programs.

1969

March 3: The Supreme Court, in a decision expanding its interpretation of the 1965 Voting Rights Act, rules that the law was aimed at "the subtle, as well as the obvious" state regulations that deny blacks the right to vote.

April 2: 21 members of the Black Panther Party in New York are indicted on charges of conspiracy to bomb several department stores, a police station and other public buildings.

April 19: 100 black students, armed with rifles and shotguns, seize the student union building at Cornell University in Ithaca, N.Y.

May 1: James Forman, director of the National Black Economic Development Conference and a former SNCC leader, demands that U.S. churches provide $500 million in "reparations" to black Americans.

May 1: The Civil Rights Commission charges the federal government with subsidizing racial discrimination in employment by cooperating with private firms that are in violation of the 1964 Civil Rights Act.

May 11: Led by Ralph Abernathy, major civil rights figures head a march of over 10,000 in Charleston, S.C., in support of striking hospital workers.

May 13: Charles Evers, brother of the slain civil rights leader Medgar Evers, is elected mayor of Fayette, Miss.

June 16: In *Powell v. McCormack,* the Supreme Court rules that the House of Representatives unconstitutionally excluded Adam Clayton Powell from membership in 1967.

June 26: Attorney General John Mitchell announces that the Nixon Administration will oppose an extension of the 1965 Voting Rights Act.

July 9: The New York City Board of Higher Education adopts an "open admissions" policy covering all graduating high school seniors in the city for the city colleges in an effort to expand college enrollment among minorities.

September 12: The Civil Rights Commission charges that the Nixon Administration's decisions on school desegregation are "a major retreat" in the struggle for integrated schools.

October 29: The Supreme Court unanimously rules that the "all deliberate speed" standard for school desegregation is no longer permissible. It declares that every school district must end dual school systems "at once."

November 21: The Senate rejects by a vote of 55–45 the nomination of Clement F. Haynsworth to the Supreme Court after heavy lobbying against him by civil rights groups and labor unions.

1970

February 28: A memo by presidential adviser Daniel Patrick Moynihan urges a policy of "benign neglect" toward blacks.

March 30: The Southern Regional Council reports that nearly 1,500 blacks hold elective office in the United States.

April 8: The Senate rejects by a vote of 51–45 the nomination of G. Harrold Carswell to the Supreme Court after intensive lobbying by civil rights organizations.

April 20: The Yale student body votes to boycott classes in support of Bobby Seale, the Black Panther Party chairman, who faces murder charges in New Haven. Demonstrations supporting Seale erupt on dozens of campuses.

May 14: Police kill two black students during demonstrations at Jackson State College in Jackson, Miss.

May 23: 10,000 civil rights advocates rally in Atlanta after a five-day, 110-mile "March Against Repression" through Georgia.

June 17: Congress approves a five-year extension of the 1965 Voting Rights Act over Administration opposition.

August 7: A shoot-out occurs at the Marin County Courthouse in San Rafael, Calif., in an attempt by Jonathan Jackson to seize hostages in exchange for the release of the "Soledad Brothers." Four are killed, including Jackson and a trial court judge.

September 5: The Black Panther Party convenes a "Revolutionary People's Constitutional Convention" in Philadelphia that includes members of the anti-war, student, women's liberation and gay liberation movements.

September 21: The Southern Governors Conference adopts a strongly worded resolution against busing to achieve school desegregation.

October 12: The Civil Rights Commission reports a "major breakdown" in the enforcement of laws prohibiting racial discrimination.

October 14: Black members of the House of Representatives announce the formation of a "Shadow Cabinet" to oversee the enforcement of civil rights laws. In January they reorganize themselves as the Congressional Black Caucus.

December 21: In *Oregon v. Mitchell,* the Supreme Court, ruling on amendments to the Voting Rights Act, upholds a congressional ban on the use of literacy tests as a qualification for voting.

1971

January 14: The Nixon Administration announces its plans to focus on the desegregation of Northern schools.

March 8: The Supreme Court holds that the 1964 Civil Rights Act bars the use of job tests that disproportionately disqualified blacks and that were not related to job performance.

March 25: Members of the congressional Black Caucus meet with Nixon and present him with a list of 60 legislative goals.

April 20: A unanimous Supreme Court rules that district court judges may make use of busing to eliminate school desegregation.

April 29: Ralph Abernathy conducts a sit-in at HEW offices and then leads a mule train to the White House to dramatize the grievances of poor blacks and whites.

May 13: A New York jury acquits Black Panther Party members of all charges of conspiracy to bomb police stations, department stores and other public places.

June 14: In a 5–4 decision, the Supreme Court rules that Jackson, Miss., officials had not denied equal protection when they closed all public swimming pools to avoid desegregation.

July 26: The Census Bureau reports that blacks lag far behind whites in economic prosperity, educational advancement and social gains and that the gap between white and black income levels is widening.

August 30: Arsonists destroy school buses in Pontiac, Mich., that were to be used for busing students to achieve school integration.

October 26: The Supreme Court declines to hear an appeal by the Pontiac, Mich., school board of a lower court order to bus students to achieve racial integration.

1972

January 10: A federal judge in Richmond orders busing across city lines to achieve school desegregation.

March 10–12: 3,300 black political leaders convene in Gary, Ind., and form the National Black Political Convention to set directions for black political action.

March 17: Nixon sends Congress a message urging legislation to deny courts the power to order busing to achieve school integration.

October 12: The Senate fails to end a filibuster by Northern liberals against a House-passed bill to limit school busing.

November 7: Andrew Young of Georgia and Barbara Jordan of Texas become the first blacks elected to Congress from the South in the 20th century.

1973

January 17: In a unanimous decision, the Supreme Court rules that a defendant has the right to question potential jurors about possible racial prejudice.

February 12: The Voter Education Project reports that 1,144 blacks hold elective office in the South, more than 10 times the number before passage of the 1965 Voting Rights Act.

1974

July 25: In a 5–4 decision, the Supreme Court strikes down a plan to desegregate Detroit schools by busing children across city lines.

July 31: Congress passes an aid to education bill with restrictions on busing of students to achieve integration.

September 12: Scattered violence and a successful boycott mar the opening of Boston's public schools under a court-ordered busing plan.

October 15: Massachusetts Gov. Francis Sargent mobilizes the National Guard as violence continues in Boston over the busing of school children.

1975

August 6: Ford signs a seven-year extension of the Voting Rights Act that includes a provision broadening its coverage to Spanish-speaking Americans and other linguistic minorities.

1976

May 1: The Congressional Black Caucus releases its legislative platform making full employment legislation its highest priority.

June 25: The Supreme Court rules that the 1866 Civil Rights Act prohibits racial discrimination by private nonsectarian schools.

1977

January 23–30: "Roots," a television dramatization of Alex Haley's fictionalized story of a black family's history, receives the largest audience in television history.

January 26: Andrew Young is confirmed by the Senate as U.S. ambassador to the United Nations, the first black ever to hold that post.

September 2: The Labor Department reports that the black unemployment rate is 14.5%, the highest since World War II. Among black youth the rate exceeds 40%.

Bibliography

Southern Society and Politics

An understanding of Southern politics and society is indispensable as background to the civil rights movement. Throughout most of America's history, the white South has had a distinct cultural and political tradition that has set it apart from the rest of the nation. The starting point for studying the South remains V. O. Key, Jr., *Southern Politics in State and Nation* (New York, 1949). Elegantly written and brilliant in its analysis, it is still, a generation after publication, the classic work on Southern politics. A valuable complement to Key is Wilbur J. Cash, *The Mind of the South* (New York, 1941), which focuses on Southern culture and its intellectual tradition. James W. Silver, *Mississippi: The Closed Society* (New York, 1964), written on the eve of the fiercest phase of the civil rights struggle in the deep South, offers a searing indictment of the state that for many came to symbolize the white South's resistance to integration. William C. Havard and Loren P. Bath have provided a model state study of Southern politics with *The Politics of Mis-Representation: Rural-Urban Conflict in the Florida Legislature* (Baton Rouge, 1962), a work whose significance is broader than the title would suggest. Some of the problems and limitations of Southern white liberalism are revealed in Edward Haas, *DeLesseps S. Morrison and the Image of Reform* (Baton Rouge, 1974).

Other Sources

Barnard, William D., *Dixiecrats and Democrats: Alabama Politics, 1942–1950* (University, Ala., 1974).

Bartley, Numan V., *From Thurmond to Wallace: Political Tendencies in Georgia, 1948–1968* (Baltimore, 1970).

Billington, Monroe Lee, *The Political South in the Twentieth Century* (New York, 1975).

Black, Earl, *Southern Governors and Civil Rights* (Cambridge, Mass., 1976).

Cortez, A.M. Ewing, *Primary Elections in the South: A Study in Uniparty Politics* (Norman, Okla., 1953).

Grantham, Dewey W., *The Democratic South* (Athens, Geo., 1963).

Havens, Murray Clark, *City Versus Farm?: Urban-Rural Conflict in the Alabama Legislature* (Tuscaloosa, Ala., 1957).

Kousser, J. Morgan, *The Shaping of Southern Politics* (New Haven, 1974).

Heard, Alexander, *A Two–Party South?* (Chapel Hill, 1952).

Leiserson, Avery, ed., *The American South in the 1960s* (New York 1964).

Lester, Jim, *A Man for Arkansas: Sid McMath and the Southern Reform Tradition* (Little Rock, 1976).

Morris, Willie, ed., *The South Today: 100 Years after Appomattox* (New York, 1965).

Peirce, Neal R., *The Deep South States* (New York, 1974).

Sherrill, Robert, *Gothic Politics in the Deep South* (New York, 1968).

Sindler, Allen P., ed., *Change in the Contemporary South* (Durham, N.C., 1963).

Vance, Rupert B. and Nicholas, J. Demerath, eds, *The Urban South* (Chapel Hill, 1954).

Wilkinson, J. Harvie III, *Harry Byrd and the Changing Face of Virginia Politics, 1945–1966* (Charlottesville, Va., 1968).

Zinn, Howard, *The Southern Mystique* (New York, 1964).

Black Life in the South: The Impact of "Jim Crow"

Until the civil rights revolution of the 1950s and 1960s, Southern blacks found their daily lives circumscribed by a web of laws and extra-legal institutions that reduced Negroes to a caste. Gunnar Myrdal's massive two-volume study, *An American Dilemma: The Negro Problem and American Democracy* (New York, 1944), remains the classic work about race relations on the eve of the civil rights movement. Its thorough research, meticulous attention to detail, and its assessment of broad social trends make it an indispensable source for an understanding of black life in the South under Jim Crow. C. Vann Woodward, *The Strange Career of Jim Crow* (3rd rev. ed., New York, 1974), is a well-written, provocative essay on the rise and fall of segregation. Harry S. Ashmore, *The Negro and the Schools* (Chapel Hill, 1954), carefully examines the state of black education in the South on the eve of the Supreme Court's momentous school desegregation decision. A good analysis of the economic impact of segregation on the Southern Negro is Gary S. Becker, *The Economics of Discrimination* (Chicago, 1957), while Alvin L. Bertrand, *Agricultural Mechanization and Social Change in Rural Louisiana* (Baton Rouge, 1957), examines the effects of the technological revolution in Southern agriculture on rural blacks. Frederick D. Ogden, *The Poll Tax in the South* (University, Ala., 1958), offers an in-depth study of one of the many devices used to disenfranchise Negroes in the South.

Other Sources

Aiken, Charles, ed., *The Negro Votes* (San Francisco, 1962).

Davis, Allison W. and John Dollard, *Children of Bondage* (Washington, 1940).

Dollard, John, *Caste and Class in a Southern Town* (New Haven, 1937).

E. Franklin Frazier, *The Negro in the United States* (Rev. ed., New York, 1957).

Friedman, Leon, ed., *Southern Justice* (New York, 1965).

Henderson, Vivian W., *The Economic Status of Negroes* (Atlanta, 1963).

Johnson, Charles S., *Growing Up in the Black Belt* (Washington, 1941).

Landis, Kenesaw M., *Segregation in Washington: A Report of the National Committee on Segregation in the Nation's Capital* (Chicago, 1948).

Lewis, Hylan, *Blackways of Kent* (Chapel Hill, 1955).

Logan, Rayford W., ed., *What the Negro Wants* (Chapel Hill, 1944).

President's Committee on Civil Rights, *To Secure These Rights* (Washington, 1947).

Price, Hugh D., *The Negro in Southern*

Politics: A Chapter in Florida History (New York, 1957).

Price, Margaret, *The Negro and the Ballot in the South* (Atlanta, 1959).

_____, *The Negro Voter in the South* (Atlanta 1957).

Rubin, Morton, *Plantation County* (Chapel Hill, 1951).

Silberman, Charles E., *Crisis in Black and White* (New York, 1964).

Swanson, Ernst W. and John A. Griffin, eds., *Public Education in the South Today and Tomorrow* (Chapel Hill, 1955).

Thompson, Daniel C., *The Negro Leadership Class* (Englewood Cliffs, N.J., 1963).

U.S. Commission on Civil Rights, *Racial Isolation in the Public Schools*, 2 vols. (Washington, 1967).

_____, *Voting in Mississippi* (Washington, 1965).

Memoirs, Personal Reminiscences and Autobiographies

The civil rights movement constitutes one of the most dramatic chapters in modern United States history. The struggle for racial equality brought out almost heroic qualities in many Americans and inspired millions to commit themselves to political activism. A number of participants, including both the leaders as well as local activists, have written about the experience. Their accounts provide some of the best reading on the day-to-day reality of the movement and the social conditions which gave rise to it. Martin Luther King, Jr.'s, *Stride Toward Freedom* (New York, 1958), tells the story of the Montgomery bus boycott which played such an important role in the development of the direct action phase of the movement. *Down the Line: The Collected Writings of Bayard Rustin* (Chicago, 1971) offers important insights into the thinking of a man whose career spans the entire history of the movement and who was involved in most of the critical civil rights campaigns. Anne Moody gives a deeply moving account of what it was like to grow up black in Mississippi and why she became involved in the movement in *Coming of Age in Mississippi* (New York 1968). Charles Morgan, Jr., a liberal white lawyer from Birmingham, shows that the white South was not monolithic in its opposition to integration in his memoir, *A Time to Speak* (New York, 1964). *The Making of Black Revolutionaries* (New York, 1972), by SNCC leader James Forman, details the shift in thinking of Southern black militants in the mid and late 1960s that led many to abandon nonviolence. *The Autobiography of Malcolm X* (New York, 1965) is indispensable reading for an understanding of the appeal of the Black Muslims and their philosophy of black nationalism.

Other Sources

Bates, Daisy, *The Long Shadow of Little Rock: A Memoir* (New York, 1962).

Belfrage, Sally, *Freedom Summer* (New York, 1965).

Blossom, Virgil T., *It Has Happened Here* (New York, 1959).

Bond, Julian, *A Time to Speak, A Time to Act* (New York, 1972).

Brown, H. Rap, *Die, nigger, die!* (New York, 1969).

Cleaver, Eldridge, *Soul on Ice* (New York, 1968).

Davis, Angela Yvonne, *Angela Davis: An Autobiography* (New York, 1974).

East, P. D., *The Magnolia Jungle* (New York, 1960).

Farmer, James, *Freedom—When?* (New York, 1966).

Forman, James, *Sammy Younge, Jr.: The First Black College Student to Die in the Black Liberation Movement* (New York, 1968).

Gregory, Dick, *Nigger: An Autobiography* (New York, 1964).

_____, *Up From Nigger* (New York, 1976).

Hays, Brooks, *A Southern Moderate Speaks* (Chapel Hill, 1959).

Holt, Len, *The Summer That Didn't End* (New York, 1965).

King, Coretta Scott, *My Life with Martin Luther King, Jr.* (New York, 1970).

King, Martin Luther Jr., *Why We Can't Wait* (New York, 1964).

Kunstler, William M., *Deep in My Heart* (New York, 1966).

McKissick, Floyd, *Three-Fifths of a Man* (New York, 1969).

Meredith, James, *Three Years in Mississippi* (Bloomington, Ind., 1966).

Nash, Diane, "Inside the Sit-Ins and Freedom Rides," in Matthew Ahman, ed., *The New Negro* (Notre Dame, Ind., 1962).

Newton, Huey P., *Revolutionary Suicide* (New York, 1973).

—————————, *To Die for the People: The Writings of Huey P. Newton* (New York, 1972).

Peck, James, *Freedom Ride* (New York, 1962).

Proudfoot, Merrill, *Diary of a Sit-In* (Chapel Hill, 1962).

Seale, Bobby, *A Lonely Rage: The Autobiography of Bobby Seale* (New York, 1978).

Sutherland, Elizabeth, ed., *Letters from Mississippi* (New York, 1965).

Watters, Pat, *Down to Now: Reflections on the Southern Civil Rights Movement* (New York, 1971).

White, Walter Francis, *How Far the Promised Land?* (New York, 1955).

The Civil Rights Movement: Leaders, Organizations, and Campaigns

A definitive history of the civil rights movement remains to be written. Anyone interested in exploring further the history of the movement will need to consult a number of works in order to obtain a balanced overview. A good starting point is David L. Lewis, *King: A Critical Biography* (2nd ed., Chicago, 1978). A sympathetic yet also perceptively critical account of the career of the most illustrious civil rights leader, Lewis's work also covers much of the movement's history and reveals many of the differences between King and other leaders of the movement. August Meier and Elliott Rudwick, *CORE: A Study in the Civil Rights Movement, 1942-1968* (New York, 1973), is a masterful, thoroughly documented study of the most important direct action organization whose history reflected the ups and downs of the movement as a whole. A forthcoming book on SNCC by Clayborne Carson should shed much light on that organization's history. Benjamin Muse, *The American Negro Revolution: From Non-Violence to Black Power, 1963-1967* (Bloomington, 1968), details the critical years of the mid 1960s when the movement abruptly shifted course. A model study of one of the most important issues of the civil rights struggle is Steven F. Lawson, *Black Ballot: Voting Rights in the South, 1944–1969* (New York, 1976).

Other Sources

Barrett, Russell H. *Integration at Ole Miss* (Chicago, 1965).

Bennett, Lerone, Jr., *Confrontation: Black and White* (Chicago, 1965).

—————————, *The Negro Mood* (Chicago, 1964).

Braden, Anne, ed., "The Southern Freedom Movement in Perspective," *Monthly Review*, July–August, 1965.

Brooks, Thomas R., *Walls Come Tumbling Down: A History of the Civil Rights Movement, 1940–1970* (Englewood Cliffs, N.J., 1974).

Carmichael, Stokely and Charles V. Hamilton, *Black Power* (New York, 1967).

Clark, Kenneth B., "The Civil Rights Movement: Momentum and Organization," *Daedalus* (Winter 1966), 239–267.

Dorman, Michael, *We Shall Overcome* (New York, 1964).

Draper, Theodore, *The Rediscovery of Black Nationalism* (New York, 1970).

Garfinkel, Herbert, *When Negroes March: The March on Washington Movement in the Organizational Politics of the FEPC* (Glencoe, Ill., 1959).

Harding, Vincent, "Black Radicalism: The Road from Montgomery," in Alfred E. Young, ed., *Dissent: Explorations in the History of American Radicalism* (DeKalb, Ill., 1968).

Huie, William Bradford, *Three Lives for Mississippi* (New York, 1965).

Kahn, Tom, "The 'New Negro' and the New Moderation," *New Politics,* 1 (Fall 1961), 61–76.

Kesselman, Louis C., *The Social Politics of FEPC: A Study in Reform Pressure Movements* (Chapel Hill, 1948).

Killiam Lewis M. and Charles Grigg, *Racial Crisis in America* (Englewood Cliffs, N.J., 1964).

Lewis, Anthony and the New York Times, *Portrait of a Decade: The Second American Revolution* (New York, 1964).

Lomax, Louis, *The Negro Revolt* (New York, 1962).

McCord, William, *Mississippi: The Long Hot Summer* (New York, 1965).

Matusow, Allen J., "From Civil Rights to Black Power: The Case of SNCC, 1960–1966," in Barton J. Bernstein and Allen J. Matusow, eds., *Twentieth Century America: Recent Interpretations* (New york, 1969).

Moore, Gilbert Stuart, *A Special Rage* (New York, 1971).

Muse, Benjamin, *Ten Years of Prelude: The Story of Integration Since the Supreme Court's 1954 Decision* (New York, 1965).

Ross, B. Joyce, *J.E. Soingarn and the Rise of the NAACP* (New York, 1972).

St. James, Warren D., *The National Association for the Advancement of Colored People: A Case Study in Pressure Groups* (New York, 1958).

Saunders, Doris E., *The Day They Marched* (Chicago, 1963).

Silverman, Corinne, *The Little Rock Story* (University, Ala., 1959).

Sobel, Lester A., *Civil Rights, 1960–1966* (New York, 1967).

Westin, Alan F. ed., *Freedom Now!: The Civil Rights Struggle in America* (New York, 1964).

Wright, M.A., "Sit-in Movement: Progress Report and Prognosis," *Wayne Law Review,* 9 (1963), 445–57.

Zinn, Howard, *SNCC: The New Abolitionists* (Boston, 1964).

The Southern Resistance Movement

The pervasive, widespread resistance to integration that swept the South in the 1950s provides a fascinating example of grass-roots political movements. In many respects, the intense, often violent, opposition to desegregation represented the last gasp of a dying social order. The best general account of this chapter in Southern history is Numan V. Bartley, *The Rise of Massive Resistance* (Baton Rouge, 1969). Bartley covers a wide terrain, from the Citizens' Councils and the Ku Klux Klan to the complex responses of each Southern state's political power structure. Neil R. McMillen, *The Citizens' Council: Organized Resistance to the Second Reconstruction, 1954–1964* (Urbana, Ill., 1971) offers a detailed analysis of the most important grassroots organization of the resistance. A solidly researched local study is Robbins L. Gates, *The Making of Massive Resistance: Virginia's Politics of Public School Desegregation, 1954–56* (Chapel Hill, 1962) which focuses on the state that provided the early leadership for the resistance to the *Brown* decision.

Other Sources

Campbell, Ernest Q. et. al., *When A City Closes Its Schools* (Chapel Hill, 1960).

Carter, Hodding III, *The South Strikes Back* (Garden City, N.Y., 1959).

Cook, James Graham, *The Segregation-ists* (New York, 1962).

Crain, Robert L. and Morton Inger, *Desegregation in New Orleans: A Comparative Study of the Failure of Social Control* (Chicago, 1966).

Graham, Hugh Davis, *Crisis in Print: Desegregation and the Press in Tennessee* (Nashville, 1967).

Lord, Walter, *The Past That Would Not Die* (New York, 1965).

Muse, Benjamin, *Virginia's Massive Resistance* (Bloomington, Ind., 1961).

Newby, I.A., *Challenge to the Court: Social Scientists and the Defense of Segregation, 1954–1966* (Baton Rouge, 1969).

Shoemaker, Don, ed., *With All Deliberate Speed: Segregation–Desegregation in Southern Schools* (New York, 1957).

Smith, Bob, *They Closed Their Schools: Prince Edward County, Virginia, 1951–1964* (Chapel Hill, 1965).

Tumin, Melvin M. et. al., *Desegregation: Resistance and Readiness* (Princeton, N.J., 1958).

Vander Zanden, James W., "The Klan Revival," *American Journal of Sociology*, 65 (1960), 456–462.

Wakefield, Dan, *Revolt in the South* (New York, 1960).

Williams, Robin M., Jr., and Margaret W. Ryans, eds., *Schools in Transition: Community Experiences in Desegregation* (Chapel Hill, 1954).

The Supreme Court and the Federal Judiciary

The judicial branch of the government played a critical role in the unfolding drama of the civil rights movement. The Supreme Court's decisions provided a firm constitutional foundation from which to carry on the struggle for racial equality, while the federal district courts had to rule on the day-to-day implementation of desegregation plans and the attempts to evade the high court's pronouncements. Richard Kluger's fast-paced and thoroughly researched study, *Simple Justice* (New York, 1976), will undoubtedly remain the definitive work on the *Brown* decision for some time to come. *The Warren Court* (Cambridge, Mass., 1968) by Archibald Cox offers a perceptive analysis of the Supreme Court under Chief Justice Earl Warren and includes a chapter assessing the court's accomplishments in the field of civil rights. For the full texts of Supreme Court decisions concerning racial justice consult Joseph Tussman, ed., *The Supreme Court on Racial Discrimination* (New York, 1963). Charles V. Hamilton provides a careful examination of the judiciary's role in securing the vote for Southern blacks in *The Bench and The Ballot: Southern Federal Judges and Black Voters* (New York, 1973). Stephen L. Washby et. al. *Desegregation from Brown to Alexander: An Exploration of Supreme Court Strategies* (Carbondale, Ill., 1977) is a recent, wide-ranging collection of essays.

Other Sources

Atkinson, David N., "Justice Sherman Minton and the Protection of Minority Rights," *Washington and Lee Law Review*, 34 (1977), 97–117.

Bickel, Alexander M., *Politics and the Warren Court* (New York, 1965).

Blaustein, Albert P. and Clarence Clyde Ferguson, Jr., *Desegregation and the Law* (New York, 1962).

De Lacy, G.L., "Segregation Cases and the Supreme Court," *Nebraska Law Review*, 38 (1959), 1017–1038.

Friedman, Leon, ed., *Argument: The Oral Argument Before the Supreme Court in Brown v. Board of Education of Topeka, 1952–1955* (New York, 1969).

Goldberg, Arthur J., *Equal Justice: The Warren Era of the Supreme Court* (Evanston, Ill. 1971).

Greenberg, Jack, *Race Relations and American Law* (New York, 1959).

Harris, Robert J., *The Quest for Equality: The Constitution, Congress and the Supreme Court* (Baton Rouge, 1960).

Konvitz, Milton R., *The Constitution and Civil Rights* (New York, 1962).

Lefberg, Irving F., "Chief Justice Vinson and the Politics of Desegregation," *Emory Law Journal*, 24 (1975), 243–312.

McCord, John H., ed., *With All Deliberate Speed* (Urbana, Ill. 1969).

Miller, Loren, *The Petitioners: The Story of the Supreme Court of the United States and the Negro* (New York, 1966).

Peltason, J.W., *Fifty-Eight Lonely Men: Southern Federal Judges and School Desegregation* (New York, 1962).

Spicer, George W., "The Federal Judiciary and Political Change in the South," *Journal of Politics*, 26 (1964), 154–176.

Strong, Donald S., *Negroes Ballots and Judges: National Voting Rights Legislation in the Federal Courts* (University, Ala., 1968).

Vines, Kenneth N., "Federal District Judges and Race Relations in the South," *Journal of Politics*, 26 (1964), 337–357.

Vose, Clement E., *Caucasians Only: The Supreme Court, the NAACP, and the Restrictive Covenant Cases* (Berkeley, 1959).

The President, Congress, and the Politics of Race

The problem of racial inequality grew in importance during the post World War II era until it became in the early 1960s the overriding issue in national politics. Allan Wolk's *The Presidency and Black Civil Rights: Eisenhower to Nixon* (Rutherford, 1971), assesses the varying policies of several presidents in the area of civil rights. Carl M. Brauer, *John F. Kennedy and the Second Reconstruction* (New York, 1977) is a carefully researched, balanced appraisal of the young, liberal president. Harvard Sitkoff's forthcoming study on federal civil rights policies during the 1940s should be exhaustive and will undoubtedly shed much light on the era in which civil rights first became a national issue. Neil Hickey and Ed Edwin illuminate the career of the most highly visible elected black official until the late 1960s in *Adam Clayton Powell and the Politics of Race* (New York, 1965).

Other Sources

Anderson, John W., *Eisenhower, Brownell, and the Congress: The Tangled Origin of the Civil Rights Bill of 1956–1957* (Montgomery, 1964).

Berman, Daniel, *A Bill Becomes Law: Congress Enacts Civil Rights Legislation* (2nd ed., New York, 1966).

Berman, William C., *The Politics of Civil Rights in the Truman Administration* (Columbus, 1970).

Bernstein, Barton J., "The Ambiguous Legacy: The Truman Administration and Civil Rights," in Bernstein, ed., *Politics and Policies of the Truman Administration* (Chicago, 1972).

Billington, Monroe, "Freedom to Serve: The President's Committee on Equality of Treatment and Opportunity in the Armed Services, 1949–1950," *Journal of Negro History*, 51 (1966), 262–274.

Billington, Monroe, "Civil Rights, President Truman and the South," *Journal of Negro History*, 58 (1973), 127–139.

Carr, Robert S., *Federal Protection of Civil Rights: Quest for a Sword* (Ithaca, 1947).

Dalfiume, Richard M., *Desegregation of the U.S. Armed Forces* (Columbia, Mo., 1969).

Dixon, R.G. Jr., "Civil Rights in Transportations and the I.C.C.," *George Washington Law Review*, 31 (1962), 198–241.

Dulles, Foster Rhea, *The Civil Rights Commission, 1957–1965* (East Lansing, Mich., 1968).

Elliff, John T., "Aspects of Federal Civil Rights Enforcement: The Justice Department and the FBI, 1939–1964," *Perspectives in American History,* 5 (1971).

Harry Golden, *Mr. Kennedy and the Negroes* (Cleveland, 1964).

Harvey, James C., *Civil Rights During the Kennedy Administration* (Hattiesburg, Miss., 1971).

Havens, Charles W. III, "Federal Legislation to Safeguard Voting Rights: The Civil Rights Act of 1960," *Virginia Law Review,* 46 (1960), 945–975.

McCoy, Donald R. and Richard T. Tuetten, *Quest and Response: Minority Rights and the Truman Administration* (Lawrence, Kan., 1973).

Marshall, Burke, *Federalism and Civil Rights* (New York, 1964).

Middleton, Russell, "The Civil Rights Issue and Presidential Voting among Southern Negroes and Whites," *Social Forces,* 40 (1962), 209–215.

Morgan, Ruth P., *The President and Civil Rights: Policy Making by Executive Order* (New York, 1970).

Nichols, Lee, *Breakthrough on the Color Front* (New York, 1954).

President's Committee on Equality of Treatment and Opportunity in the Armed Forces, *Freedom to Serve* (Washington, 1950).

Ruchames, Louis, *Race, Jobs and Politics: The Story of FEPC* (New York, 1953).

Sitkoff, Harvard, "Harry Truman and the Election of 1948: The Coming of Age of Civil Rights in American Politics," *Journal of Southern History,* 37 (1971), 597–616.

Whitehead, Don, *Attack on Terror: The FBI Against the Ku Klux Klan in Mississippi* (New York, 1970).

Northern Blacks and the Ghetto Riots

Until the mid 1960s, civil rights forces concentrated the bulk of their efforts on racial injustice in the South, a tendency encouraged by the blatant nature of discrimination there. Not until the urban ghettoes exploded in violence did the plight of Northern blacks receive the attention it deserved. Myrdal's work, already cited, contains much valuable information on black life in the North. St. Clair Drake and Horace R. Cayton, *Black Metropolis: A Study of Negro Life in a Northern City* (New York, 1945) is the classic study of the experience of blacks in the urban North. The distinguished black educator, Kenneth Clark, offers an insightful analysis of the effect of ghetto life upon its black residents in *Dark Ghetto* (New York, 1965). A valuable complement to Clark's work is Claude Brown, *Manchild in the Promised Land* (New York, 1965), an autobiographical account of growing up in New York City's Harlem. By far the most thorough examination of the ghetto riots and the conditions which led to them is the Report of the National Advisory Commission on Civil Disorders (New York, 1968). C. Eric Lincoln, *The Black Muslims in America* (Boston, 1961) offers an inside view of one of the most influential groups among Northern blacks. B.J. Widick, Jr., *Detroit: City of Race and Class Violence* (Chicago, 1972) dissects the social, political and economic conditions that underlay the most serious outbreak of urban violence in the 1960s.

Other Sources

Abrams, Charles, "The Housing Problem and the Negro," *Daedalus,* 95 (Winter 1966), 64–76.

Boesel, David and Peter H. Rossi, eds., *Cities Under Siege: An Anatomy of the Ghetto Riots, 1964–1968* (New York, 1971).

Boskin, Joseph, "The Revolt of the Urban Ghettoes, 1964–1967," *Annals of the American Academy* (Washington, 1969).

Connery, Robert H., ed., "Urban Riots: Violence and Social Change," *Proceedings of the Academy of Political Science,* 29 (1968).

Conot, Robert, *Rivers of Blood, Years of Darkness* (New York, 1968).

Drotning, Phillip and Wesley South, *Up from the Ghetto* (New York, 1970).

Duncan, Otis D. and Beverly, *The Negro Population of Chicago: A Study of Residential Succession* (Chicago, 1957).

Eishkowitz, Miriam and Joseph Zikmund II, *Black Politics in Philadelphia* (New York, 1973).

Essien-Udom, E.U., *Black Nationalism: A Search for an Identity in America* (Chicago, 1962).

Gilbert, Ben W. et. àl., *Ten Blocks from the White House: Anatomy of the Washington Riots of 1968* (New York, 1968).

Glazer, Nathan, "School Integration Policies in Northern Cities," *Journal of the American Institute of Planners*, 30 (August 1964), 178–188.

Grier, Eunice and George, "Obstacles to Desegregation in America's Urban Areas," *Race*, 6 (July 1964), 3–17.

Grier, William H. and Price M. Cobbs, *Black Rage* (New York, 1968).

Hayden, Tom, *Rebellion in Newark* (New York, 1967).

Higham, Robin, ed., *Bayonets in the Streets: The Use of Troops in Civil Disturbances* (Lawrence, Kan., 1969).

"Housing and Minorities," *Phylon*, 19 (Summer 1958), 8–124.

Johnson, Reginald A. *Racial Bias and Housing* (New York, 1963).

Lee, Frank, F., *Negro and White in a Connecticut Town: A Study in Race Relations* (New York, 1961).

Marine, Gene, *Black Panthers* (New York, 1969).

Maslow, Will and Richard Cohen, *School Segregation, Northern Style* (New York, 1961).

Michael, Donald, *The Next Generation* (New York, 1965).

Moore, Gilbert, *A Special Rage* (New York, 1971).

National Advisory Commission on Civil Disorders, *Supplemental Studies* (Washington, 1968).

Parris Guichard and Lester Brooks, *Blacks in the City: A History of the National Urban League* (Boston, 1971).

Taeuber, Karl E. and Alma F., *Negroes in Cities* (Chicago, 1965).

Weaver, Robert C., "Class, Race and Urban Renewal," *Land Economics*, 36 (August 1960), 235–51.

Wilson, James Q., *Negro Politics: The Search for Leadership* (Glencoe, Ill., 1960).

Zannes, Estelle, *Checkmate in Cleveland: The Rhetoric of Confrontation During the Stokes Years* (Cleveland, 1972).

Southern Politics and the Second Reconstruction

The civil rights movement had a profound impact upon Southern life. Historians and analysts of American politics have dubbed it the "Second Reconstruction." The changes in Southern politics have already attracted the attention of many students and, as the contours of the new order in the South become clearer, the number of works on the subject will undoubtedly increase. Some valuable works have already appeared. William C. Havard, ed., *The Changing Politics of the South* (Baton Rouge, 1972) is thus far the best resource on the subject. The essays in the collection, written by some of the most knowledgeable students of Southern politics, provide a thorough analysis of the still incomplete revolution in Southern politics. Numan V. Bartley and Hugh D. Graham, *Southern Politics and the Second Reconstruction* (Baltimore, 1975), offers a good overview. A valuable local study is Frederick M. Wirt, *The Politics of Southern Equality* (Chicago, 1970), which examines the impact of the civil rights movement on a black belt county in Mississippi. Gary Orfield, *The Reconstruction of Southern Education: The Schools and the 1964 Civil Rights Act* (New York, 1969) represents an early effort to assess the effects of desegregation on the Southern educational system.

Other Sources

Bartley, Numan V. and Hugh Davis Graham, "Whatever Happened to the Solid South?" *New South,* 27 (Fall, 1972), 28–34.

Davidson, Chandler, *Biracial Politics: Conflict and Coalition in the Metropolitan South* (Baton Rouge, 1972).

Diamond, M. Jerome, "The Impact of the Negro Vote in Contemporary Tennessee Politics," *Tennessee Law Review,* 54 (1967), 435–481.

Highsaw, Robert B., ed., *The Deep South in Transformation* (University, Ala., 1964).

Hollingsworth, Harold M., ed., *Essays on Recent Southern Politics* (Austin, 1970).

Holloway, Harry, *The Politics of the Southern Negro: From Exclusion to Big City Organization* (New York, 1969).

Keech, William R., *The Impact of Negro Voting* (Chicago, 1968).

Matthews, Donald R. and James W. Prothro, *Negroes and the New Southern Politics* (New York, 1966).

Roland, Charles P., *The Improbable Era: The South Since World War II* (Lexington, Ky., 1975).

Sarratt, Reed, *The Ordeal of Desegregation: The First Decade* (New York, 1966).

Tindall, George Brown, *The Disruption of the Solid South* (Athens, Ga., 1972).

Vander Zanden, James W., *Race Relations in Transition* (New York, 1965).

Watters, Pat and Reese Cleghorn, *Climbing Jacob's Ladder: The Arrival of Negroes in Southern Politics* (New York, 1967).

Index